# APPLIED C

# APPLIED  C

## STRAWBERRY SOFTWARE, INC.

Edited by
Bonnie Derman

**VNR** VAN NOSTRAND REINHOLD COMPANY
—————————————————————— New York

Published by Van Nostrand Reinhold Company Inc.
115 Fifth Avenue
New York, New York 10003

Van Nostrand Reinhold Company Limited
Molly Millars Lane
Wokingham, Berkshire RG11 2PY, England

Van Nostrand Reinhold
480 Latrobe Street
Melbourne, Victoria 3000, Australia

Macmillan of Canada
Division of Gage Publishing Limited
164 Commander Boulevard
Agincourt, Ontario M1S 3C7, Canada

15 14 13 12 11 10 9 8 7 6 5 4 3 2 1

**Library of Congress Cataloging-in-Publication Data**
Main entry under title:

Applied C / Strawberry Software, Inc.

   Includes index.
   1. C (Computer program language)   I. Strawberry
Software, Inc. (Firm)
QA76.73.C15A66  1986       005.13'3       85-23403
ISBN 0-442-28217-6

WITHDRAWN

# Preface

In recent years, the C language has become the standard for mini- and micro-computer development. The proliferation of UNIX, the system for which C was developed, has contributed to this popularity. C's combination of high-level language features, such as structured programming, and low-level language features that enable the programmer to manipulate individual bytes has also contributed heavily to the language's popularity.

A number of excellent texts teach the basics of the C language.* There is a gap, however, between the syntax of the language and the knowledge required to complete real-world applications in C. It is this gap that *Applied C* addresses.

The gap arises from three major considerations: Applications tend to be much longer than introductory exercises, they must place a major emphasis on the user interface, and they will likely involve programming problems that have already been solved (e.g., by C toolmakers).

In real-world applications, the development cycle itself needs to be considered: In a program substantially larger than the 50-line examples in an introductory text, how is the task most efficiently broken down? This question is addressed by the organization of this book. The five major sections of program development—planning the application, choosing data types, organizing code, writing the algorithms and code for major tasks, and creating bug-free executable code—are the five major sections of this book. Within each section, the steps of software development are further broken down into chapters.

User interface design is considered very early in the book, and should be considered very early in the creation of an application. A later chapter discusses some of the methodology for implementing a user interface.

The utilities and tools commercially available to aid in C development also merit consideration. Throughout this book, the emphasis is on practical imple-

---

*The C Programming Language* by Kernighan and Ritchie is the standard introductory C text. Many others are also available. We do not list them here due to space considerations.

mentation, which means that commercial products are discussed in the context of any task in which they are useful. While the book discusses how the individual programmer can implement many tasks with solely the language as a tool, it also takes into account constraints on time and money, and thus indicates where commercial products may help save either.

*Applied C* is not a comprehensive discussion of every conceivable element of writing applications in C. Rather, it is a compendium of topics deemed most important and most valuable to our readers, by the collection of its contributors, reviewers, and editors. *Applied C* is unique in its multiplicity of viewpoints, and the practicality of its approach. Both these features derive from the source of the information presented: more than a dozen C tool makers, utility makers, and experienced, expert programmers. Each chapter represents the views of at least two sources, often conflicting. Thus the reader is not presented with one "recipe" for developing in C, but the collected ideas, opinions, and experiences of many professional real-world C programmers.

Some topics covered in *Applied C* are relevant to any real-world application: organizing and expressing program operation in a specification, designing a user interface, and many aspects of debugging, for example. Other topics are applicable to a subset of languages, including C: functions and modularity, for example. For the most part, however, this book is specific to the use of C in professional, end-user application development.

The first section, Designing the Application, discusses writing a specification, designing a user interface, and thinking about coding style.

The second section, Choosing Data Types, provides a brief review of C's elementary data types, covers the more confusing aspects of structures, arrays, pointers, and addresses, then goes on to explain some of the more complex data types you can create and implement in C. Stacks, linked lists, queues, sets, and more are defined, implemented in C, and used in sample C programs.

The third section, Code Organization, discusses the planning of the code itself. Modularity and flow control are considered, as are the division of tasks into functions, the use of commercial libraries, and the considerations for (and pitfalls in) creating portable code.

The fourth section, Coding Specific Tasks, discusses some of the algorithms and tools for performing major programming tasks: receiving user input, parsing, and indexing.

The fifth section, Producing the Executable, deals with the process of turning source code into executable: linking, overlaying, debugging, testing, and revising. Commercial linkage editors, debuggers, syntax checkers, and the like are all described in terms of their functionality and contribution to efficient software development.

# Acknowledgments

As a cooperative project, *Applied C* would not have been possible without the efforts of its many contributors and reviewers. In addition, *Applied C* gained a great deal from the insights of Ann Briggs and John Hutchinson of Solution Systems and The Programmer's Shop, Michael St. Hippolyte of Xor Corporation, P.J. Gardner of Techwrights, Mark A. Clarkson of Concept Software Design, and Tim Farlow and Art Shane of Strawberry Software, Inc.

## Disclaimers

### Code:

While we have taken care to ensure that the code samples within this book are valid and will perform as described, we can make no guarantees. Feel free to use any of the code printed in *Applied C*, but please be sure to test it yourself.

### ANSI Standard:

As this book goes to press, the ANSI standard has not yet been finalized. We have made statements about the ANSI standard based on that committee's progress so far. Any inaccuracies in our description of the ANSI standard are due to changes made to the standard after *Applied C* was printed.

# Contents

## 14. Make and Lint Utilities / 254

## APPENDIX: C Programming Aids / 267

## Index / 277

# APPLIED C

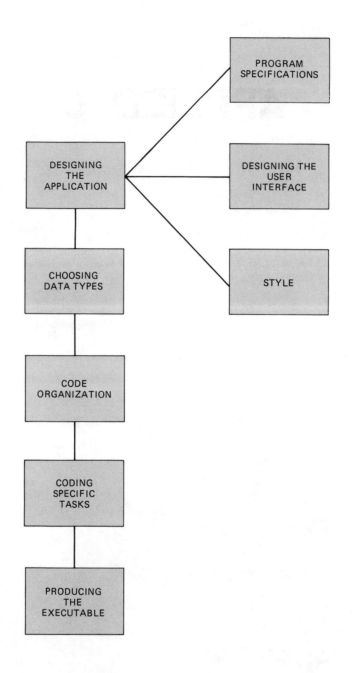

# Section A

# DESIGNING
# THE APPLICATION

The programmer who comes to real-world C programming with only classroom experience in the language will soon find that a major difference between classroom and professional programs is size. Invariably, professional software development entails large, multi-person, long-term projects. The final source code may literally represent reams of paper. For an application of such size and scope, the planning phase involves a good deal more than mentally envisioning the algorithm before writing two pages of code.

The programmer who comes to C from professional experience in other languages likely knows the planning process and its importance. He or she may also be aware, however, that this crucial first step is often underemphasized in practice. Program specifications are ambiguous and incomplete. User interfaces are complicated, inconsistent, or simply inappropriate. Code becomes cumbersome, difficult to read, debug, and maintain, as major design changes are made well into the development cycle.

Carefully planning any application is essential. Specifications, whether written by programmers or others, must be clear and unambiguous. Design must take the user as well as the machine into consideration at the inception of the project. Prototypes are often much more useful than text in expressing and reviewing design ideas. Before any code is written, a complete (though not iron-clad) blueprint must be formed.

The following chapters discuss program specifications and user interface design—two of the most important aspects of planning an application. A chapter on coding style is also included in this section, which discusses many of the considerations for creating clear, legible code.

# 1
# Program Specifications

*Reviewer:* Bob Saunders of UNITECH Software, Inc.

## INTRODUCTION

### Why Write Specifications?

One of the most important and most neglected aspects of software creation is specification. For all but the most trivial programs, careful planning reduces errors, revisions, maintenance, and plainly ill-conceived software. And for all but the most complex and formal programs, this planning process is often all but ignored.

Unless you are working alone from initial idea to final product, you will need to communicate with others to arrive at a mutually agreeable conception of your program. Anyone who has ever written a program in a professional environment knows that such communication often goes awry. People change their minds, disagree about what they meant, neglect to consider many aspects of the program, and often have no record of previous design decisions to consult. The program specification (''spec'') is designed to alleviate these problems. A program spec reflects careful thought on the functions and limitations of the program. Well written, it is a clear description of what the program should be. It provides reference for the designer, the programmer, the maintainer, and the potential user.

### Chapter Organization

This chapter discusses two separate specification documents: the requirements document and the software specification. These documents serve two different (although related) purposes, and are aimed at two different audiences. The requirements document states the purpose of the program, defining those functions that the system must perform, and is aimed at the user. The software specification is the first step in defining the implementation of the system. It associates abstract software components with each section of the system, and is aimed at the programmer. Many systems are not complex enough to require two separate specification documents. While the actual documents may be combined into one, their purposes should be kept separate, since they represent two different phases in design. To emphasize the different functions of these documents, we will discuss them separately in this chapter.

## THE REQUIREMENTS DOCUMENT

The first step in creating a piece of software is to specify what it will do. Such a specification is known as a requirements document or a functional specification. We will use the former term to avoid confusion, since the term "functional specification" is often used for other parts of the spec, discussed later in this chapter.

The requirements document describes, usually in natural language, what the program is supposed to do. It lists those properties or constraints that the program must satisfy. Such requirements must be specific enough to be testable: "easy to use" is a poor requirement; "user will give any command by selecting it from a menu," on the other hand, is a valid one.

The requirements document is aimed at the user, although in many practical instances the programmer will have no access to the user until the software has been written, tested, and marketed. But creating a user-oriented document in the first stages of designing a program has several advantages. Since software is created for user needs (as opposed to programmer capabilities), satisfying user needs is the first criterion of a software project. A user-oriented approach allows you to consider those needs before considering implementation. Review of the requirements document allows you to find and change many flaws in satisfying user needs before you write any code. And the user-oriented, functional approach is probably the easiest way to think about the project as a whole. Only after you have determined what the program will do are you prepared to determine how the program will do it.

One author sets forth the following criteria for a requirements document.* A requirements document should:

1. Specify only external system behavior, that is, describe the system as the user will see it.

---

*K. L. Heninger, "Specifying software requirements for complex systems. New techniques and their applications," *IEEE Transactions on Software Engineering*, **SE-6**(1), 2–13 (1980).

2. Specify constraints on the implementation, that is, describe the limits imposed by the hardware, and constraints on speed, size, and the like.
3. Be easy to change. This criterion suggests that a list or outline format is preferable to full sentences and paragraphs.
4. Serve as a reference tool for system maintainers. It should include a useful index and table of contents, and should be carefully organized.
5. Record forethought about the life cycle of the system, that is, reflect plans and predictions about later revisions of the system.
6. Characterize acceptable responses to error conditions, specifying when a simple error message is sufficient, and how and when the system should recover from errors.

With these criteria in mind, another author proposes an outline for a requirements document, shown in Figure 1-1.*

Introduction
    The need for the system
    Structure of the remainder of the document
    Notations used

Hardware
    Description of particular hardware to be used
              OR
    Minimal and optimal configurations on which the system will execute

The Conceptual Model
    Major services provided by the system, and their relationships to
        each other. Often best expressed graphically.

Functional Requirements
    The services provided to the user. This section includes any
        requirements about the nature of the user interface. Screen pictures
        are often very useful in this section, specifying clearly and
        precisely how the system will appear to the user.

Database Requirements
    The logical organization of the data used by the system and their
        relationships to each other

**FIGURE 1-1**

---

*I. Sommerville, *Software Engineering,* 2nd Ed., Addison-Wesley, Boston, 1985.

Nonfunctional Requirements
The constraints under which the software must operate, in relation to
the functional requirements, for example, speed and size
limitations

Maintenance Information
Fundamental assumptions on which the system is based
Anticipated changes (changing hardware, changing user needs, etc.)

Glossary
Definitions of technical terms used in document

Index

**FIGURE 1-1** (*Continued*)

In a requirements document, information is best understood presented one
point at a time. Abandon narrative flow in favor of a clear list of separate, well-
defined items. An outline format is often the best option.

A requirements document is a statement of what the program will do, not
how. Although implementation is, to some extent, inseparable from functionality, keeping the two as distinct as possible in the early stages provides maximum flexibility. Assuming a particular implementation may unnecessarily limit
your design. Whether the code will be written by you or by someone else, allow
as much room for the programmer's creativity as possible. Where some specifics of implementation must be assumed, be sure to note that fact.

## The Conceptual Model

The conceptual model is the highest level abstraction of the system. Although
such a model can, in principle, be described in text or even in a formal, logical
notation, it is often easiest to describe and to understand when expressed graph-
ically. Simple labeled boxes connected by arrows often suffice to describe the
major components of the system and their relationships to each other and to the
user. A conceptual model of a simple address book application is shown in
Figure 1-2.

The conceptual model can be further refined to conceptual models for each
component, if necessary. For example, you could construct a second-level conceptual model for the "Display Names and Addresses" component of Figure
1-2. This model would include components for displaying the entire address
book, displaying a detail screen for a single name/address, and the like. In
general, the more complex the system, the more levels of conceptual modeling
you will find useful.

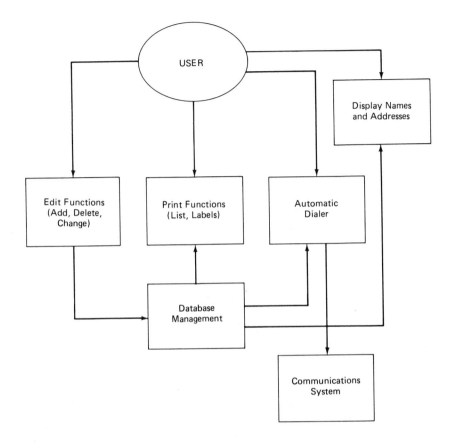

**FIGURE 1-2**

## Functional Requirements

The functional requirements section states each service provided to the user by the system. Optimally, this section should be complete—it should list all services provided to the user—and consistent—no one requirement should conflict with any other. In practice, both completeness and consistency at this early phase in software development are difficult to attain. They are, however, useful goals.

You can avoid many of the problems of writing specifications in natural language by avoiding free-form paragraphs. Instead, state each point separately. Organize requirements by functionality, perhaps using the individual components sketched out in the conceptual model as your major divisions. As in any part of a program specification, sacrifice narrative flow for clarity. Tedium and redundancy are preferable to ambiguity.

Figure 1-3 specifies the functional requirements for the "Edit Functions" component of the address book (modeled in Figure 1-2), in an outline format. You may notice that the functional requirements refer to the user "selecting" various options. The method by which the user selects these options must be documented, but for the sake of brevity, we will assume that it is documented earlier in the requirements document.

EDIT FUNCTIONS

The user selects any one of the following EDIT FUNCTIONS from the MAIN DISPLAY:
    ADD AN ENTRY
    DELETE AN ENTRY
    CHANGE AN ENTRY

I.   ADD AN ENTRY

The program displays a blank template, with instructions including (but not limited to) the following:
    Press ENTER when all the information is correct.
    Press ESC to cancel ADDing this entry.
    A. If the user presses ENTER:
        1. The template disappears
        2. The new information is added to the database
        3. The user is returned to the MAIN DISPLAY
        4. The new information is displayed on the MAIN DISPLAY
    B. If the user presses ESC:
        1. The template disappears
        2. The new information is NOT added to the database
        3. The user is returned to the MAIN DISPLAY

II.  DELETE AN ENTRY

The program will prompt the user to select an entry to DELETE.
    A. If the user selects an entry:
        1. The program displays a confirmation message, instructing the user to press ENTER to DELETE, or ESC to cancel.
        2. If the user presses ENTER:
            a. The confirmation message disappears
            b. The entry is removed from the database
            c. The user is returned to the MAIN DISPLAY
            d. The entry is removed from the MAIN DISPLAY
        3. If the user presses ESC:
            a. The entry is NOT removed from the database
            b. The user is returned to the MAIN DISPLAY

**FIGURE 1-3**

B. If the user presses ESC:
  1. The prompt disappears
  2. The user is returned to the MAIN DISPLAY

III. CHANGE AN ENTRY

The program prompts the user to select an entry to CHANGE.
  A. If the user selects an entry:
    1. The program displays the template containing that entry's information, with instructions for the user to change that information.
    2. If the user presses ENTER:
      a. The template disappears
      b. The changed information is added to the database
      c. The user is returned to the MAIN DISPLAY
      d. The changed information is displayed on the MAIN DISPLAY
    3. If the user presses ESC:
      a. The template disappears
      b. The changed information is NOT added to the database
      c. The user is returned to the MAIN DISPLAY
  B. If the user presses ESC:
    1. The prompt disappears
    2. The user is returned to the MAIN DISPLAY

**FIGURE 1-3** (Continued)

## Database Requirements

The requirements document should also describe the necessary database for the system. This description should encompass the required data items and their logical relationships. Tables are often useful for this section of the requirements document. You can construct one table for each related set of data items. Such a table is illustrated in Figure 1-4, which specifies the data for the address book application modeled in Figure 1-2.

| LName | FName | Street | City | State | Zip | Phone |
|-------|-------|--------|------|-------|-----|-------|
| Derman | Bonnie | 1 Elm | Boston | MA | 02115 | (617) 926-2625 |
| Farlow | Tim | 2 Main | Boston | MA | 02114 | (617) 549-4829 |
| Gregory | Keith | 10 Cross | Hartford | CT | 06604 | (203) 268-8243 |
| Gruneau | Justin | 5 Main | L.A. | CA | 90016 | (818) 238-4958 |
| Pendzick | Rick | 12 Birch | Austin | TX | 78766 | (512) 234-4593 |
| Shane | Art | 5 Stepney | Closter | NJ | 07092 | (201) 589-6843 |

**FIGURE 1-4** The data provided in a table like this one are samples, for the purpose of illustration.

## Nonfunctional Requirements

The nonfunctional requirements of a system are the restrictions or constraints on the program's performance. These include considerations of speed, memory, and operating systems, as well as more detailed considerations like available character sets and graphics capabilities.

Nonfunctional requirements tend to be particularly sensitive to hardware capabilities. If you are designing a long-term project, it is likely that hardware capabilities will expand by the time the project is completed. Nonfunctional requirements often anticipate greater hardware capabilities than are currently available. If you do anticipate, be careful to state explicitly the assumptions you are making about future capabilities.

Nonfunctional requirements often present trade-offs with functional requirements, most notably the execution speed versus storage space trade-off. These trade-offs should be clearly pointed out for consideration in the implementation stage, perhaps in the form of a matrix. Such a matrix lists program properties like run speed and maintainability on one axis, and requirements such as size limitations on the other. The cells of the matrix then contain comments detailing the relevant trade-offs and identifying the requirements and properties that conflict with each other.

## Requirements Validation

A truly useful requirements document should be validated by a potential user or by someone assuming the role of a potential user. Just as a beta version of a program should be tested and evaluated, a requirements document should be evaluated against true user needs. A completed requirements document should contain no internal contradictions, should describe all functionality that will be provided to the user, and should be as realistic about user needs and system capabilities as possible. Establishing the requirements document as a clear, complete, and realistic statement of what the program should do is likely to save significant amounts of program revision and maintenance.

## THE SOFTWARE SPECIFICATION

The next step in program design is the software specification, also known as the design specification. The software spec is written for the programmer. Its purpose is to present a preliminary view of the program's implementation.

The software spec is the first step in defining how the program will accomplish its purpose. For each service or group of services specified in the requirements document, the software spec introduces an abstract software component. In general, writing the software spec is the first step in creating program functions and modules. The software spec provides a finer breakdown of system behavior than the requirements document, specifying the actions taken by and the effects of individual program procedures.

## Formalism in Specifications

The software specification provides the guidelines from which the programmer writes code. It must therefore be as clear and unambiguous as possible in setting forth every criterion with which the program must comply. For very large systems, especially those for which the software specification is considered a contract, many software engineers find the use of a formal specification language necessary. Natural language is inherently ambiguous, and in attempting to remove ambiguity from software specs, designers have developed several formalisms. Generally, these are highly structured languages employing logical symbols, and resemble pseudocode. Formalism in specifications provides two basic advantages: The specifications can only be interpreted in one way, and definitions are likely to be more rigorous because of the impositions of the formal language. Incompleteness is easily hidden in natural language; within a formal structure, incompleteness is readily apparent. In cases where complete compliance with the specification is important, software can be tested against a formal spec.

While this level of formalism is beyond the needs of this discussion, we will introduce some general concepts in writing formal specifications. Considerations of formalism are presented to encourage you to think about clearly communicating the essential aspects of software design. Throughout this section on software specifications, examples will employ some degree of formalism. More rigorous formalisms have been developed, but we avoid them here because they are unnecessarily complex.

## Parts of a Software Specification

The software specification often consists of two distinct parts: the nonfunctional specification, which describes system constraints, and the functional specification, which describes the effects of each program module, and may describe the data types used. We will first discuss the nonfunctional portion of the software specification, then the functional portion. We will treat the description of data types as a separate topic, discussed in a third section.

## Nonfunctional Specification

The software spec often includes a specification of the nonfunctional aspects of the program: those constraints under which it must operate. The difference between the description of constraints in the software spec and the corresponding description in the requirements document is a difference in audience. The software spec is written for the programmer.

## Functional Specification

The functional description of the program is the major component of the software spec. The functional description identifies the effect of each module on its environment: its inputs, its outputs, and its effects on global information. In this context, "module" refers to any procedure isolated at this point in the system design. In the final product, modules are likely to be further divided, and some procedures identified as modules in the spec will become single functions within modules.

You can identify modules for the functional specification by breaking down your conceptual model. The level of detail you use is a matter of individual judgment, dependent upon the complexity of your application and the degree of specificity you feel you need. Once you refine your conceptual model to its final level of detail, consider each bottom-level "box" a module.

A module's functional specification often provides some guidance on implementation, in the extreme case consisting of pseudocode for the procedure. At the other extreme, a functional spec can treat the procedure as a black box, describing only its external effects.

The functional specification also includes data abstractions, where necessary. Data abstractions define the data types used in a program by defining the operations that can be performed on that type, and the behavior of those operations. While you can create data abstractions for any data type, we consider such a degree of formalism beyond our requirements. Data abstractions are useful in describing new data types that your program will define, however.

**Procedural Abstraction.** The functional specification for each procedure, often called a procedural abstraction, at the very least identifies the procedure's inputs, outputs, and effects. At its most concrete, a procedural abstraction may consist of actual pseudocode for the procedure described.

*I/O Specification.* The black box perspective, whereby a procedure is described only in terms of its inputs, outputs, and effects, is generally known as an I/O specification. The I/O spec states that given the input constraints, the output will conform to the output constraints. An I/O spec for a function to return the factorial of its input is presented in Figure 1-5.

FACT(X : integer) $->$ integer
    input $0 < X < 8$
    output FACT $= X!$

**FIGURE 1-5**

The I/O spec in Figure 1-5 describes the effect that this procedure will have on its environment. The first line establishes the name of the procedure (FACT), the type of input (integer), and the type of output (integer). The second line states the input constraint: The input must be greater than 0 and less than 8 (8! is greater than the maximum integer on many machines). The third line states the output constraint: The output will be the factorial of the input. Notice that all details of how the factorial is to be computed are left out.

This I/O spec fully defines the effects of the procedure, if it is provided with valid input. The spec is not complete, however, since it does not define the effect of the procedure given invalid input. Any procedural abstraction should define the effects of the procedure for every possible class of invalid input. The modified I/O spec for this procedure, describing the error case, is shown in Figure 1-6.

```
FACT(X : integer)  − > integer
        N-state
            input 0 < X < 8
            output FACT = X!
        E-state
            input X < = 0 or X > = 8
            output ERROR CODE
```

**FIGURE 1-6**

The I/O spec in Figure 1-6 is complete. The first line is identical to that of Figure 1-5. The second line specifies that the following description is for a normal state, that is, valid input. The third and fourth lines are taken directly from the spec in Figure 1-5. The fifth line signifies an error state, that is, invalid input. In this case, only one E-state is described, since only one error class is possible. (We assume that the input is of the proper data type.) In the event that the input does not conform to the input constraint ($>0$ and $<8$), an ERROR CODE is returned.

For complex procedures with many classes of possible inputs and outputs, an I/O spec can become as large and complex as the actual code. I/O specifications are generally useful for simple procedures. For more complicated modules, an operational specification is often easier to write and to understand.

*Operational Specification.*   I/O specs present the most abstract view of a procedure. At the other extreme, a procedural abstraction may consist of pseudocode to perform that procedure. This near-implementation is known as an operational specification. It differs from actual code in that it is designed for clarity as opposed to efficiency. To some degree, it defines implementation, although it is usually much less concrete than actual code. An operational spec for the factorial function specified in Figures 1-5 and 1-6 is shown in Figure 1-7.

```
FACT(X : integer) - > integer
if X < = 0 return ERROR CODE
if X > = 8 return ERROR CODE
if X < = 2 return X
return (X * FACT(X-1))
```

**FIGURE 1-7**

Figure 1-7 illustrates the use of references to procedures within a procedural abstraction. In this case, the reference is a recursive one, but a procedural abstraction can also reference a different function. Any referenced function, of course, must have its own procedural spec. The use of references makes procedural abstractions more concise, and easier both to write and to understand.

The operational spec in Figure 1-7 implies a particular implementation. An iterative implementation could also be used, the operational spec for which is shown in Figure 1-8.

```
FACT(X : integer) - > integer
if X < = 0 return ERROR CODE
if X > = 8 return ERROR CODE
let FACT = 1
for all i, 2 < = i < = X do
     FACT = FACT * i
```

**FIGURE 1-8**

The operational specs shown in Figures 1-7 and 1-8 are practically valid code, and each restricts the programmer to a particular implementation. For this procedure, the I/O spec is both sufficient and preferable: It provides all the necessary information, does so with a minimum of complexity, and does not unnecessarily constrain the programmer. For more complex procedures, however, the I/O spec is often cumbersome, and an operational spec can define the procedure more clearly.

*A Mixture of Methods.*   For most real world applications, you will find I/O specs preferable in some places, operational specs in others, and natural language descriptions best in still other places. Mixing these methods is a perfectly valid way to construct a program specification, and is often the best way to construct that specification. As we stated at the outset, the primary goal of a program spec is clarity. The method that presents the clearest picture of any part of the program is the correct method for specifying that part of the program.

*Data Abstraction.*   For new data types that your program will define, you may find it useful to include a data abstraction in your software spec. A data abstraction defines a data type by the scope and behavior of the operations performed on it. It thus avoids restricting the programmer in his or her implementation of the data type, but completely describes the necessary characteristics of that data type. A data abstraction for a queue of integers is presented in Figure 1-9.*

```
queue of I
        Interface
                create  - > queue of I
                put (queue of I, I)  - > queue of I
                get (queue of I)  - > I
                is_empty (queue of I)  - > boolean
                remove (queue of I)  - > queue of I
        Axioms
                1. is_empty (create) = true
                2. is_empty (put(q,v)) = false
                3. get (create) = ERROR
                4. get (put(q,x)) = if is_empty (q) then x else get (q)
                5. remove (create) = ERROR
                6. remove (put(q,x)) = if is_empty (q) then create else put
                                       (remove(q), x)
```

**FIGURE 1-9**

In Figure 1-9, the Interface section lists each function, along with its input(s) and output. The Axioms section defines the behavior of each function.

Axioms 1 and 2 define the is_empty operation. Axiom 1 states that a newly created queue is always empty, and Axiom 2 states that a queue created by a put operation is not empty.

Axiom 3 states that it is an error to attempt to get an item from an empty queue.

Axiom 4 recursively states that the get function returns the last item put on the queue.

Axioms 5 and 6 define the remove operation, which yields the input queue with the first item removed. (The remove function is the "remainder" of the get function.) Axiom 5 states that removal from an empty queue is an error. Axiom 6 is similar to Axiom 4, recursively stating that the last item put on the queue is the one removed.

The specification in Figure 1-9 completely and unambiguously states what a queue is and how it should behave, without any mention of how a queue is to be implemented.

---

*I. Sommerville, *Software Engineering,* 2nd Ed., Addison-Wesley, Boston, 1985.

## CONCLUSION

Program specification is the first, and often most neglected, phase of software design. This chapter has presented some justification and suggestions for writing a program spec.

In all but the most trivial cases, careful planning reduces costly and frustrating errors, revisions, and maintenance. The program specification is a systematic method for planning and communicating the goals and methods of an application.

Careful thought about the functions and limitations of the program are necessary to create the specification. This thought process alone can reduce errors and revisions. Well written, the specification clearly describes what the program should be, providing reference for the designer, the programmer, the maintainer, and the potential user.

The program spec is divided into two major components: the requirements document and the software specification. The requirements document is intended for the user, and describes what the program will do. It makes as little mention as possible of internal implementation, specifying only what the user will see. The software specification, on the other hand, is intended for the programmer. It describes constraints on the software, and associates some measure of design with each component of the system. The functional part of the software spec describes, at least, the input, output, and global effects of each procedure; at its most detailed, it describes the method for implementing that procedure.

Program specifications can be written on any level of detail, with any level of formalism. The choice of how much formalism and detail are necessary depends on the nature of the application and the communications requirements of those involved in creating the application.

# 2

# Designing the User Interface

*Contributor:* Michael St. Hippolyte of Xor Corporation
*Reviewer:* Francis Fedele of Essential Software, Inc.


## INTRODUCTION

Software development is an art based on a science. The science consists of an understanding of the control structures and data structures, simple and complex, which arise out of the way computers work. But this science does not yet (and perhaps never will) extend to the point that any but the most simple of programming tasks has a readily visible optimal solution. Wherein comes the art.

No aspect of programming is more of an art than the design of the user interface. The object of all software is manipulation of data or devices, but the object of a user interface is interaction with a particularly unique and unpredictable device: a person. The data manipulation that occurs in a user interface is seldom more involved than capturing keystrokes and displaying strings on the screen. The hard part is not the writing of such routines, but determining how to use them: deciding which keystrokes to capture, what strings to put on the screen, and when to put them there.

The implementation of these routines, then, is not the subject of this chapter. Implementation, specifically in terms of commercial tools, will be treated in Chapter 9, Receiving User Input. This chapter is a qualitative discussion of the difficult aspect of the user interface: its design.

Not surprisingly, one finds that the usual methods and tools of software design are no longer sufficient when it comes to designing a user interface. Structured programming says nothing of what happens outside of the computer. A program is assumed to have the proper input, and the job is considered done once the proper output is generated. But any program is just one part of a larger system: The input to the program must come from somewhere and the output must go somewhere. Getting the input and providing the output are precisely the functions of a user interface.

There exists, at present, no widely accepted procedure specifically for creating user interfaces, no hard and fast rules guaranteed to work for every program. Rather, knowledge and experience in this field take the form of a body of technique. As with any technique, there is little that can be usefully expressed as rigid rules. It is possible, however, to seek something that in any case must always precede technique: an understanding of the medium. A deeper understanding of what a user interface is will lead to better design (and implementation). Such an understanding is the goal of this chapter.

## WHAT IS A USER INTERFACE?

"User interface" refers not to a part of a program, but to a view of a program, namely the view of a human user. Most programs do have specific routines that are directly responsible for processing input and output, but it is generally misleading to consider these routines as comprising the user interface. The user interface derives from the overall organization of the program as well as the specific input and output routines. A simple example may illustrate this point.

Consider a hypothetical data retrieval program called DELPHI. DELPHI accepts questions from the user, analyzes and assembles a response screen, and then displays the response screen. Only three details of the program's operation are necessary for our discussion:

1. Sometimes the process of assembling the data requires a noticeable amount of time.
2. Keyboard input is received by the operating system, loaded into a buffer, and passed to the program as requested.
3. The user exits the program by hitting the escape key.

We examine two variations on the logical structure of DELPHI. In the first variation (see Figure 2-1), a top-level loop contains calls to four routines:

1. **get_input()**, which removes the next key from the buffer and returns its value;
2. **esc_key()**, which searches the keyboard buffer for an escape key and returns a true value if one is found, regardless of any other unprocessed keys ahead of it;
3. **process_data()**, which analyzes the question, generates the response, and returns some nonzero answer code;
4. **put_screen()**, which generates a screen on the basis of this answer code and displays any error or other special messages called for.

```
main()
{
    int key,check,code;

    initialize();
    while (1)
    {
        key = get_input();
        check = esc_key();
        if (check)
        {
            break;
        }
        code = process_data(key);
        put_screen(code);
    }
    exit();
}
```

**FIGURE 2-1** DELPHI (first version)

With the call to **esc_key()**, the program checks the buffer for a possible escape key before processing the key retrieved by **get_input()**. This way, the user does not have to wait for all keys ahead of an escape key to be processed before the program can exit. The user may have to wait, however, for the complete processing of up to one keystroke, if the escape key is pressed in between the call to **esc_key()** and the call to **process_data()**.

In the second variation, we have changed the function **process_data()** as well as the top-level structure of DELPHI (see Figure 2-2).

The function **process_data()** now breaks longer tasks into parts. A defined constant (not shown) sets a maximum level of processing allowed at one time. When called with a key value that requires more than this defined amount of processing, **process_data()** performs only part of the task, and returns a zero value. The next time the function is called, it ignores any passed argument and continues with the unfinished task. Unless it completes the processing, on the next call it again returns false, proceeding in this fashion as long as necessary. The structure of the top-level loop of the program has been modified to accommodate the new **process_data()** by the insertion of a new loop. This new loop contains the call to **process_data()** and breaks only when **process_data()** returns a nonzero value.

Notice an interesting feature of the new structure: The call to **esc_key()** has been moved, along with **process_data()**, into the inner loop. The maximum wait for the program to respond to the escape key is thus limited to the defined amount of processing that **process_data()** performs per call.

```
main()
{
    int key,check,code;

    initialize();
    while (1)
    {
        key = get_input();
        while (1)
        {
            check = esc_key();
            if (check) break;
            code = process_data(key);
            if (code) break;
        }
        if (check) break;
        put_screen(code);
    }
    exit();
}
```

**FIGURE 2-2** DELPHI (second version)

The functions that interact in any way with the user (**get_input()**, **esc_key()**, and **put_screen()**) are identical in the two versions of the program. But to the user, the two versions and indeed their user interfaces appear to be different. The second version is more responsive, so the user is likely to find it more "friendly." Yet the differences are purely in overall structure and in a routine (**process_data()**) with no user interaction.

The above example demonstrates that the user interface depends on many aspects of a program. For this reason, the designer cannot help but consider it from the very start. But to do so systematically requires a conceptual foundation, a way to think about a user interface not as a refinement of a program's structure but as its premise. With the proper conceptual tools, a designer may visualize the user interface and even its inner workings at a very early stage in the project. Without such a clear visualization, the design process is liable to run into serious obstacles.

## PRINCIPLES OF USER INTERACTION

It is possible to state certain principles that describe, in general terms, the nature of the interaction between computer programs and users. These principles point to useful considerations for user interface design.

1. A program is a part of a larger system.
2. Virtually all user input to a program is initiated by output from that program.
3. The interactions of a program fall into two groups: those that concern the state of the program, and those that represent some portion of the data.

The first principle states the obvious, perhaps, but the implications are nevertheless often ignored. The standard methods of software design work in an inward direction: Various parts of the program are isolated early, and details within them resolved as much as possible independently of the other parts. The programmer progresses toward greater and greater detail. But a program cannot dependably be isolated in this fashion from the system of which it is a part: the user and his or her working environment. The structure of the larger system is not determined by the programmer, nor can this structure ever be known in all its detail. Changes in the larger system, both during the development process and after, are outside of the power of either the program or the programmer to contain. It is therefore dangerous to attempt to define the larger system. Yet it is impossible to avoid doing so, implicitly if not explicitly.

In practice, the designer must strike a balance. The program must be flexible enough to handle some of the variability of the larger system, but it must forego some flexibility in order to operate in a well-defined manner.

The system that exists logically above the program consists of the program plus the user. While you can specify very little about the user, you can influence the user's behavior via the program's behavior. In fact, this influence is essential: The user cannot be expected to behave in the ''proper'' way (i.e., know exactly how to run the program) without the influence of the program.

This relationship is summarized in the second principle: The output from the program (input to the user) initiates the input to the program (output from the user). On a trivial level, any user input can be said to be caused by the prompt from the program that precedes it. More meaningfully, this principle holds because the user gains knowledge from the output of the program and uses this knowledge in making decisions, including the decision as to what input should be entered next.

The implication of the first two principles taken together is that the control structures we see in our program truly extend beyond the program into the user's world. Therefore a proper analysis of the logic of a program requires knowledge of the logic external to the program: the logic of the user. Otherwise, we are looking at just one routine of the system.

In practical terms, know your audience. Anticipate the user's needs to the best of your knowledge. Having done that, then give the user as much flexibility to differ from your anticipations as possible.

To demonstrate the significance of this perspective, we have changed our data retrieval program DELPHI once more (see Figure 2-3).

```
main()
{
    int key,check,code;

    initialize();
    while (1)
    {
        key = get_input();
        check = esc_key();
        if (check)
        {
            break;
        }
        while (1)
        {
            code = process_data(key);
            if (code)
            {
                break;
            }
            check = esc_key();
            if (check)
            {
                break;
            }
        }
        if (check)
        {
            reset();
        }
        put_screen(code);
    }
    exit();
}
```

**FIGURE 2-3** DELPHI (third version)

The first modification is a new call to **esc_key()** in the outer loop, right after the call to **get_input()**. Thus the program checks for an escape key before it enters the inner loop, and breaks to exit the program if it finds one. Inside the inner loop, we switched the order of the call to **esc_key()** and the call to **process_data()**, so that the latter is now called first. (This is why we now need an escape key check before the inner loop. Otherwise, the program might call **process_data()** with an escape key in the buffer.) Logically, so far, this version is equivalent to the previous one.

Notice, however, that immediately after the inner loop we have replaced a **break** statement with a call to a new function: **reset()**. In the previous version of DELPHI, the outer loop break covered the inner loop break in response to an escape key. Now, an escape key detected in the inner loop will not exit the program. The new function, **reset()**, contains logic to drop any question still being processed and prepare for a new question. A final change is in the routine **put_screen()**, enabling it to process a passed output code of zero, which previously could not happen. The function **put_screen()** handles a zero code by simply resetting the screen.

The net effect of the changes we have made is to alter the way the escape key works. In our new version of DELPHI, the escape key has two functions, depending on whether it is pressed while a question is being processed (the inner loop) or while DELPHI is waiting for a new question (the outer loop). Only in the latter instance does the escape key cause the program to exit. If DELPHI is in the middle of working on a question, the escape key merely interrupts it and causes it to go on to the next question.

Is the new version of DELPHI an improvement over the previous version? One drawback is that the user must work harder (i.e., press the escape key twice) to exit the program in certain cases. But in terms of "external logic" as discussed above, we see clear evidence of improvement. The DELPHI-user system operates as a loop: The user asks a question, DELPHI processes the question and presents an answer. With our latest enhancement, we have expanded the external logic. Now our external loop has two paths: the original one, ask-answer, and a new one, ask-ask. The decision of which path to follow is up to the user. If the new path is of any value to the user, it easily outweighs the extra key sometimes required for exiting.

In other words, the program, as a result of our change, handles a potential user goal that was not accommodated before. Our cycle of interaction is broader.

This brings us to the third and final principle, which sets forth a primary functional distinction among the interactions of a program: Interactions concern either the program state or streams of data. Stated in a slightly different way, a user of a program perceives the program as doing two things:

1. It operates in some way on a stream of data which is independent of the program.
2. It displays the program status and mode, which are internal to the program but change in predefined ways according to user actions and other outside events.

We will explore the meaning of this for user interface design shortly. First, though, we turn to examine something we have referred to repeatedly: the perception of the user.

## PERCEPTION AS REALITY

It is no surprise that the principles that underlie the user interface appear more clearly when viewed from the perspective of the user. It is this perspective that defines the user interface. The user interface is a perception. If a programmer scrambles the functions that drive the user interface, but the program looks just the same to the user, then the user interface has not changed. Conversely, a minor program change that leads to a significant difference in the way the program looks to the user is a major change in the user interface.

This is the source of many problems when user interface design is treated as simply another aspect of program design. In many cases a programmer must make major changes in a program just to correct a seemingly small problem in the user interface. To go back to an earlier example, consider the changes we first made in the program DELPHI to make it more responsive. Remember that we had to modify the function **process_data()** to break up its processing activities into parts. In practice this could well have been a very difficult program modification.

There is another important implication of the perception-as-reality nature of the user interface: Much is perceived which is not explicit. Human perceptions are the product not just of sensory input but of a high degree of internal processing. Sensory input is filtered, processed, and reinforced in such a way as to support a certain coherent world view. Many cultural and psychological factors are included in the processing, and much of what is perceived is not really "there."

This principle works at many levels in a user interface. At the lowest level, the various symbols and colors employed for user input and output are full of cultural and psychological content, which can support or contradict their meaning in the program. At intermediate levels, a user interface designer must take into account the numerous conventions of human communication, such as the way time, dates, dollar amounts, and other kinds of data are expressed, the semantics of messages, the aesthetics of screen composition, and the meaning of various directions, orientations, and forms.

Most of us are easily made aware of these considerations, and do not find it difficult to incorporate them properly in a design. In some cases, the way in which we incorporate them is just a matter of personal style. It is at the highest level that the nature of perception holds both the most promise and the most difficulty for user interface design. At the highest level, a user personifies the program: He perceives it to be an agent of some degree of intelligence, with a purposeful behavior.

This perception contrasts sharply, of course, with the reality. Any intelligence and coherence in a program must result from very complex and careful design, and as of yet purposeful behavior can only be simulated. This is undoubtedly the cause of much of the frustration reported by users. Where a programmer sees a certain amount of intelligence, a user may see a complementary lack of intelligence.

Yet the user's expectations may be turned into a positive force, as well. Since we, the programmers, are people too, we can understand these expectations and use them very effectively in the design process. We can design the personality of a program, before we even think about its structure. Even if we cannot endow a program with a true personality, we can take advantage of the user's expectations and simulate one.

Simulating a personality is not necessarily a difficult programming task, but it is, invariably, a difficult creative task. It takes a good set of display and keyboard routines, a willingness to experiment, and, above all else, the ability to assume the user's perspective.

The user of a program naturally endows the program with certain values. To simulate a personality, the designer's major task is to prevent the program from showing that it lacks these values. Examples of such values are consistency, sincerity, and a sense of proportion.

Consistency means that a program does not contradict itself or confuse the user—in similar situations the program behaves in similar ways. Sincerity means more than not stating untruths (which presumably would be a logical error in the program as well as a shortcoming in the user interface design). It means truly pursuing the goal of service to the user. A sense of proportion means always reacting at an appropriate level, neither over-emphasizing minor activities or situations nor under-emphasizing major ones. A program that manages to conserve these values will be seen to be well intentioned and relatively intelligent, even if it cannot do everything that the user would like.

These are not guidelines for user interface design as much as they are the general goals of such guidelines. To derive guidelines for design, we must investigate a bit further the principles of user interaction.

## MANIPULATING DATA: THE WINDOW

The user, states our third principle, sees a program as doing two things:

1. Operating on data
2. Communicating the status and modes of the program.

Regardless of the organization of the program, this division dominates the design of the user interface. Let us examine why.

A user always has a reason for running a program. Some specific goal is to be achieved: numerical computation, the retrieval of data, the generation of data, or even entertainment. The program exists simply as the means for achieving this goal. Ideally, the program would not require any input from the user to accomplish the goal. But in all except the most trivial of applications, this is impossible. In general, a user must prepare a program for a task, give it frequent instructions, and monitor it as it functions. The user must, in short, communicate with the program.

At various points, when the proper communication has occurred and everything is in order, the program actually accomplishes some part of the task requested by the user. If the user's involvement in accomplishing the task is sufficiently direct and immediate, then the user will perceive that he or she is directly manipulating the data rather than communicating with the program.

Thus, a user perceives him or herself as engaging in two activities:

1. Communicating with the program
2. Manipulating data.

These activities correspond directly with the user's perception of the program's activities, which are:

1. Reporting its state (i.e., communicating with the user)
2. Processing data.

The design of the user interface determines, ultimately, which functions of the program are associated with which activity. Interactions that are transparent to the user will be seen as part of his or her manipulation of the data; interactions that are not transparent will be seen as part of the communication between program and user.

Consider a process that occurs in some form in nearly every program: echoing characters to the screen in response to keystrokes. A user inevitably perceives this as direct data manipulation. In truth, the program is intervening with processing like searching for special keys, advancing the cursor, performing word wrap, and so on. The characters on the screen are not the data being manipulated at all; they are simply a display for the benefit of the user. The data themselves are somewhere in memory or on disk.

But for the user, the characters on the screen really are the data being manipulated. The way a program chooses to display them will determine the user's view of the data. The more something on the display screen appears to be data, the less it appears to be the program. This illusion is reinforced to the extent that the boundaries between data and program are clear. If the boundaries of a section of the screen are clear and the contents of that section coherent, then the program has succeeded in creating what is generally referred to as a "window."

A window, by our definition, is a space generated by the program which is perceived to contain something other than the program (i.e., data). It need not be the well-known box on the screen; it can be any shape, or it can be the entire screen, as long as the presence of the program within it is hidden from the user.

The power of windows derives from this illusion of transparency. As we observed above, interactions between the program and the user which are transparent to the user will be experienced as a direct manipulation of data. Thus, the more powerful such transparent interactions are, the more power the user will experience.

A user interface designer can utilize the transparency of windows to cover many data manipulation functions, and in this way extend the illusion of transparency. As an illustration, consider the difference between line editors and full-screen editors, from a user's perspective. With a line editor, the user must edit a file line by line. With a full-screen editor, the user can edit a full screen of data at one time. To the user, the full-screen editor is vastly more powerful.

Yet the functions a user can perform with these two programs are not necessarily different. Any data operation that can be accomplished by a full-screen editor could be accomplished as well by a sufficiently powerful line editor. Despite what the user sees, the amount of data a program can manipulate at one time, the kinds of operations it can perform, and the speed at which it can perform them are functions of the hardware and of the algorithms used for processing.

This contradiction between the user's perception of the power of a program and the real limits of that power is not really a paradox, if viewed in the light of the principles of user interaction. Software cannot ultimately increase a computer's computational power, speed, or storage capacity. But software can increase, through a well-designed user interface, the performance of the computer-plus-user system. In our example, the full-screen editor enhances the performance of the computer-plus-user system by making more operations transparent, that is, making the user feel more powerful. To edit a particular line in a file using a line editor, the user must specify the line by entering an appropriate instruction, that is, by communicating with the program. With a full-screen editor, the user must also specify the line to be edited, but can do so by "directly" moving a cursor to the line. While pressing a key to move a cursor involves no less communication with the program than typing a line number, the illusion of direct control is complete.

This illusion of direct control need not be limited to moving a cursor. There are many other program functions that can similarly be "given" to the user by making the role of the program transparent. The way it is done is no mystery, and follows naturally from the concepts we have discussed. The first point to realize is that the representation of a function is different from the function itself, just like the characters on a screen are different from the data being processed in memory. It is the representation of a function, and not the function itself, which allows or prevents transparency. Avoiding any representation (making a function not transparent but invisible) is not usually a solution, since any user has to know what his or her program is doing.

Once we have focused on the representation of a function, we can list some properties of such representations that reinforce their transparency:

1. Continuity. The more a function appears to be continuous, the stronger the illusion of transparency. The world of human perception is continuous, and our visual processing often interpolates discrete perceptions into a continuous image, as film and television strikingly prove. A window works by providing a continuous space for data to reside in. A function can be made to appear to operate on a continuous space, and in the process be made transparent. Motion, in particular, is a naturally continuous activity, and if a function (such as specifying a line for editing) is represented by motion (such as the movement of a cursor), its transparency is reinforced considerably. The motion can be of an object (as in moving a cursor or some data) or of a space (as in scrolling a window) or of the boundaries of a space (as in moving a window).

2. Feedback. If every time a user presses a certain button he or she hears a beep, that user will naturally assume that pressing the button causes the beep. Since the user decides when to press the button, he or she is in control of the beep. This simple dynamic can be used to reinforce the transparency of many functions. The feedback may or may not be part of the ''actual'' representation of the function (i.e., what the user thinks is the function). In the case of moving a cursor, the visible motion of the cursor itself provides the necessary feedback. This feedback is part of the representation. In other cases, a sound or other signal accompanying the representation can be just as effective. The substance of the feedback (a sound, a motion, a flashing light) is less important than its relationship to the user. If the causal connection between the input and the feedback is naturally perceived, then the user may in fact feel in control.

3. Timing. The speed at which a function appears to operate can either strengthen or weaken the transparency of that function, depending on how it corresponds to the user's expectations. Timing plays a crucial role in the effectiveness of both feedback and motion, for example. Feedback that is too slow may not be perceived as feedback. Motion that is too fast may cease to appear continuous. The speed of the function itself is not at issue; merely the speed and rhythm of its representation.

4. Graphics. A picture is worth a thousand words simply because words, though we may be quite accustomed to them, are very difficult to process. For a word, visual recognition is just the beginning; this must be followed by complex, context-sensitive, and very likely ambiguous semantic processing, as any programmer involved in a natural language project would

readily attest. Graphic images in many cases can provide the same information more immediately and therefore more transparently. (Graphics in this sense includes changing the color or intensity of text as well as pictorial graphics.) A cursor, for instance, is nothing but a graphic image; so is depicting a section of data in reverse video to indicate that it has been "selected."

None of the above properties by itself is either necessary or sufficient to make a function transparent. Their effectiveness depends on their application to an appropriate function and in an appropriate combination. Moreover, they require the proper object for their operation: a transparent data space perceived to contain the actual data being manipulated, that is, a window.

## COMMUNICATING WITH THE PROGRAM:
## THE CONTROL PANEL

Windows are an avenue for one kind of interaction—the processing of data—but as our third principle states, another kind of interaction exists. A program must have predefined instructions for the user. These instructions are nontransparent interactions: communication between the user and the program concerning the status and modes of the program. Fortunately, this requirement is not a drawback.

The nontransparent interactions of a program are inherently stable and predictable, since they follow from the predefined aspect of a program. This stability is complemented by malleability: They can be crafted by the designer into virtually any shape. These interactions are malleable for the very reason that they are nontransparent: Since they need not be made to appear to be data or anything else in particular, they can be made to appear to be almost anything.

Because they are nontransparent, these interactions have forms that are readily perceived by the user, which leads to many possibilities both in terms of aesthetics and performance. Complex interactions, through intelligent design, can be made simple and therefore easier for the user. A program can even be made enjoyable to operate—which for most users also translates into easy to use.

The above potential of nontransparent interactions can be clearly seen in one of the most common forms of such interactions: the menu. The idea of any menu is to present a user with a number of options, and allow one to be selected. The way the options are listed (horizontally, vertically, in text, with icons, etc.) as well as the way an option is selected (number key, cursor keys, mouse, etc.) vary enormously. A good program will generally use one form throughout, but occasionally it is helpful to distinguish groups of functions by giving them special menus.

There should be a very close correspondence between the nontransparent interactions of a program and the program's instruction manual. The instruction manual, ideally, explains completely the options available to the user in the operation of the program and describes exactly the means for communicating the choice of options to the program. Probably most of this communication must be nontransparent, especially if the program is at all complex, since the more things a program can do, the more nontransparent communication is required.

Thus it is not surprising that many of the same criteria apply to both the writing of an instruction manual and the design of the nontransparent part of a user interface. Clarity, for both, is the greatest virtue. The goal is to make the necessary communication between user and computer as simple in form and clear in effect as possible. The generally unattainable ideal is a user interface that makes obvious the method for accomplishing anything the program is capable of doing.

Approaching such a goal requires more from a user interface than clarity of design. It also requires unity and balance. Unity means that the user can follow a common logic and form in communicating various choices to the program and in interpreting various types of status information from the program. The effort spent learning how to communicate one choice or interpret one state will not have to be repeated for the next. Balance means negotiating the trade-off between the complexity of choices the user faces at any one moment and the immediate availability of as many options as possible.

These considerations are very general, and do not provide us with concrete guidelines for specific situations. Such guidelines are difficult to set forth, for the reason that designs in this area come in an abundance of forms and continue to evolve rapidly. Nevertheless, we will present a model for the nontransparent aspect of user interface design.

A control panel, like a window, is an archetypal image. Any culture that knows machines knows control panels. A control panel is the avenue through which a user communicates with a machine. Complex machines have complex control panels. A complex control panel is either intimidating (as on most electronic equipment) or alluring (as in a Cadillac). On a computer, the choice belongs to the software designer, because a computer is a different machine every time it runs a different program.

The significance of the concept of a control panel, like that of a window, rests not in the details of its implementation, which can take many forms, but in the perception it creates. As the illusion of windows is transparency, the illusion of control panels is simplicity. The power of this illusion is that it allows a program to accomplish more without necessarily becoming more complicated to use.

A good control panel will be organized in a way that reflects the functioning of the machine it controls. If the machine is complex and has many major functions, each one might be represented by a different part of the control panel, each one containing functionally specific controls and indicators. On the other hand, if the functions are exclusive in operation but similar in form, the machine would best be served by a single set of switches and indicators that can be used in turn for every function.

Many control panels hide various switches and indicators. Switches that are used very rarely (like horizontal hold on a television) are often relegated to the back of the machine or behind a hinged panel. Status indicators, likewise, are often designed to be invisible when not in operation, like the idiot lights in a car. This is generally not just for aesthetic reasons. The less a user is confronted with, the clearer will be that which is presented. Minimalism is the optimal design philosophy for control panels.

A software designer has in general a more complex task but a greater scope of possibilities than the designer of a conventional control panel. The substance of the task is nevertheless the same. What might seem to be aesthetic considerations, such as the layout of a menu or the way error messages are displayed, are in fact of the utmost practical importance. The user will naturally assume that the way he or she communicates with the program—the design of its control panel—reflects the capabilities and the limitations of the program. If user-computer communication can be simplified without reducing the capabilities of the program, the program itself may not become more powerful, but the user-plus-program system certainly will.

The relevance of the idea of a control panel to user interface design is both literal and conceptual. On a literal level, a program's user interface can benefit from mimicking the indicator lights, switches, wording of messages, and even gauges of a well-designed control panel. (Gauges are not yet popular in software, but the ease with which the linear LED gauge common on stereo systems, for instance, can be simulated in software means that gauges probably have a place in programs to come. Indicating the extent of memory used by a program at any point is just one possible function for a software gauge.)

On a conceptual level, the model of a control panel helps the designer by emphasizing the more-than-just-aesthetic questions of layout and form. Since the control panel of a program should reflect accurately its functioning, it is wholly appropriate to design the control panel before the program—as soon as the functional specifications have been determined, for example. One effective method of avoiding some costly design changes later in a development effort is to implement a dummy control panel for a program as a first step in the project. Such a prototype serves two equally important functions: it helps designers discover potential deficiencies of a program long before the program is ready for testing, and it also clarifies the most useful hierarchy and interrelations of functions, thereby suggesting the most appropriate logical structure for the program.

## CONCLUSION

This chapter has studied the problem of designing a user interface, starting with a theoretical understanding of user interaction in software and then examining the practical implications of the theory.

We began by looking carefully at the nature of a user interface. We observed that a user interface is a perception. We also laid out a set of principles which underlie the user interaction of a program. On the basis of these principles, we analyzed various aspects and requirements of user interface design, and thereby arrived at practical concepts and considerations: the window and the control panel. We used these concepts to generate specific guidelines and models for successful user interface design.

One general conclusion that arose from our investigation is the importance of tackling user interface design early in a software development project, in some cases even before the task of the logical design of the program.

The justification for the path we have followed in this chapter lies in the gap we see today in user interface design between potential and reality. Too often, the approach of a designer consists of the application of various techniques without a deep understanding of the medium. The techniques themselves are well known. Relating these techniques to a theory, we hope, will lead to the innovation of new techniques and the better application of existing ones.

# 3
# Style

*Contributors:* Kenneth Pugh of Pugh-Killeen Associates
Robert H. Jones IV of Amber Systems, Inc.
*Reviewer:* James F. Gimpel, Ph.D. of Gimpel Software

## INTRODUCTION

Because of its flexibility, C allows the programmer to write unreadable code. Clarity and simplicity of coding style are of paramount importance, however. In any substantial application, source code must be read after it is written, to accommodate changes in functionality, debugging, maintenance, and the like. Aesthetically clear code is inherently easier to read. Discipline to a particular style of coding will make programs both more readable and more maintainable.

We can view coding style on three levels: visual aesthetics, clarity, and design. The visual level of style, while superficial, is the first that any reader will notice. Code that is neatly laid out, makes good use of white space, and uses a consistent comment format is easily read because it is aesthetically pleasing. Clarity in style involves the use of simple, easily understood expressions rather than compact and obtuse ones. If the reader can not look at a line of code and understand what it does, it lacks clarity. Style of design involves a broader picture: appropriate algorithms representing the programmer's clear understanding of the task at hand. Such clear algorithms make the programming task look simple to the reader, and hence make the code easier to modify and maintain.

Following are some specific suggestions for maintaining good style on all three levels.

## NAMES
### Conventions

Adopt a consistent set of naming conventions for the various types in C. A typical set of conventions, representing just one possibility in naming conventions, is presented in Table 3-1. Whatever your rules, carefully comment any deviations you may need to make from them.

### Table 3-1

Function names: always in lower case, and never more than 8 characters
Variable names: always in lower case
      External (global) variables: always begin with a particular letter
                (such as ''x'')
**#defines:** always in upper case, except where the define is used to replace
      a function call
Structure and union types: always begin with a particular letter (such as
              ''s'' or ''u'')

## Name Length

Although most compilers only recognize the first eight characters of a variable or function name, most will also allow you to write longer names. Longer names often make code more readable, and are thus quite useful. Be sure, however, that the first eight characters of any name are unique.

## Reusing Variable Names

Although you can reuse a variable name at any point after the next opening brace, try not to take advantage of this opportunity. Recycling variables is very confusing to anyone reading the code. If, for example, the statement **i=0;** appears in one portion of the code, a reader might assume that the statement **if (i==0)** is true. If **i** is re-declared in the intervening lines, however, this assumption would be false.

## Using the Static Storage Class

Within modules, declare as **static** all function names and external variables used by the functions within the module. This practice prevents conflict of local names between modules and also reduces linking time.

## INDENTATION AND BRACES

Several different styles of brace placement and indentation are shown in Table 3-2. All are acceptable, as are other styles not presented here. More important than which style you choose is that you use one style consistently. Although omitting the braces in a one-statement **while** or **for** loop is permissible, using braces creates a consistent format. Braces also allow you to insert debug statements easily.

**Table 3-2**

Kernighan and Ritchie style:
```
while (i < 0) {
    i++;
}
```

Alignment of braces with the loop statements:
```
while (i < 0)
    {
    i++;
    }
```

Alignment of braces with the control statement:
```
while (i < 0)
{
    i++;
}
```

A combination of the above:
```
while (i < 0) {
    i++;
    }
```

## DEFINES

### Using Defines

In general, no numeric constants other than 0 (and perhaps 1) should appear in the body of a function. All other constants should appear as **#defines**. Sizes of arrays might either be stated symbolically, as in

**#define SCHRARR 30**
**...**
**char chrarr[SCHRARR];**

or deduced (if the size is governed by an initializer), as in

**#define SCHRARR sizeof(chrarr)/sizeof(chrarr[0])**
**...**
**char chrarr[] = "ABCDEF";**

Any **for** loops would use **SCHRARR** as the size for the end test, for example,

**for (i=0;i<SCHRARR;i++) {.....**

#define file names, such as:

**#define NAMEFILE "B:NAMEFIL.DAT"**
**#define WRITEMOD "w"**

**filepnt=fopen(NAMEFILE,WRITEMOD);**

This simplifies switching between operating systems with different file naming conventions.

## Defining Literal Strings

It is often useful to **#define** literal strings, such as error messages:

**#define FOPENERR "Can't find file."**

This allows you to localize the text for such messages, making them easier to edit and examine for consistency.

## Defining Functions

C allows you to **#define** functions, as in

**#define max(a,b) ((a) > (b) ? (a) : (b))**

This practice is dangerous, however. A **#defined** function is not really a function at all, but a simple substitution. The danger arises when a **#defined** function is mistaken for a real function, and expected to behave as such. For example, according to the above definition, the statement

**m = max(x++,y);**

will cause the variable **x** to be incremented twice if **x** is greater than **y**.

## HEADER FILES
### Using Header Files

Header files should contain any definitions needed by more than one module, keeping the definitions consistent and easy to find for modifications. One good practice is to declare all **extern** variables in a single header file. (The corresponding definitions of these **extern** variables should be kept in one source file). The C compiler typically uses a header file to contain machine-dependent input/output information, such as the file control block. Localizing such details in a header file promotes a "black box" theory of programming, whereby the programmer can ignore the inner workings of such functions and simply use them.

## Define Header Files

A **#define** file that renames functions will be particularly useful if your compiler supports longer function names than those allowed by your linker. For example

    **#define AscToStr(x,y) atos(x,y)**

## GLOBAL VARIABLES

### The Pros and Cons of Globals

Global variables may be either external (i.e. program-wide) or static (declared only within a source file). Global variables decrease execution time and make coding a bit simpler, since you do not have to pass global parameters to functions. Global variables should be avoided, if possible, however. Tracing modifications made to global variables can get quite confusing, making programs difficult to debug.

### Constructs That Avoid Globals

The code in Figure 3-1, for example, uses a global variable:

```
int mode=0;                              /* global */
...
if (mode= =0)...
```

**FIGURE 3-1**

You can avoid the global variable by coding functions to change and retrieve the value of this variable. This prevents you from inadvertently changing the value of **mode**. To use or change its value, you must invoke the functions **putmode()** and **getmode()**, as in Figure 3-2.

```
static int mode;

putmode(value)                          /* sets the value of mode */
int value;
{
    mode=value;
    return;
}
getmode()
{
    return mode;
}
```

**FIGURE 3-2**

The code presented in Figure 3-1 above would then read as shown in Figure 3-3.

```
putmode(0);
    ...
if (getmode() ==0) ...
```

**FIGURE 3-3**

This method provides two advantages in debugging:

1. A single print statement in **putmode()** would allow you to track any changes to **mode**.
2. If the code were erroneously typed as **(getmode()=0)...**, the compiler would signal an error. (This would not be the case if the error had been **if (mode=0)....**)

After the program is thoroughly debugged, the advantages listed above are no longer necessary. The addition to the header file, shown in Figure 3-4, will then allow you to avoid the overhead of the function calls.

```
extern int mode;
    #define putmode(x)   mode=(x)
    #define getmode()    (mode)
```

(**mode** would have to be defined as an external variable in some source file).

**FIGURE 3-4**

The code in Figure 3-4 defines the functions **putmode()** and **getmode()**, which are specific to the variable **mode**. If you want to use this scheme to manipulate other variables, as well, you can use the macro shown in Figure 3-5.

```
#define getprefix() get
#define putprefix() put

#define getput(name,type) putprefix()name (value)\
    type value; {name = value;}\
    type getprefix()name () {return name;}
```

**FIGURE 3-5**

The third macro in Figure 3-5 defines the function **getput()**. At the begining of a file, call **getput()** for every variable you will want to treat as the example above has treated **mode**. The function **getput()** takes the name of the variable to be manipulated and its type, and defines two new functions: a get function and a put function. These get and put functions are just like **getmode()** and **putmode()**, except that they are specific to the variable name and type passed to **getput()**.

## FUNCTIONS

Because functions are so common in C, it is particularly important that they be readable and understandable. Some guidelines for writing functions are presented below:

In general, no function should exceed two printed pages.

### Comments

Use a consistent style for commenting code. One format is illustrated in Figure 3-6. Note that each variable is declared on a separate line to allow room for comments.

```
funcexm(parm1,parm2)
/* this is the purpose of the function on one line */
int parm1;                    /* this describes the first parameter */
char *parm2;                  /* this describes the second parameter */
                             /* the return value, if any, is described here */
{
    int var1;                /* this describes the purpose of var1 */
    char var2;               /* this describes the purpose of var2 */
```

**FIGURE 3-6**

### Grouping Functions

In general, keep related functions in the same source file. Be aware, however that source files get linked in as a package, and that the entire source file must be re-compiled whenever any of its component functions changes. In partitioning your functions among source files, consider data sharing, usage as a library, related functionality, and time to re-compile.

### Flow Control

**Goto Statements.** While C allows the use of the **goto** statement, few programmers take advantage of it. Redirecting program flow via a **goto** statement destroys the block structure of C (as discussed in detail in Section D, Code Organization). The **goto** statement may be useful, for example, in handling critical errors that require a drastic detour of program execution. For nearly all purposes, however, the **goto** statement is best avoided.

**Return Statements.** Limit the number of **return** statements in any function, since multiple **returns** make it difficult to trace program flow. According to traditional structured programming, each "black box," that is, each function, should have one point of entry (the call) and one point of return. This ideal is not always practical, however. Often, multiple **return** statements in the middle of functions correspond to real-world constraints: an error has occurred, a boundary condition has been exceeded, and the like. The ability to leave a function that cannot be correctly executed is one of C's advantages over other structured languages. Keep clarity of flow control in mind when coding **return** statements, however, and use them sparingly.

At least in the preliminary stages, return a variable rather than a constant value, that is, **return(x)** rather than **return(5)**. This allows a debug statement to print the value just before it is returned.

**The Exit() Function.** Like multiple **return** statements, the **exit()** function (a **return** statement for the entire program) violates traditional structured programming style. It is often useful, however, for the same reason that mid-function **returns** are useful: In real-world applications, errors occur, and program execution should sometimes be terminated. Use the **exit()** function carefully, but take advantage of it where appropriate.

### Pagination

If your editor supports pagination commands, you can include them as comments between the functions. For example, in WordStar, the following will separate printed functions by page:

```
/*
.pa
*/
funcnew()
```

## Using the Static Storage Class

Variables common to related functions should be **static**. This ensures that other functions will not affect the values of these variables.

## COMPACTNESS

Code can be made reasonably compact without sacrificing clarity. Since a major portion of many functions is calling other functions, long function parameter lists can use up code space rapidly. You can often make parameter lists more compact by passing pointers to structures that contain the parameters rather than the individual parameters themselves. In many cases, the code can be made more clear by the use of a structure, which will indicate the "package" of parameters instead of a long and confusing list of specific ones. The example in Figure 3-7 writes a string to a cursor position on the screen.

```
strout(row,col,str)
                    /* writes a string on the screen at a cursor position */
int row;                                              /* row position */
int col;                                           /* column position */
char *str;                                        /* string to write out */
```

**FIGURE 3-7**

The function defined in Figure 3-7 might be called by

**strout(5,7,"Hi there");**

Using structures, the routine could alternately be written as shown in Figure 3-8.

```
struct sstr
{
    int row;                                          /* row position */
    int col;                                       /* column position */
    char *str;                                    /* string to write out */
};
```

**FIGURE 3-8**

```
    strout(str)
                              /* writes a string on the screen at a cursor position */
    struct sstr *str;                      /* struct of string to write out */
```

**FIGURE 3-8** (*Continued*)

The function in Figure 3-8 would be called by

**static sstr out = {5,7,"Hi there"};**

**strout(&out);**

Suppose **strout()** were called several times in the program. Then two more bytes per call could be saved by defining **sstr** as shown in Figure 3-9.*

```
    struct sstr
    {
      char row;                            /* row position */
      char col;                            /* column position */
      char *str;                           /* string to write out */
    };
```

**FIGURE 3-9**

If **strout()** were called several times in a row, then further code could be saved by defining a function as shown in Figure 3-10.

```
    scrout(scr,nscr)
    /* writes a number of strings onto the screen */
    struct sstr scr[];                     /* array of strings to write */
    int nscr;                              /* number of strings */
    {
      while (nscr--)
      {
        strout(scr);
        scr++;
      }
      return;
    }
```

**FIGURE 3-10**

---

*This code is only valid if the maximum values of **row** and **column** are both less than 256.

The function in Figure 3-10 might be called by the code shown in Figure 3-11.

```
#define NSCR sizeof(scr)/sizeof(struct sstr)
static sstr scr[] =
{
    {5,10,"Hi there"},
    {6,11,"So long"},
};
    ...
scrout(scr,NSCR);
```

**FIGURE 3-11**

Notice that other output could be added to the screen without changing the call to **scrout()**. Performing screen input and output in this manner, content is separated from code. This is similar to the way the Macintosh system is designed: The screen text (resource files) is separate from the code.

Using parameters in this way also permits additional parameters to be added without affecting previously written code. For example, if color were added to the lines, then **sstr** could be redefined as shown in Figure 3-12.

```
struct sstr
{
    char row;                    /* row position */
    char col;                    /* column position */
    char *str;                   /* string to write out */
    char color;                  /* color to write string in */
};
```

**FIGURE 3-12**

The function **strout()** would be modified to switch colors if the value of **str->color** were nonzero. All previously written code could be recompiled without changing the source, and it would work as before, since the value of an uninitialized static is 0.

## CONCLUSION

C coding style has no standardized prescription. What is essential about your coding style is that it be clear and easy to read, both for you and for other programmers. This chapter has presented suggestions in several areas for attaining clear, legible code. There are, of course, many others. Keep in mind, as you write applications, that performing the required tasks is not the only function of your code. It must also be understood, maintained, and likely modified, and therefore stylistically sound, as well.

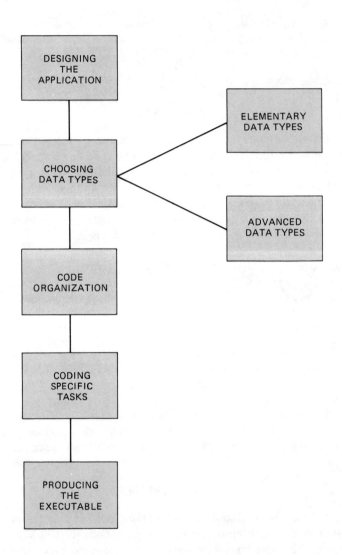

# Section B

# CHOOSING DATA TYPES

Good C programmers select data types early in the development process, often before planning individual algorithms. While you are still envisioning the application as a whole, start thinking about what the code will look like in terms of data types. In general, the tasks to be performed may dictate which data types should be used, which in turn may dictate the algorithms used. Time and memory trade-offs are often addressed by data types, both because of data type sizes and methods of storage and access.

Close attention to data types is critical to good programming. Poorly chosen types will greatly complicate the programming effort. In many cases, convoluted code can be directly traced to the use of data types that are inappropriate to the task.

The chapters that follow discuss both elementary data types (those provided by the C language) and advanced data types (those that you can define and then use in C). The advanced data types are discussed in terms of their definitions, purpose, and implementation in C.

# 4
# Elementary Data Types

*Written for* Applied C *by:* Roger Sessions of Prime Computer, Inc.
*Reviewer:* Steve A. Hersee of Lattice, Inc.

## INTRODUCTION

This chapter introduces the various data types, and discusses how they are used in C. In the examples in this chapter, we will for the sake of clarity ignore the arbitrary limitation of eight significant characters for variable names. These examples are designed for legibility, often at the expense of efficiency. Many could be condensed into fewer lines of code.

## FUNDAMENTAL DATA TYPES

C contains a relatively sparse collection of fundamental data types, that is, data types predefined by the compiler. It provides, instead, considerable flexibility in designing your own types. All of these fundamental types are covered in K&R and any introductory C book; we provide only a brief overview in the interest of completeness.

### Variables

A variable is a storage location for one piece of data. The data types a variable can hold are **char**, **int**, **short int**, **long int**, **unsigned int**, **float**, and **double**. They are all described in introductory texts.

The scope of a variable determines which sections of code have access to that variable. The scope is defined both by the section of code in which the variable is declared and the form of the declaration: **static** or **external**.

A variable declared with no prefix in the global section of a file is potentially available to all functions in all files. Another file must declare it **external** in its global section in order to use the same variable. A variable declared **static** in the global section is available only to functions in the file in which it is declared. A variable declared **static** in a function is available only to the function in which it is declared. A variable declared with no prefix within a function, called an **auto** variable, is available only to that function. **Auto** variables are stored on the stack. They therefore use no memory, but can cause stack overflow.

These rules are summarized in the example in Figure 4-1.

```
File 1:

int start;
static int next;
main ()
{
    int last;
    last = 1;
    start = 2;
    next = 3;
    printf ("In main\n");
    printf ("    last: %3d  start: %3d  next: %3d\n", last, start, next);
    proc1a ();
    proc2a ();
    proc2b ();
    printf ("In main\n");
    printf ("    last: %3d  start: %3d  next: %3d\n", last, start, next);
}

proc1a ()
{
    int last;
    printf ("In proc1a \n");
    last = 11;
    start = 12;
    next = 13;
    printf ("    last: %3d  start: %3d  next: %3d\n", last, start, next);
}


File 2:


extern int start;
static int next;
```

**FIGURE 4-1**

```
    proc2a()
    {
        int last;
        static int here;
        printf ("In proc2a\n");
        last = 21;
        start = 22;
        next = 23;
        here = 24;
        printf ("    last: %3d   start: %3d   next: %3d   here:
                      %3d\n", last, start, next, here);
    }

    proc2b ()
    {
        printf ("In proc2b\n");
        start = 32;
        next = 33;
        printf ("    start: %3d   next: %3d\n", start, next);
    }
```

Output
--------
```
In main
    last:   1    start:   2    next:   3
In proc1a
    last:  11    start:  12    next:  13
In proc2a
    last:  21    start:  22    next:  23    here:  24
In proc2b
    start:  32    next:  33
In main
    last:   1    start:  32    next:  13
```

FIGURE 4-1 (Continued)

In Figure 4-1, **start** is the same variable for functions in files 1 and 2. If **proc2a()** modifies it, the modification is effective in all functions in both files.

The variable **next** is different in file 1 than in file 2, although each is known to all functions within their own files. If **proc2a()** modifies **next**, the modification is effective in **proc2b()**, but not in **proc1a()**.

The variable **last** is local to both **main()** and **proc2a()**. Either function can modify the variable without affecting any other functions. The variable **here** is also local to **proc2a()**. The difference between **here** and **last** in **proc2a()** is that the value of **here** will remain constant (i.e., static) after **proc2a()** is completed, retaining its value until it is modified again in **proc2a()**. The value of **last,** on the other hand, reverts to some unpredictable value upon exit from **proc2a()**.

## Defined Constants

A statement such as **#define TOO_FAR 100** is a message to the compiler to replace any instance of the string "TOO_FAR" with the string "100", except when it is encountered in a quoted string, such as **printf("THEY TRAVELED TOO_FAR TODAY\n");**.

The defined constant can then be used anywhere a regular constant can be used. The sample code segment shown in Figure 4-2 is very common.

```
#define TOP 0
#define BOTTOM 22
#define LEFT 0
#define RIGHT 80

main ()
{
    int cursor_row, cursor_column;
    cursor_row = check_row();
    cursor_column = check_column();

    if (cursor_column > RIGHT)
    {
        cursor_column = LEFT;
    }
    if (cursor_column < LEFT)
    {
        cursor_column = RIGHT;
    }
    if (cursor_row > BOTTOM)
    {
        cursor_row = TOP;
    }
    if (cursor_row < TOP)
    {
        cursor_row = BOTTOM;
    }

    update_cursor(cursor_row, cursor_column);
}
```

FIGURE 4-2

Defining constants allows you to modify programs very easily. It can also serve as self-documentation. To maintain clarity and flexibility, avoid referencing any constant but a declared constant. Capitalizing constant names allows them to be quickly distinguished from variables. Most well-written programs also group constant definitions where they are easily located. When the same constants are referenced in many files, they can be placed in a dedicated header file which can be **#included** wherever needed.

Remember that a constant can not be used to store results. It is strictly a string replacement command. Code such as

**#define length 1**
**length = length + 1;**

will be translated by the compiler as

**1 = 1 + 1;**

which has no meaning.

## Constants Versus Variables

It is sometimes difficult to decide whether to use a constant or a variable. Values that will be modified at run time must be stored in variables, but it is not always obvious in early design stages that values will change.

The example in Figure 4-2 could have been written as shown in Figure 4-3.

```
static int top=0, bottom=22, left=0, right=80;
main ()
{
    int cursor_row, cursor_column;

    cursor_row = check_row ();
    cursor_column = check_column ();

    if (cursor_column > right)
    {
        cursor_column = left;
    }
    if (cursor_column < left)
    {
        cursor_column = right;
    }
```

**FIGURE 4-3**

```
if (cursor_row > bottom)
{
  cursor_row = top;
}
if (cursor_row < top)
{
  cursor_row = bottom;
}

update_cursor (cursor_row, cursor_column);
}
```

**FIGURE 4-3** (*Continued*)

The code in Figure 4-3 provides a major advantage if you discovered that you need to run our program on a new terminal type that is 120 columns wide. If **top**, **bottom**, **left**, and **right** are global variables, code can be added to check the terminal type and to adjust the values at run time. Constants can never be adjusted at run time.

Defined constants, besides being easier to understand, are somewhat more efficient. They use less memory and fewer CPU cycles than similar statements with variables. The gain in efficiency, however, is usually inconsequential, and constants are primarily used to improve readability.

## Addresses Versus Pointers Versus Values

In addition to being one of the basic data types, a variable can be declared as a pointer to any allowable type.

| | |
|---|---|
| **int number1;** | /* This is an integer variable */ |
| **int number2;** | /* This is another integer variable */ |
| **int *numpnt;** | /* This is a pointer to an integer variable, perhaps number1 */ |

A pointer is a variable that contains the address of another variable. The relationship between values, addresses, and pointers can be confusing. Examine the oversimplified memory map shown in Figure 4-4, and the effects of the C statements.

| Memory Location | Contents | Variable |
|---|---|---|
| 001 | ?? | number1 |
| 002 | ?? | number2 |
| 003 | ?? | numpnt |

**FIGURE 4-4**

```
                    ↓
                    ↓ number1 = 10; number2 = 20;
                    ↓
001               ⁎ 10                number1
002                 20                number2
003                 ??                numpnt
                    ↓
                    ↓ numpnt = &number1;
                    ↓
001                 10                number1
002                 20                number2
003                 01                numpnt
                    ↓
                    ↓ *numpnt = 100;
                    ↓
001                100                number1
002                 20                number2
003                 01                numpnt
```

**FIGURE 4-4** (*Continued*)

## Structures

What we have discussed so far are the elementary data building blocks. C gives you several ways to associate these into higher level data types. One of these is called a **structure**.

**Declaration.**   A structure can be thought of as a logical grouping of related elements. The statement shown in Figure 4-5 declares a new data type to exist which is to be referred to as "**box_type**".

```
struct box_type
{
  int top_row;
  int bottom_row;
  int left_column;
  int right_column;
};
```

**FIGURE 4-5**

You can declare and use such a variable with the code shown in Figure 4-6. The declaration of the structure types is often found in a globally available header file, which can be **#included** in all files making use of such types. The variable declaration is made in the individual files, and follows the same scope rules as other variables.

```
struct box_type
{
  int top_row;
  int bottom_row;
  int left_column;
  int right_column;
};
main()
{
  struct box_type box1;

  box1.top_row = 10;
  box1.bottom_row = box1.top_row + 10;
  box1.left_column = 15;
  box1.right_column = box1.left_column + 5;

  printf ("Top: %d  Bottom: %d  Left: %d  Right: %d\n",
       box1.top_row, box1.bottom_row, box1.left_column,
       box1.rightcolumn);
}
/ ***********************************************************
** Output
*********************************************************** /
Top: 10   Bottom: 20   Left: 15   Right: 20
```

**FIGURE 4-6**

**Passing Structures.**   While UNIX III and ANSI C allow structures to be passed as arguments to functions, some compilers allow you to pass only the addresses of structures. You can pass the address of a structure in either of the equivalent ways shown in Figure 4-7.

```
struct box_type box1;                    /* A variable of type box */
    ...
draw_box (&box1);
    or

struct box_type box1;                    /* A variable of type box */
struct box_type *box_pnt;                /* A pointer to a variable of type
                                                                box */

    ...
box_pnt = &box1;
draw_box(box_pnt);
```

**FIGURE 4-7**

**Receiving Structures.**   Regardless of how the address of the structure is passed into the function, the function has no choice about how it receives it. The correct syntax is

**draw_box(box)**
**struct box_type \*box;**
**{**
 **...**
**}**

The function **draw_box()** can refer to the elements of the box in one of two different ways, however. Remember that it does not have the variable, only the address of the variable. Thus it should refer to

**(\*box).top_row**

But more commonly the equivalent and much easier C syntax is used:

**box − > top_row**

This is a general syntax rule useful in other situations as well.

**(\*something).other  ⟺  something − > other**

**Elements of Structures.**   A structure is allowed to contain as one of its elements any of the other data types. A very important element is a pointer to another structure of the same type. Constructs such as that shown in Figure 4-8 are common in higher-level data manipulation.

```
struct box_type
 {
 int top_row;
 int bottom_row;
 int left_column;
 int right_column;
 struct box_type *next_box;
 };
```

**FIGURE 4-8**

A structure is allowed to contain other structures, although such constructs lose usefulness in complexity.

**Allocation of Memory for Structures.**   Compile Time Versus Run Time.
When you use a structure type statement, such as

**struct boxtype**
**{**
 **...**
**};**

no memory is being allocated. This is strictly a message to the compiler saying
that should a structure be created of type **box_type**, this is what it will look
like, and this is how much memory it will require.

When you give the statement

**struct box_type box1;**

you have now told the compiler that you want to allocate memory for one of
these **box_types**, that you want to interpret this memory as a **box_type**, and
that you want to refer to this piece of memory as ''**box1**''.

The statement

**struct box_type *box_pnt;**

is telling the compiler that you want to allocate enough memory to contain the
address of a **box_type**, and that you want to refer to this piece of memory as
''**box_pnt**''.

If you know when you are writing the program that you are going to need
exactly two boxes, there is nothing wrong with allocating the memory with

**struct box_type box1, box2;**

If you do not yet know how many boxes you will need, however, you may not
want to allocate the memory for the boxes when the program is compiled.

C allows you to allocate memory at run time through function calls. This is
a useful technique, especially when you can not predict what your needs will
be. The details of this run-time allocation differ slightly from machine to
machine.

Run-time allocation makes use of the standard C functions **malloc()** and
**free(),** which are responsible for managing memory allocation.

The function **malloc()** takes as its argument the number of bytes of memory
you want and returns a pointer to the first byte. It is responsible for locating
that much consecutive available memory and marking it as unavailable for future

uses. The function **free()** takes as its argument the same pointer, and makes the memory available again for further calls.

The function **malloc()** is internally defined as returning a **char** pointer. If you will need a different type of pointer (which you usually will), typecast the pointer that **malloc()** returns.

The function **malloc()** is often used in conjunction with the compiler directive **sizeof()**. The directive **sizeof()** takes as its argument a data type, and returns the number of bytes which that data type uses.

In general, run-time memory allocation looks very similar to the code shown in Figure 4-9.

```
struct box_type            /* Tell the compiler what a box looks like */
{
    ...
};
struct box_type *box_pnt;            /* Create a pointer to a box */
                                      /* Allocate memory for a a box */
box_pnt = (box_type*) malloc (sizeof(box_type));
...                                   /* Use the box for whatever */
free (box_pnt);                       /* Free the box to free its memory */
```

**FIGURE 4-9**

## Arrays

The variables we have been talking about contain only single data types. The data type may be composed of many parts, as in a structure, but still a variable contains only one of them. Arrays are variables that can contain more than one of the same data type. The syntax to declare an array is

**type array_name[array_size];**

Figure 4-10 shows various legal array declarations.

```
int numbers[100];            /* A 100 element array of numbers */
char name[30];               /* A 30 element array of characters */
#define MAXBOXES 10
struct box_type boxes[MAXBOXES];            /* A 10 element array of
                                                               boxes */

struct box_type *boxes[MAXBOXES];           /* A 10 element array of
                                                    pointers to boxes */
```

**FIGURE 4-10**

The difference between the last two lines in Figure 4-10 should be clearly understood. An array of structures and an array of pointers to structures are very different, and require different amounts of memory to implement. In Figure 4-11, we examine their memory requirements in detail, as much to clarify the difference between arrays of pointers and arrays of their values as to discuss efficient memory management.

STRUCTURE

MEMORY
REQUIREMENTS
(Bytes)

```
struct box_type
{
    int top_row; ................................. 2
    int bottom_row; ........................... 2
    int left_column; ........................... 2
    int right_column; ......................... 2
    struct box_type *next_box; .............. 4
};                                         --------
                                              12


    struct box_type *box_pnt ................... 4
    struct box_type boxes[10]; .... 10 * 12 = 120
    struct box_type *boxes[10]; .. 10 *  4 =  40
```

**FIGURE 4-11**

One might conclude from Figure 4-11 that an array of pointers requires less memory than an array of the actual data types, especially if those data types are structures. The data types pointed at must exist in memory, too, however. If, in addition to these pointers, you also have ten boxes in memory, then the actual memory cost of using the array of pointers is (10 * 12) + (10 * 4), or 160. Arrays of pointers retain their memory advantage if the array has a significant number of null pointers, that is, pointers that are not being used and hence have no corresponding memory used for the data type.

Another advantage to using arrays of structure pointers rather than arrays of structures is the ease of assigning the data in one structure to another structure. In Figure 4-12, look at the difference between the code required to "place" a box on these two different arrays.

We will use this rapid "data movement" frequently when we discuss higher-level data manipulation.

Arrays are often used to contain pointers to strings, especially strings containing globally accessible messages. This facility is useful in storing error messages, as in Figure 4-13.

Example I.

```
struct box_type boxes[10], newbox;
boxes[1].top_row = newbox.top_row;
boxes[1].bottom_row = newbox.bottom_row;
boxes[1].left_column = newbox.left_column;
boxes[1].right_column = newbox.right_column;
boxes[1].next_box = newbox.next_box;
```

Example II.

```
struct box_type *boxes[10], newbox;
boxes[1] = &newbox;
```

**FIGURE 4-12**

```
static char *err_msg[]=
{
  "*** File I/O completed normally",
  "*** Error during attempt to open file",
  "*** Error during I/O operation"
};

main()
{
    int result;
    result = io_operation();
    printf ("%s\n", err_msg[result]);
}

io_operation()
{
/* Do the file operation */
    return (0);
}
```

```
/ **********************************************************
** Output
********************************************************** /
```

*** File I/O completed normally

**FIGURE 4-13**

Arrays allow you to find things very quickly, as long as you know which element you are looking for. This speed makes them useful in storing and retrieving tabular data. Consider Table 4-1, which translates ASCII codes to their equivalent EBCDIC codes.

**Table 4-1**

| Character | ASCII | EBCDIC | Character | ASCII | EBCDIC |
|-----------|-------|--------|-----------|-------|--------|
| A | 065 | 193 | N | 078 | 213 |
| B | 066 | 194 | O | 079 | 214 |
| C | 067 | 195 | P | 080 | 215 |
| D | 068 | 196 | Q | 081 | 216 |
| E | 069 | 197 | R | 082 | 217 |
| F | 070 | 198 | S | 083 | 218 |
| G | 071 | 199 | T | 084 | 219 |
| H | 072 | 200 | U | 085 | 220 |
| I | 073 | 201 | V | 086 | 221 |
| J | 074 | 209 | W | 087 | 222 |
| K | 075 | 210 | X | 088 | 223 |
| L | 076 | 211 | Y | 089 | 224 |
| M | 077 | 212 | Z | 090 | 225 |

You could translate the codes algorithmically, as in Figure 4-14.

```
main()
{
    printf ("ebcdic: %d\n", (int)trans('A'));
    printf ("ebcdic: %d\n", (int)trans('Z'));
}
char trans(ascii)
char ascii;
{
    char newchr;

    newchr = (ascii < = 'I') ? (ascii + 128) : (ascii + 135);
    return (newchr);
}

/ ********************************************************
** Output
******************************************************** /

ebcdic: 193
ebcdic: 225
```

**FIGURE 4-14**

A table lookup will be both faster and more flexible, however, allowing you to use the same method to translate different coding schemes.

You declare and initialize the array as shown in Figure 4-15.

```
char ascii_2_other[26] =
{
193, 194, 195, 196, 197, 198, 199, 200, 201, 209, 210,
211, 212, 213, 214, 215, 216, 217, 218, 219, 220, 221,
222, 223, 224, 225
};
```

**FIGURE 4-15**

You can now quickly find the EBCDIC code for any ASCII character. Figure 4-16 uses this method to translate whole strings.

```
char ascii_2_other[26] =
{
    193, 194, 195, 196, 197, 198, 199, 200, 201, 209, 210, 211,
    212, 213, 214, 215, 216, 217, 218, 219, 220, 221, 222, 223,
    224, 225
};

main()
{
    char char_string [50];
    char *nxtchr;
    int n, length;
    strcpy(char_string, "ABCXYZ");

    translate(char_string);

    length = strlen(char_string);
    for (n=0; n<length; n++)
    {
        printf("%d ", (int)char_string[n]);
    }
}

translate(string)
char *string;
{
```

**FIGURE 4-16**

```
    while (*string + +)
    {
        *string = ascii_2_other[*string - 65];
    }
}
```

**FIGURE 4-16** (*Continued*)

Multi-dimensional arrays are also used in C, but much less frequently than in languages such as FORTRAN or BASIC, which do not allow arrays of pointers or structures.

## CONCLUSION

This chapter has presented the standard data types that C provides. In the next chapter, we discuss some higher-level data types, and show you how to use C to create and manipulate them.

# 5
# Advanced Data Types

*Written for* Applied C *by:* Roger Sessions of Prime Computer, Inc.
*Reviewer:* Dr. Michael Pearce of Pearce Associates

## INTRODUCTION

While C provides you with the standard data types, several more advanced types may be useful in your code. This chapter begins with a discussion of the steps necessary to create and implement a new data type in C, illustrated with the creation and implementation of a sample data type. The chapter then discusses some of the data types you may want to create, defines their operation, and implements them in C.

## CREATING NEW DATA TYPES

Creating a new data type requires four basic steps:

1. Decide how the data type will behave
2. Decide on a basic set of operators needed to manipulate the data type
3. Represent your new data type in terms of the standard C data types
4. Create a library of functions to provide the basic operators for this type.

Our example will follow these steps in creating a sample data type.

### Design

C provides a full set of bitwise operators for working on any of the standard scalar (as opposed to array) variables. But the standard variables give us at most 32 bits to work with. We would like to be able to work with very large numbers of bits.

**Step 1.** The new data type will be 200-300 bits long, and will respond to operations similar to the standard C bitwise operations. The data type will be named "**big_word_type**".

**Step 2.** The example will define operators to do the following:

1. Print a **big_word**.
2. Clear a **big_word**.
3. Set or clear a specified bit in a **big_word**.
4. Logically AND two **big_words** together to get a third.
5. Logically OR two **big_words** together to get a third.
6. Check a specified bit in a **big_word**.
7. Determine if a **big_word** is true.

## Implementation

**Step 3.** We define the new data type in terms of standard C data types as follows:

```
#define MAX_BITS 200
#define MAX_BYTES (MAX_BITS/8) + 1
typedef char big_word_type[MAX_BYTES];
#define byte_location(A) (A/8)
```

**Step 4.** We write the specified operations as shown in Figure 5-1.

```
#define NBITS 64              /* The number of bits in a big word */
#define NBYTES (NBITS/8)+1
typedef char bigword_type[NBYTES];

/ ************************************************************
Big Word Utilities
---- ------ ----------
This file contains procedures for doing bit manipulations on arbitrarily
large words. The bit mappings are (for a character array):
  bigword bit     array element     bitnumber
      0               0                 0
      5               0                 5
     10               1                 2
                    etc.
************************************************************ /
```

**FIGURE 5-1**

```
/ **********************************************************
** Function printit()
** Print a big word in hex format showing bit 0 at far right.
********************************************************** /
printit(word)
char word[];
{
    int n;
    for (n=NBYTES-1; n> =0; n--)
    {
        printf ("%2x", (unsigned)word[n]);
    }
    printf ("\n");
}


/ **********************************************************
** Function clear_all()
** Clear all of the bits in a big word.
********************************************************** /
clear_all(word)
char word[];
{
    int n;
    for (n=0; n<NBYTES; n++)
    {
        word[n] = 0;
    }
}


/ **********************************************************
** Function set_bit()
** Set a specific bit in a big word.
********************************************************** /
set_bit(word, bitno)
char word[];
int bitno;
{
    char mask;
    int index;
    mask = (1 < < (bitno % 8));
    index = bitno / 8;
    word[index] |= mask;
}
```

Figure 5-1 (Continued)

```
/ **********************************************************
** Function clear_bit()
** Clear a specific bit in a big word.
********************************************************** /
clear_bit(word, bitno)
char word[];
int bitno;
{
    char mask;
    int index;
    mask = ~(1 << (bitno % 8));
    index = bitno / 8;
    word[index] &= mask;
}


/ **********************************************************
** Function and_bits()
** Logically AND two big words together.
********************************************************** /
and_bits (word1, word2, result)
char word1[], word2[], result[];
{
    int n;
    for (n=0; n<NBYTES; n++)
    {
        result[n] = word1[n] & word2[n];
    }
}


/ **********************************************************
** Function or_bits()
** Logically OR two big words together.
********************************************************** /
or_bits (word1, word2, result)
char word1[], word2[], result[];
{
    int n;
    for (n=0; n<NBYTES; n++)
    {
        result[n] = word1[n] | word2[n];
    }
}
```

Figure 5-1 (Continued)

```
/ ***********************************************************
** Function true()
** See if a big word is true.
*********************************************************** /
true (word)
char word[];
{
    int n;
    for (n=0; n<NBYTES; n++)
    {
        if (word[n])
        {
            return (1);
        }
    }
    return(0);
}
/ ***********************************************************
```

**Figure 5-1** (*Continued*)

Once these functions are complete, using this data type is easy. All of the hard work has already been done. You can now write code like that shown in Figure 5-2, with no regard to the implementation details.

```
#define NBITS 64                 /* The number of bits in a big word */
#define NBYTES (NBITS/8)+1
typedef char bigword_type[NBYTES];

main ()
{
    bigword_type word1, word2, word3;

    clear_all (word1);
    clear_all (word2);

    set_bit (word1, 0);
    set_bit (word1, 4);
    set_bit (word1, 10);
    printf ("          word1: ");
    printit (word1);
```

**FIGURE 5-2**

```
    set_bit (word2, 0);
    set_bit (word2, 1);
    set_bit (word2, 2);
    set_bit (word2, 3);
    printf ("          word2: ");
    printit (word2);
    printf ("word1 AND word2: ");
    and_bits (word1, word2, word3);
    printit (word3);

    printf (" word1 OR word2: ");
    or_bits (word1, word2, word3);
    printit (word3);

    clear_all (word3);
    if (true(word1))
    {
        printf ("word1 is true\n");
    }
    if (true(word2))
    {
        printf ("word2 is true\n");
    }
    if (true(word3))
    {
        printf ("word3 is true\n");
    }
}
```

OUTPUT

```
            word1:  0 0 0 0 0 0 0 411
            word2:  0 0 0 0 0 0 0 0 F
word1 AND word2:  0 0 0 0 0 0 0 0 1
word1 OR word2:  0 0 0 0 0 0 0 41F
word1 is true
word2 is true
```

**Figure 5-2** (*Continued*)

Taking the time to construct proper operator functions for your data types can not be over-emphasized. It will make your code much easier to understand, cut down substantially on debugging time, and allow you to build up a library of data types you can reuse in new situations with, at most, minor modification.

In the following sections, we discuss a few useful data types you can create, and illustrate their implementation in C.

## STACKS

### Definition

A stack is a data type used for temporarily storing things and then retrieving them. Visualize a stack as a vertical pile of data. The order that things come off a stack is the reverse of the order in which they went in: New items are placed on the top of the stack, and items can only be removed from the top of the stack. This is often referred to as LIFO (Last In, First Out).

There are two kinds of stacks. A simple stack makes no provision for the number of things that can be on the stack at any given time. If you attempt to push too many things on a simple stack, results are unpredictable, and often disastrous. A constrained stack does make provision for overload. If you push too many things on a constrained stack, the items at the bottom of the stack are discarded.

A simple stack is one of the easiest data types to implement, and one of the most commonly used. It is so common that many computers, including the IBM family of PCs, have a stack built into the hardware with machine language instructions for manipulating it.

Simple stacks are the standard mechanism for parameter passing among functions in languages that allow recursion (like C). The calling function pushes the parameters, one at a time, onto a globally available stack, and the called function pops them back off in the reverse order.

Constrained stacks are often used to remember the state of things. A database program might use a constrained stack to remember the last three states of a record as it is being modified, so that if anything goes wrong, the user can return to any one of them. If the record is modified more than three times, the program will only remember the most recent three states.

Constrained stacks are implemented very much like queues, a data type that will be discussed later. In this section, therefore, we will only discuss simple stacks.

### Implementation

We require only two things of a stack. We want to push things onto it, and pop things off of it. The code need be no more complicated than Figure 5-3.

```
#define STK_TYPE int
#define STK_SIZE 100
static STK_TYPE stack[STK_SIZE];
static int stk_pnt = 0;


/ **********************************************************
** Function push()
** Push something onto the stack.
********************************************************** /
push (element)
STK_TYPE element;
{
    stack[stk_pnt] = element;
    stk_pnt++;
}


/ **********************************************************
** Function pop()
** Pop something off of the stack.
********************************************************** /
STK_TYPE pop ()
{
    stk_pnt--;
    return (stack[stk_pnt]);
}
```

The following sample code uses the stack created above:

```
main()
{
    push (1);
    push (2);
    push (3);
    printf ("%d\n", pop());
    printf ("%d\n", pop());
    printf ("%d\n", pop());
}
```

OUTPUT
3
2
1

FIGURE 5-3

## LINKED LISTS

### Definition

A linked list, like an array, is a data type that holds other data types. It differs from an array in the manner in which these items are stored and accessed. The linked list is an important data type because it is used as a building block to other, higher-level data types, specifically queues and trees, discussed later in this chapter.

The organization of items in a linked list is like a train. A train is made up of cars, each of which can contain people, and each of which has two doors: one leading to the next car, the other to the previous car. If you wanted to find someone in a train, you would start in the first car, and see if she were there. If she is, you are finished with your search. If she is not, you try to open the door to the next car. If that door is locked, you are also finished: she is not on the train. (We assume that a door is locked only because there are no further cars). If the door is open, you move to the next car and start again.

Like this train in which you hunt for your friend, a linked list is an ordered sequence of elements (cars), each of which may contain an item (people), and one of which may contain the item for which you are looking (your friend). In order to ensure that you will not miss the item in your search, you must proceed through the elements in order, either forward or backward, through the doors provided.

The items in a linked list are the ''storage elements'': elements such as we have seen in previous data types. These elements are the data we will access. In a linked list, the storage elements are each accompanied by at least one ''structural element'': a pointer that allows you to find the next or previous element. In a linked list, the doors between cars—pointers to the next and previous items— are the structural elements.

To clarify this qualitative definition of a linked list, examine Figure 5-4, illustrating a linked list as a series of items connected by pointers to the next item.

A one-way linked list is like a train with doors that lock behind you as you move from the front to the rear of the train. A two-way linked list allows you to move either forward or backward through the train, that is, doors do not lock behind you.

The two-way linked list is more common in C. Therefore we will detail the implementation of this data type. We will require the following of our two-way linked list:

1. Given a particular item (e.g., #3 in the list), we will be able to retrieve the next item in the list (#4).
2. Given a particular item (e.g., #3 in the list), we will be able to retrieve the previous item (#2).

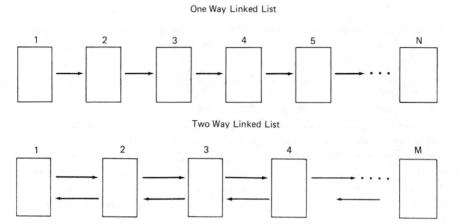

FIGURE 5-4

3. We will NOT be able to access directly any item in the list without going through the list sequentially to find it. This is an important distinction between linked lists and arrays.
4. Given a particular item, we will be able to link a new item to it at any time, regardless of the original item's position in the list.
5. We will be able to remove any item from the list.

The function we write will free us from the details of maintaining the data type. We will only have to deal with updating the storage elements, or informational content of the data type.

## Implementation

Sample code for implementing a two-way linked list is shown in Figure 5-5.

```
#include "stdio.h"
#define STR_LEN 50

struct link_type
{
    struct link_type *next;                          /* Next link */
```

FIGURE 5-5

```
      struct link_type *previous;              /* Previous link */
      char string[STR_LEN];                    /* The string in this link */
   };
   struct link_type *head = NULL;              /* The head of the list */
   struct link_type *tail = NULL;              /* The tail of the list */
   char *malloc();


   / ***********************************************************
   ** Function print_list()
   ** Print the list
   *********************************************************** /
   print_list(list)
   struct link_type *list;
   {
      while (list != NULL)
      {
         printf ("%s\n", list->string);
         list = list->next;
      }
   }

   / ***********************************************************
   ** Function init_list()
   ** Initialize the list with this string.
   *********************************************************** /
   struct link_type *init_list (newstring)
   char *newstring;
   {
      struct link_type *create_link();

      head = tail = create_link (newstring);
      return (head);
   }


   / ***********************************************************
   ** Function find_link()
   ** Returns a pointer to the requested link
   *********************************************************** /
   find_link (start, search_string)
   struct link_type *start;                    /* Where to start looking */
   char *search_string;                        /* String to look for */
   {
      int status;
      while (start != NULL)
```

**Figure 5-5**  (*Continued*)

```
      {
         status = strcmp (start- >string, search_string);
         if (status = = 0)
            {
               return (start);
            }
         else
            {
               start = start- >next;
            }
      }
   return (NULL);
}


/ ***********************************************************
** Function delete_link()
** Logically deletes the link from the list, and
** frees the space.
*********************************************************** /
delete_link (link)
struct link_type *link;
{
   struct link_type *previous_link, *next_link;

   previous_link = link- >previous;
   next_link = link- >next;
   if (link = = head)
      {
         head = next_link;
      }
   if (link = = tail)
      {
         tail = previous_link;
      }

   if (previous_link != NULL)
      {
         previous_link- >next = next_link;
      }
   if (next_link != NULL)
      {
         next_link- >previous = previous_link;
      }
   free (link);
}
```

**Figure 5-5** (Continued)

```
/ **********************************************************
** Function insert_link()
** Inserts a new link into this location.
********************************************************** /
insert_link (string, place)
struct link_type *place;
char *string;
{
    struct link_type *next_link, *newlink;

    newlink = create_link(string);          /* Create link with
                                                     this string */
    next_link = place- >next;               /* This is the old tail */

    place- >next = newlink;                 /* Describe relationship
                                                between new link */
    newlink- >previous = place;             /* and original link. */

    if (next_link != NULL)                  /* If there was originally a tail */
    {                                       /* reattach the tail to the new link. */
        newlink- >next = next_link;
        next_link- >previous = newlink;
    }
    else
    {
        tail = newlink;                     /* Reset tail pointer */
    }
}


/ **********************************************************
** Function create_link()
** Allocates memory for a link, sets up string and
** pointers, and returns pointer to the link. Used
** internally by insert_link and init_list.
********************************************************** /
struct link_type *create_link(newstring)
char *newstring;
{
    struct link_type *newlink;

    newlink = (struct link_type *) malloc(sizeof(*newlink));
    newlink- >next = NULL;
    newlink- >previous = NULL;
    strcpy(newlink- >string, newstring);
    return (newlink);
}
```

Figure 5-5 (Continued)

# QUEUES

## Definition

Queues are similar to stacks in that they are used for temporary storage. In a queue, however, items are retrieved in the same order as they were entered. Queues derive their name from the type of queue we see at a ticket line for a theater: Like a patron in the ticket line, the next item retrieved from a queue is the item that has been on the queue the longest. This data storage and retrieval method is called FIFO (First In, First Out).

The keyboard buffer on many computers is an example of a queue. As keys are typed, they are placed on a queue. When the program expects a character, it requests one from the queue. Characters are then passed to the program in the same order in which they were typed at the keyboard. This keyboard buffer queue allows the user to type characters faster than they can be processed by the program. If the user types fast enough, he will fill the queue. When this happens on the IBM PC, he is warned with a beep, and additional characters are ignored.

A printer queue is another example familiar to most programmers and users alike. With many operating systems, particularly multi-user operating systems, when a user requests a print job, the job is entered on a queue. The program responsible for coordinating print output requests jobs from this queue and prints them in the same order as they were entered.

Queues are a little more complicated to implement than stacks, so if no advantage will be gained by storing data in a queue, a stack is usually preferred.

## Implementation

You can implement a queue in several different ways. The example in Figure 5-6 uses a linked list implementation, allowing us to use code developed earlier in this chapter. The queue will hold character strings (although a queue can hold any data type).

The operations necessary are:

1. Push a string onto the queue.
2. Pull a string off the queue, and return it in the buffer specified.

```
#include "stdio.h"
#define STR_LEN 50
struct link_type
{
    struct link_type *next;                    /* Next link */
```

**FIGURE 5-6**

```
        struct link_type *previous;              /* Previous link */
        char string[STR_LEN];                /* The string in this link */
};
extern struct link_type *head, *tail;         /* The head and tail
                                                 of the list */

extern struct link_type *find_link();


/ ************************************************************
** Function push()
** Push a string on the queue
************************************************************ /
push (newstring)
char *newstring;
{
    if (head = = NULL)
    {
        init_list (newstring);
    }
    else
    {
        insert_link (newstring, tail);
    }
}


/ ************************************************************
** Function pull()
** Pull a string off the queue, and return in provided
** buffer.
************************************************************ /
pull (oldstring)
char *oldstring;
{
    strcpy (oldstring, head- >string);
    delete_link (head);
}
```

The code below uses the queue defined above:

```
main ()
{
    char string[50];

    push ("Element 1");
    push ("Element 2");
    push ("Element 3");
```

**Figure 5-6** (Continued)

```
    pull (string);
    printf ("%s\n", string);

    pull (string);
    printf ("%s\n", string);

    pull (string);
    printf ("%s\n", string);
}
```

OUTPUT

Element 1
Element 2
Element 3

**Figure 5-6** *(Continued)*

## A BRIEF NOTE ON CREATING STACKS AND QUEUES FOR MORE COMPLEX DATA TYPES

Throughout the discussion on stacks and queues, we have been assuming that the stored elements are simple data types such as integers, characters, or pointers. With just some minor modification, we can also make our stacks and queues work for arrays and structures.

When we stored (or retrieved) elements from the stacks created in the previous section, we used a statement such as

**stack[stk_pnt] = element;**                    /* Store element in the stack */

The assignment operator ("=") is only valid for these simple data types. To generalize these stacks and queues to accommodate arrays and structures, you need only create an applicable assignment function. You can do this in one of two ways.

You can create an assignment function that will work on any data type, and therefore need not be changed when you change the stored data type. This assignment function is a move memory instruction like that shown in Figure 5-7.

```
equal (from, to)
QUE_TYPE *from, *to;
{
    movmem (from, to, sizeof(QUE_TYPE));
}
```

**FIGURE 5-7**

Unfortunately, such a routine is compiler specific, since no move memory instruction is defined in the standard library.

An alternative is to create an assignment function that will work on any compiler, but is specific to the stored data type. For the **box_type** that we discussed much earlier, this might look like Figure 5-8.

```
equal (from, to)
QUE_TYPE *from, *to;
{
        to- >top_row = from- >top_row;
        to- >bottom_row = from- >bottom_row;
        to- >left_column = from- >left_column;
        to- >right_column = from- >right_column;
}
```

**FIGURE 5-8**

## SETS

### Definition

The set as a data type resembles its mathematical counterpart in that it is a collection of objects with the following characteristics:

1. The order of the collection has no significance.
2. No two items in the collection are identical.

As a data type, a set has a third characteristic:

3. The collection is usually small.

In designing a bibliographic database to store abstracts of articles, for example, you might want a collection of the keywords for each article. These keywords would allow you to search for articles about certain topics. A set is suited to this type of data storage: a given article might have many keywords, but each item—the combination of article title and keyword—should nót be repeated, and the order of the items has no significance.

### Implementation

Set implementation can get quite complicated. Often, however, you can make do with only a few of the more easily implemented formal set operator functions. A reasonably complete collection of set operator functions includes:

**chk_set()**: takes an item and a set and returns true if the item is contained within the set.

**add_to_set()**: adds an item to a set.

**intersection()**: takes two sets and returns a new set containing all of the objects found in both of the input sets.

**setunion()**: takes two sets, and returns a new set containing all of the items found in either of the input sets.

The set definition and operator functions are shown in Figure 5-9.

```
#include "stdio.h"
#define STR_LEN 50

struct link_type
{
    struct link_type *next;           /* Next link */
    struct link_type *previous;       /* Previous link */
    char string[STR_LEN];             /* The string in this link */
};
extern struct link_type *find_link();


/ ************************************************************
** Function chk_set()
** Return true if this element is in the set, false otherwise
************************************************************ /
chk_set (set, newstring)
struct link_type *set;
char *newstring;
{
    if (find_link(set, newstring) != NULL)
    {
        return (1);
    }
    else
    {
        return (0);
    }
}
```

**FIGURE 5-9**

```
/ ***********************************************************
** Function add_to_set()
** Adds a string to a set, returns a pointer to the beginning
** of the set (this is useful if this string initializes the
** set). If the string is already in the set, does nothing.
*********************************************************** /
struct link_type *add_to_set (set, newstring)
struct link_type *set;
char *newstring;
{
   if (set = = NULL)
   {
      return (init_list (newstring));
   }
   else if (!chk_set(set, newstring))
   {
      insert_link (newstring, set);
      return (set);
   }
   else
   {
      return (set);
   }
}


/ ***********************************************************
** Function intersection()
** Returns a pointer to a new set, the intersection of two
** sets.
*********************************************************** /
struct link_type *intersection (set1, set2)
struct link_type *set1, *set2;
{
   struct link_type *link, *set3;
   if (set1 = = NULL || set2 = = NULL)
   {
      return (NULL);
   }

   link = set1;
   set3 = NULL;
   while (link != NULL)
   {
      if (chk_set(set2, link- >string))
```

Figure 5-9 (Continued)

```
        {
            set3 = add_to_set(set3, link->string);
        }
        link = link->next;
    }
    return (set3);
}



/ **********************************************************
** Function setunion()
** Returns a pointer to a new set, the union of two sets.
********************************************************** /
struct link_type *setunion (set1, set2)
struct link_type *set1, *set2;
{
    struct link_type *link, *set3;
    if (set1 == NULL && set2 == NULL)
    {
        return (NULL);
    }

    set3 = NULL;
    link = set1;
    while (link != NULL)
    {
        set3 = add_to_set(set3, link->string);
        printf ("........\n");
        print_list(set3);
        link = link->next;
    }

    link = set2;
    while (link != NULL)
    {
        set3 = add_to_set(set3, link->string);
        printf ("........\n");
        print_list(set3);
        link = link->next;
    }
    return (set3);
}
```

**Figure 5-9** (*Continued*)

The code below uses the set defined above:

```
#define set_type link_type
struct set_type *set1=NULL, *set2=NULL, *set3=NULL;

main()
{
   set1 = add_to_set(set1, "Element 1");
   add_to_set(set1, "Element 2");
   add_to_set(set1, "Element 3");
   printf("set1:\n");
   print_list (set1);

   set2 = add_to_set(set2, "Element 2");
   add_to_set(set2, "Element 3");
   add_to_set(set2, "Element 4");
   printf("set2:\n");
   print_list(set2);

   printf("intersection set1, set2\n");
   print_list(intersection(set1, set2));

   printf("union set1, set2\n");
   print_list(setunion(set1, set2));
}
```

OUTPUT

```
set1:
Element 1
Element 3
Element 2
set2:
Element 2
Element 4
Element 3
intersection set1, set2
Element 3
Element 2
union set1, set2
Element 1
Element 4
Element 2
Element 3
```

**Figure 5-9** (*Continued*)

# RECURSION

## Definition

Recursion is a special programming technique in which a procedure or a problem is defined in terms of itself. It is widely used in higher-level data manipulation, and is essential for creating trees, a data type presented in the next section.

Many familiar activities can be defined recursively. Figure 5-10 is an example of a common recursive action.

```
search_for_lost_object()
{
    hiding_place = hiding_place_you_have_not_looked_in();
    if (hiding_place == NONE_LEFT)
    {
        return (CANT_FIND_IT);
    }
    else if (object_is_in(hiding_place))
    {
        return (hiding_place);
    }
    else
    {
        return (search_for_lost_object());
    }
}
```

**FIGURE 5-10**

This function finds a lost object. It continues looking until either

1. There is no place left to look.
2. The object is found.

Examine how this works in a room with three possible hiding places: a box, a bag (which contains the object), and a cupboard. The program invokes **search_for_lost_object()** (label this "invocation 1"). It retrieves a new **hiding_place**, for example, the cupboard. The program checks **if (object_is_in (cupboard))**, which is false. So the function returns with the value of **search_for_lost_object()**. What is the value of **search_for_lost_object()**? The program invokes it to find out.

The function **search_for_lost_object()** is invoked again (label this "invocation 2"). It retrieves a new **hiding_place**, for example, the bag. It checks **if** (object_is_in(bag)), which is true. So invocation 2 returns with the value of **bag**. To what does it return? It returns to the function that called it, that is, invocation 1.

The function **search_for_lost_object()** (invocation 1) now knows the value it wants to return - **bag**. So it returns with that value to the procedure that called it.

Every recursive function has two things in common with all other recursive functions.

1. At least one condition causes it to return without calling itself. This is the "terminating condition."
2. At least one situation causes it to invoke itself, either directly or indirectly. This is the "recursive condition."

In Figure 5-10, there are two terminating conditions. The function terminates when it has either run out of hiding places or found the object. The recursive condition is the default: The function has not run out of hiding places, nor has it found the object. A recursive function must have at least one terminating condition so that, at some point, it will leave the recursion.

A terminating condition does not in itself guarantee that the function will terminate. Usually, the function is designed with the real world in mind, and a terminator guarantee is built in. In this example, we know the function will terminate, since the number of hiding places in which it can look before it runs out of them is finite.

In Figure 5-11, we see a situation which, although it has a terminating condition, is not guaranteed of terminating.

```
find_friends_house_when_lost()
{
    if (look_for_house() == SPOTTED)
    {
        return (LOCATED);
    }
    else
    {
        make_a_random_turn();
        go_a_block();
        return (find_friends_house_when_lost());
    }
}
```

**FIGURE 5-11**

One final caution: Every time a function is called in C, some information is pushed onto the system stack (see previous discussion on stacks). This is true for recursive functions as well. A recursive function that calls itself too many times will eventually overrun the stack, yielding unpredictable results.

The example **find_friends_house_when_lost()** is a recursive function that can only return one thing: **LOCATED**. If the search continues too long, the stack will overflow, causing the program to, in some way, break down.

## Implementation

Now that we have explained the principles of recursive programming, we will examine how recursion can be applied to higher-level data types.

Searching for a particular object in a linked list is a typical problem with a recursive solution. Examine the problem of returning a pointer to the element of a linked list containing a particular item.

Given a pointer to the head of the linked list to be searched, there are several possibilities. First, the pointer could be the null pointer, in which case the item can not exist. Second, the function could find the item in the head of the list. Otherwise, the item could exist further down the list, perhaps in the next element.

If the function has not found the item, it must check the next element (#2). But element #2 is really the head of the linked list starting with element #2. Hence the same logic applies. We can therefore write this as a recursive function.

The example in Figure 5-12 will perform this recursive function with a linked list of **box_types**. This will be a one-way list, but the principle is identical for two-way lists.

```
struct box_type
{
  int top_row;
  int bottom_row;
  int left_column;
  int right_column;
  struct box_type *next_box;
};
/ ****************************************************************
This recursive function returns a pointer to the list element containing the
requested box. It returns NULL if the box could not be located.
**************************************************************** /
```

**FIGURE 5-12**

```
    box_type *find_box(list, box)
    struct box_type *list, *box;
    {
       if (list = = NULL)
       {
          return (NULL);
       }
       if (boxes_equal (list, box))
       {
          return (list);
       }
       else
       {
          return (find_box(list - >next_box, box));
       }
    }


    / ***************************************************************
    Check two boxes for equality
    Return true if equal, false otherwise.
    *************************************************************** /
    boxes_equal (box1, box2)
    struct box_type *box1, *box2;
    {
       return (
       (box1 - >top_row = = box2 - >top_row) &&
       (box1 - >bottom_row = = box2 - >bottom_row) &&
       (box1 - >left_column = = box2 - >left_column) &&
       (box1 - >right_column = = box2 - >right_column)
       )
    }
```

**Figure 5-12** (Continued)

This same function could have been written non-recursively (that is, itera-
tively), as in Figure 5-13.

The iterative function is probably better for searching linked lists. It is faster,
and involves no danger of overloading the stack. The recursive function is presented for illustative purposes only. In the next section, however, we present a
data type that would be very difficult to implement without recursion.

```
/ ********************************************************
This iterative function returns a pointer to the list element containing the
requested box. It returns NULL if the box could not be located.
******************************************************** /
box_type *find_box(list, box)
struct box_type *list, *box;
{
    while (list - >next_box != NULL)
    {
        if (boxes_equal(list, box))
        {
        return (list);
        }
        list = list - >next_box;
    }
    return (NULL);
}
```

**FIGURE 5-13**

## TREES

A tree is a data type often used in searching and sorting. While a linked list is
a data type that can be linked to another of the same data type, a tree can be
linked to at least two others of the same data type. We refer to the relationship
between an element in a tree and the other elements to which it is linked as a
parent-child relationship.

A binary tree is a special tree in which every element can have exactly two
children.

There are many different tree applications and tree algorithms; we will discuss just one in this section. The reader who would like to pursue this subject
is refered to an advanced text on data types.

### Search/Sort Trees

**Definition.**  You can visualize the way a tree works by imagining a series of
rooms (see Figure 5-14). Each room has two doors, each of which leads to
another room, and a third door leading back to the room from which we have
just come. Each room also bears a sign in its center, containing a unique word
and its definition.

The placement of the signs has been planned such that the left door leads to
a room with a word alphabetically less than the word in this room (i.e., it

appears earlier in the dictionary). The door on the right leads to a room with a word alphabetically greater (appearing later in the dictionary). If any door is locked, no rooms exist beyond it.

Typical Room
Leads back to previous room

"BANANA"
Yellow Fruit

Leads to a room
with a word greater
than "BANANA"

Leads to a room
with a word less
than "BANANA"

**Figure 5-14**

We are looking for the definition of the word "MARMALADE." We enter the first room, and find that its word is "LICORICE." Our word is greater ("M" comes after "L" in the alphabet), so we take the right door. We enter a room whose word is "SERENADE." Our word is less, so we take the left door. The next room has "OXYMORON," so we go left. The next room has "MEALY-MOUTHED," so we go left again. The next room has "LINGERIE," so we go right. The next room has "MARMALADE," and we are finished.

There are two possible endings to this story. We can either find the word, or end up in a room in which the door we want to leave by is locked. If this happens, we know that none of the rooms contain our word.

The process here is really quite remarkable. When we left the first room, we eliminated half of the rooms in the house. When we left the second, we eliminated half of the remaining rooms, and so on. If the original house had 320,000 rooms, how many rooms would we have to go through (in the worst case) before we found our word? The answer is found in Table 5-1.

**Table 5-1**

| Room | Eliminates | Rooms left |
|------|-----------|-----------|
| 1 | 160000 | 160000 |
| 2 | 80000 | 80000 |
| 3 | 40000 | 40000 |
| 4 | 20000 | 20000 |
| 5 | 10000 | 10000 |
| 6 | 5000 | 5000 |
| 7 | 2500 | 2500 |
| 8 | 1250 | 1250 |
| 9 | 625 | 625 |
| 10 | 313 | 312 |
| 11 | 157 | 156 |
| 12 | 78 | 78 |
| 13 | 39 | 39 |
| 14 | 19 | 20 |
| 15 | 10 | 10 |
| 16 | 5 | 5 |
| 17 | 3 | 2 |
| 18 | 1 | 1 |
| We have either arrived at our word, or it does not exist. | | |

We can do something else in this house. By following a recursive procedure, we can display all of the words in sorted order, either ascending or descending. The algorithm for the ascending display is shown in Figure 5-15.

```
display_words_in_ascending_order()
{
    char word[MAX_WORD_LENGTH];
    if (left_door_is_unlocked)
    {
        walk_out_left_door();
        display_words_in_ascending_order();
    }
    display_word_in_this_room();
    if (right_door_is_unlocked)
    {
        walk_out_right_door();
        display_words_in_ascending_order();
    }
}
```

**FIGURE 5-15**

Examine how this algorithm works in a small house, illustrated in Figure 5-16.

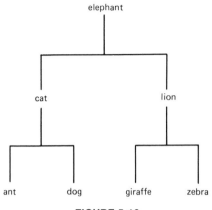

**FIGURE 5-16**

The function enters the elephant room, and invokes **display_word()** (invocation 1). It takes the left door to the cat room, and invokes **display_word()** (invocation 2).

In the cat room, the function takes the left door to the ant room and invokes **display_word()** (invocation 3). In the ant room, it finds the left door locked. So it displays "ANT," and tries the right door. The right door is locked, so the function returns to the function that called it: invocation 2, in the cat room.

Invocation 2 has now completed the first part of its task, so it displays "CAT," goes through the right door, and invokes **display_word()** (invocation 4).

The function is now in the dog room. The left door is locked. The function displays "DOG." The right door is locked. So the function returns to invocation 2.

Invocation 2 has now completed the left door, its own display, and the right door, so it is finished. It returns to invocation 1, in the elephant room.

The elephant room has now completed its left door, so it displays "ELEPHANT." And then it starts the entire process again by going through the right door.

At this point the following is displayed:

ANT
CAT
DOG
ELEPHANT

The reader is invited to complete the tracing of the algorithm and prove that the rest of the words do indeed show up in the right order.

You could modify the algorithm to display words in descending order by first leaving through the right door, printing the room's word, and then going through the left door.

To add a new word to the house, the function goes through the house as if searching for the new word. It will either find the word, in which case it does not need to add it, or it will come to a locked door. If it comes to a locked door, it unlocks the door, enters the room, and places the new word on the wall.

In the section on recursion, we discussed the system stack implications of recursive functions. Stack overload is unlikely to be a problem with trees, be-

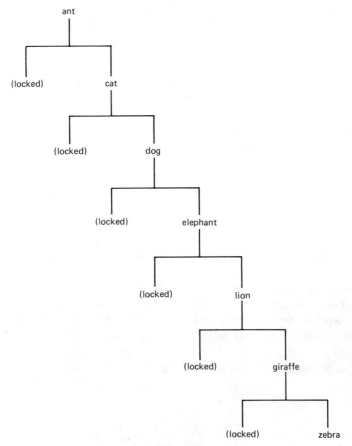

**FIGURE 5-17**

cause the maximum number of recursions which will be active at any one time is the depth of the tree. Earlier we showed that a tree of depth 18 was sufficient to plod through 320,000 rooms. Thus it seems unlikely that the system stack will be overloaded.

One note of caution is due, however. In this analysis, we have been assuming a ''balanced tree.'' In the animal room example, we could have constructed the tree as shown in Figure 5-17.

The algorithms described above are still valid for this tree, but search time is greatly increased. Our earlier statement that half the rooms are eliminated with each step is no longer valid for an imbalanced tree, and the more imbalanced the tree, the fewer the rooms eliminated with each step. A completely imbalanced tree, such as the one in Figure 5-17, is essentially a linked list, requiring the function to search sequentially through all elements until we reach our target item.

In most cases, the order of word insertion will be reasonably random, and the insertion algorithm we described will produce a reasonably balanced tree. If the insertion order is non-random, for example, the words are in alphabetical order before they are inserted, the result may well be an imbalanced tree.

If you know the words will come in non-randomly, you can often write a routine that semi-randomizes them before insertion. If you are still, for some reason, concerned about imbalanced trees, investigate some more complex insertion algorithms in an advanced text on data types. In particular, examine the tree structure known as AVL trees.

**Implementation.**  The code in Figure 5-18 implements a tree in C.

```
#include "stdio.h"
#define STRLEN 50

struct tree_type
{
    char string[STRLEN];
    struct tree_type *smaller;
    struct tree_type *bigger;
};
struct tree_type *tree;

/ **********************************************************
** Function init_tree()
** Initializes a tree
*********************************************************** /
```

**FIGURE 5-18**

```
struct tree_type *init_tree (nustring)
char *nustring;
{
   struct tree_type *new_tree;
   int size;

   size = sizeof(struct tree_type);
   new_tree = (struct tree_type *) malloc (size);
   strcpy (&(new_tree- >string[0]), nustring);

   new_tree- >smaller = NULL;
   new_tree- >bigger = NULL;
   return (new_tree);
}


/ ********************************************************
** Function add_to_tree()
** Adds an element to a tree
   ******************************************************* /
add_to_tree(tree, nustring)
struct tree_type *tree;
char *nustring;
{
   struct tree_type *next_room;
   int status;

/* If string is in this room, there is nothing to do. */

   if (!strcmp(nustring, tree- >string))
   {
      return;
   }

/* See which room to try next. */

   if ((status = strcmp(nustring, tree- >string)) < 0)
   {
      next_room = tree- >smaller;
   }
   else
   {
      next_room = tree- >bigger;
   }
```

Figure 5-18 (Continued)

```
/* If the room exists, continue there. */

    if (next_room != NULL)
    {
        add_to_tree(next_room, nustring);
    }

/* Otherwise, create that room. */

    else
    {
        if (status < 0)
        {
            tree->smaller = init_tree (nustring);
        }
        else
        {
            tree->bigger = init_tree (nustring);
        }
    }
}


/ ************************************************************
** Function print_tree()
** Prints the tree elements, in order
 ************************************************************ /
print_tree(tree)
struct tree_type *tree;
{
    if (tree->smaller != NULL)
    {
        print_tree(tree->smaller);
    }
    printf("%s\n", tree->string);
    if (tree->bigger != NULL)
    {
        print_tree(tree->bigger);
    }
}


/ ************************************************************
** Function get_string()
 ************************************************************ /
```

**Figure 5-18** *(Continued)*

```
  char *get_string()
  {
    static char nustring[STRLEN];

    printf("Word to add: ");
    scanf("%s", nustring);
    return(&nustring[0]);
  }
```

The following code uses the tree defined above:

```
main()
{
struct tree_type *tree;
char *nustring;

  nustring = get_string();
  tree = init_tree (nustring);
  for (;;)
  {
     nustring = get_string();
     if (nustring[0] == 'x')
     {
        break;
     }
     add_to_tree(tree, nustring);
  }
  print_tree (tree);
}
```

OUTPUT

Word to add: horse
Word to add: ant
Word to add: mouse
Word to add: fish
Word to add: ape
Word to add: dog
Word to add: cat
Word to add: x
ant
ape
cat
dog
fish
horse
mouse

**Figure 5-18** (Continued)

## CONCLUSION

This chapter has discussed, in detail, the implementations and applications of several advanced data types in C.More important, it has set forth a basic design tactic for defining any new data type in C:

1. Decide how the data type will behave
2. Decide on the basic set of operators needed to manipulate the data type
3. Represent the data type in terms of the standard C data types
4. Create a library of functions to provide the basic operators for the data type.

Appropriate data types are essential to an efficient application. The methodology employed in this chapter will enable you to easily create and use the data types you need.

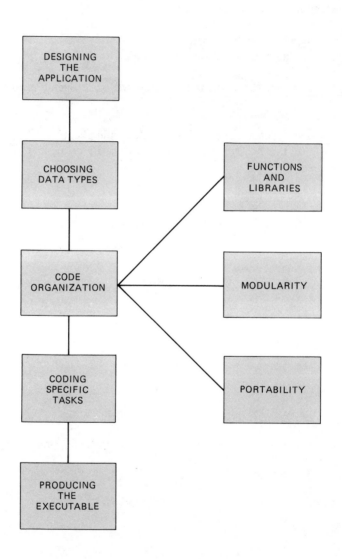

# Section C

# CODE ORGANIZATION

C, as a structured language, requires you to plan the organization of your code. Source code is not contained in a single file, nor is your program's flow coded as one continuous procedure. Rather, C programs are written in separate files, known as modules, and procedures are coded individually as functions. An efficient, easily debugged, and maintainable C application is carefully organized and divided into self-contained units. Before you begin writing your C code, you should map its operation onto functions and modules.

You will need to define the boundaries of each function, that is, decide how much of which task it will perform. You must also decide which functions should be grouped together in a module, and which functions and variables should be known to which other functions. These decisions are important tasks in creating an application in C. Well made, they will make your code much easier to write and debug, and will likely result in a collection of functions and modules that you can reuse in other applications.

The chapters in this section discuss the issues of code organization, with examples that follow the decision-making process. "Functions and Libraries" discusses the division of procedures into general-purpose functions, and provides some information on commercial libraries of functions available to the C programmer. "Modularity" defines and discusses modules, the level of code organization above individual functions. The chapter addresses the issues of the scope of variables and functions, and traces the process of dividing an application into self-sufficient, individual packages. "Portability" discusses those aspects of compilers, machines, and the C language which you need to consider in writing portable code. The chapter is a useful collection of possible problems and solutions, pointing out constructs to avoid and techniques for ensuring that your C code will be portable both among different compilers and different machines.

# 6
# Functions and Libraries

*Contributors:* Donald Killen of Greenleaf Software, Inc.
Donald K. Kinzer of Polytron Corporation
*Reviewer:* Dave Hirschman of Phoenix Software Associates, Ltd.
and Phoenix Computer Products Corporation

## FUNCTIONS

In order to maintain its portability, the C language itself does not include commands to accomplish many procedures. C, then, more so than most languages, requires functions. A function is an independent set of statements for performing some computation—a black box procedure. This black box need be written only once—by you, or by some outside manufacturer—and then can be used and reused without attention to its internal workings. The function performs the task, and the programmer need not worry again about how that task is performed.

Procedures that make good candidates for functions are those with most or all of the following characteristics:

1. The code for performing the task is confusing. Dealing with that code only once will make programming simpler.
2. The code is likely to change.
3. The task is one you will need to perform often within a single program. Writing it only once, in a function, and merely calling the function for each iteration of the task saves code.
4. The task is one you will want to perform again, in other programs. When the time comes to write those programs, part of the work will already be done.
5. The task is largely self contained, in that it requires complicated data structures, and can be used to isolate important design decisions from the remainder of the program.

## Input and Output

In order to be reusable, functions must be applicable in many different circumstances. To accomplish this generality, functions take input arguments that specify the details of each particular invocation.

Functions return information in one or both of two ways: by loading and passing a return value to the calling function, and by modifying global variables. Both returned values and modified variables can be pointers to larger blocks of memory.

## An Example: Homing the Cursor

To illustrate the writing, naming, documenting, and invoking of a function, we will use as an example a function that places the cursor in row 0, column 0. This task suits the criteria for a function stated earlier:

1. The code for homing the cursor is complicated (as will be demonstrated shortly).
2. The code is likely to change if we port it to a different computer. Cursor control is **not** consistent from one machine to the next.
3. and 4. Homing the cursor is a common, useful task that we will need to perform often within one program as well as in other programs.
5. The function will isolate the operation of the terminal, "hiding" it from the rest of the program.

Homing the cursor seems a simple task, but the C language makes no mention of cursors. Some new compilers include a function that positions the cursor, but most do not. Cursor control must be accessed through the operating system. With the IBM Personal Computer DOS (specifically the file **ansi.sys**), you can use the following C statements to position the cursor on row 0, column 0:

```
putchar( 27 );
printf("[0;0H");
```

The simple function shown in Figure 6-1, then, will home the cursor:

```
void homecursor()
{
    putchar( 27 );
    printf( "[0;0H" );
}
```

**FIGURE 6-1**

With the function in Figure 6-1 linked in with your code, a succinct call to **homecursor()** will home the cursor, and will be much more legible in your code than if the statements contained in that function were used instead.

A generalized version of this function will be more useful, however. The function **homecursor()** positions the cursor at (0,0); a generalized version will position the cursor at any row and column you specify. You will specify the particular row and column by passing them as arguments when you call the function from your code.

The function shown in Figure 6-2, **cur_set()**, will position the cursor at any row and column values specified.

```
cur_set(row,column)
int row;
int column;
{
    putchar( 27 );
    printf( "[%d;%dH", row, column);
}
```

**FIGURE 6-2**

To avoid undefined constants within the code, Figure 6-2 would be modified as shown in Figure 6-3.

```
#define ESC 27
cur_set(row,column)
int row;
int column;
{
    printf( "%c[%d;%dH", ESC, row, column);
}
```

**FIGURE 6-3**

If you use the version shown in Figure 6-3, remember to include the **#define** statement in your code before calling the function.

## Error Conditions

Because cursor positioning is a very reliable hardware operation, the functions above do not include reports of error conditions. Often, however, such reports are a valuable aid in debugging. Most error conditions on which you would want a report fall into one of three categories:

1. The function was passed an invalid parameter.
2. One of the functions called by the function returned an error code.
3. Some calculation performed by the function does not fall within the range of valid results.

If any of these conditions are likely to occur in your function, the function should check for them and return an error code indicating either the absence of error or the type of error encountered.

## Naming

Naming functions is an important part of writing them: it is the name that appears in the code, and ideally it should aid in self-documentation. The function **homecursor()**, for instance, describes by its name precisely what it does. Our generalized function, however, positions the cursor. The name **position_the-_cursor()**, while self-documenting, will be somewhat cumbersome to type each time you want to call the function. (It may be too long to be uniquely recognized by your compiler, as well.) We chose the name **cur_set()**, which is short enough to be entered easily, yet long enough to indicate the task accomplished by the function. Names like **pos_cur()** or **set_cur()** would work equally as well. Function names are based largely on your own preferences, but bear two opposing factors in mind: Keep the name short enough to be entered easily (and recognized by the compiler), but long enough to convey meaning. Names like **cs()** or **cp()** are easily entered, but will represent little to anyone else using the function.

## Functions, Declarations, and Calls

Having written and named the function, we need two more elements in order to use **cur_set()** in our code:

1. Function declaration, to appear at the top of our program.
2. Function call, to be customized when we need it.

The declaration line at the top of the program source file tells the compiler what to expect on return from a function. We therefore declare a function with the data type of the return value. If there is no return value, as in **cur_set()**, it makes no difference what type we declare: The compiler merely arranges for a return value of that type to be available. In general, functions with no return value are declared as type **int** or, if your compiler understands the term, type **void** (i.e., no return value). The relationships among functions, declarations, and calls are illustrated in Figure 6-4.

```
#define ESC 27
void cur_set();                              /* function declaration */

main()
{
    cur_set( 0, 0 );                         /* function call */
}
          .
          .
          .
cur_set(row,column)                          /* function */
int row;
int column;
{
    printf( "%c[%d;%dH", ESC, row, column);
}
```

**FIGURE 6-4**

## Documentation

Our function has now been written, (tested), declared, and called. It will operate as expected in the code. What is still missing, however, is documentation. A function without a manual page is useful, but will not be for long. Argument lists, returned values, parameters modified, and specifics of the task performed are all easily forgotten. Build a manual page, a scrap of paper, or a file on your computer describing precisely what **cur_set()** does. Write the documentation when you write the function. That way, it will correspond as closely as possible to the function itself. When you design a function, write down what you want to do, write the function, then write the manual page, while you still remember the facts. If you put it off, you may not recall a caveat, a quirk, or a suggestion that the function's users (which include you, at some later date) should know about. A function's documentation should include the function name, its type, its input arguments, its return value, any parameters it modifies, and the specific task it performs, as well as any cautions, limitations, suggestions, and the like.

## LIBRARIES

A library is a collection of object modules—independently compiled source files—all stored in a single file. You can purchase commercial libraries, containing one or more modules of functions, or, by using a librarian, you can create your own libraries from the functions you have written.

In linking together the object modules that constitute your application, the linker may discover that some variables and/or functions are referenced but not defined in any of the object modules explicitly mentioned in the linker invocation. The linker therefore searches the specified libraries for the unresolved references, and links those modules (from the libraries) that are required to resolve the references.

Note that the linker does not include individual functions or variable definitions, but individual modules. The module is the "atomic" unit to the linker. Pay attention, then, both in buying commercial libraries and in creating your own, to the organization of functions into modules. Ideally, one module should contain functions and definitions such that either all will be needed in an application, or none will be needed. Realistically, modules should be as close to this ideal as possible. Such efficient module design keeps the resulting application of minimal size: Only the code needed is included, and there is little or no "overhead" of included functions and definitions that are not referenced.

## Object Module Librarians

To build your own libraries of object modules, you can use a commercially available utility called an object module librarian. The minimum requirements for such a utility are the abilities to:

—create a new (empty) library
—add a module to an existing library

Additional features in a librarian are often useful. The following list of capabilities may help you in choosing a librarian:

—merge two libraries
—add specified modules from one library to another
—specify the position of added modules relative to modules already in the library
—replace a module with a specified module(s)
—delete a module
—copy a module to a separate object file
—change module names
—list module names
—list public names within modules
—identify modules containing publics or external references
—cross reference public and external references
—time stamp modules with creation date
—support multiple library formats

—support names specified using "wild card" characters
—support interactive, command line, and command file operational modes
—support intermixing of modes and mode nesting
—provide access to the operating system in interactive mode
—supply on-line help
—automatically (re)name modules
—provide protection from operator error and suitable overrides

## Pre-Defined Functions

Since C provides so little in the way of ready-made procedures, a programmer can spend a lot of time writing functions to accomplish all the necessary tasks to build even the simplest of applications. The job at hand, however, is to build the application. Much of the work has been done already, by independent developers marketing "C Libraries"—sets of pre-packaged functions. One approach, which many take, is to buy several of these and sort through them, selecting the functions that seem useful. Do not expect to find everything you need in a single product.

**Compiler-Provided Functions.** Every compiler comes with a set of functions. Not all compilers have the same functions, however, and no standard has yet been developed. There is a "standard I/O library," but while every compiler has I/O functions that are more or less equivalent in the tasks they perform, the particulars vary widely. The following general functions are considered the minimum requirements for any compiler for the IBM PC:

1. Low-level file I/O functions to:
   —close a file
   —create a new file
   —open a file
   —read data from a file
   —write data to a file
   —remove a file name from the file system
2. DOS level file I/O functions to:
   —open a buffered file
   —read blocks of data from a file
   —write blocks of data to a file
   —close a buffered file
   —seek to a specified file position
   —rename a file
3. Character I/O functions (to file or console) to:
   —get a character from a file

—get a string from a file
—send a character to a file

4. Memory allocation functions to:
   —allocate and clear a block of memory
   —allocate a block of memory (compatible with UNIX)
   —release a block of memory

5. Formatted I/O functions to:
   —get a character from the standard input file
   —send a character to the standard input file
   —generate formatted output (to the standard output file, to a specified file, or to a specified output string)
   —perform formatted input conversions (from the standard output file, from a specified file, or from a specified line)
   —flush the output buffer of a specified file

6. String operations to:
   —copy a string
   —compare two strings
   —measure string length
   —concatenate two strings

7. Miscellaneous functions to:
   —terminate execution of a program
   —move data to a specified buffer from a specified memory address
   —move data from a specified buffer to a specified memory address
   —determine if the parameter is an alphabetic character
   —determine if the parameter is a digit
   —determine if the parameter is upper case
   —determine if the parameter is lower case
   —convert a character to upper case
   —convert a character to lower case
   —generate random numbers

In addition to these essentials are some near-essentials provided with most compilers. These include functions to:

—check for end of file
—return the current file position
—get a character directly from the console
—send a character directly to the console
—push a character back to the console
—check for a key pressed
—perform mathematical functions
—perform data type conversion
—perform general purpose system access

**Commercial Libraries.** Many functions are still left to be found in commercial libraries, however. Since such a wide variety of library products are available, collect as much information about the products as possible. Get a list of functions for each. The following checklist of questions should help you in your search:

1. Do the functions do what you want?
2. Is there a royalty you would have to pay if you sell your application program and it employs one of the functions from the library?
3. Does the library support the compiler (version and memory model) you wish to use? Will it be updated to support possible revisions in your compiler?
4. How are the functions organized—in one file, or in a DOS library format where each function is a separate module? In the former case, every function will be included in the link. In the latter case, only those functions that are referenced are included, cutting down on program space.

(The following considerations, while phrased specifically in terms of libraries, apply to any commercial software:)

5. Is source code included (or is it available at extra cost) in case you want to modify certain functions?
6. Is competent support available quickly?
7. Is a demonstration disk available?
8. How long has this product been on the market and how many have been sold? What generally is the reputation of the firm that developed the library?
9. Is the product available now?
10. How good is the documentation? Are there examples of each function? Demo programs? Are functions named in a manner that will be easy to remember?
11. How easy will it be to install the libraries?

You may note that the above checklist contains no mention of price. The retail price of most C libraries for microcomputers is inconsequential relative to the amount of time and money it would take to duplicate even a few of its functions.

*The Greenleaf Functions.* The Greenleaf Functions is one commercial C library containing about 200 functions relevant to the IBM PC. This is typical of the many "general" library products available. This library is structured around 13 categories of functions:

1. DOS—disk-related functions.

2. Video effects, cursor, and so on.
3. Video, graphics, color graphics.
4. Display, color text.
5. String manipulation, string I/O.
6. Printer data and control.
7. Keyboard, console I/O.
8. Time and Date.
9. Serial I/O.
10. Equipment determination, register read, peeks, pokes.
11. Math (random numbers).
12. Diagnostics.
13. System interface and miscellaneous.

Note that there is no such thing as a "complete" C library, since there is always one more way to do things, and one more thing that needs to be done.

Screen display functions.  In addition to cursor positioning, this category includes functions to:

—make the cursor disappear (to eliminate the "snow" that is present when the cursor moves rapidly)
—make the cursor reappear
—change the cursor's shape
—print messages on the display faster than **printf()** does
—display strings, characters, and formatted arguments in color and with various attributes (e.g., high intensity or reverse video) to provide contrast.
—scroll the display at will
—determine the cursor position
—select color or monochrome display
—set a video mode
—set a video page
—create simple graphs or bar charts
—print some data in hex simply and rapidly (without using **printf()**)
—center or justify text on the display
—set the color palette or border color for a color display

Disk operations.  Most C compilers include file I/O functions. Some tasks still remain, however, which many compiler libraries do not address. The Greenleaf package offers C routines to access directly the disk hardware of the IBM PC.

Keyboard functions.  You can always look up the codes for function keys and cursor control (arrow) keys, but your code is clearer and easier to write as shown in Figure 6-5.

```
#include "ibmkeys.h"

if (getkey() = = F1)
{
    printf( "Help Is On The Way...");
    do_help_screen();
}
```

**FIGURE 6-5**

The **#included** header file that defines the keys and the function to retrieve the key pressed are part of The Greenleaf Functions. You will find similar pieces in other general libraries. A function like The Greenleaf Function's **kbhit()** is useful as well, to return TRUE if any key has been pressed or FALSE otherwise. Functions to determine if a shift or shift lock key is in effect are useful in keyboard processing, as well.

Time and date functions.   You may want functions to retrieve and display the system time and date. Using The Greenleaf Functions, you can write code like that shown in Figure 6-6.

```
#include "timedate.h"
struct TIMEDATE *timedate;

timedate = gettime();
printf( "The System Says it Is: %s\n", timedate- >dateline);
```

**FIGURE 6-6**

The code in Figure 6-6 will print something like:

The System Says it Is 07-Jan-85 12:15:00pm

String manipulation functions.   Common string manipulation functions include deleting, inserting, replacing, or blanking out specified characters or words, generating string pointer lists, sorting strings, retrieving keyboard input, and the like.

Printer functions.   Functions to facilitate output to the printer typically include capabilities like the following:

—write string to printer
—center string on printer

—justify string on printer
—**printf()** for printer
—center formatted arguments on printer
—set bold typeface on printer
—screen print
—print graphics

These and many more control and data functions will be useful if, for example, you write a word processor or a program that has extensive output.

Other functions. The list of other functions you may need and which exist now in commercial C libraries is a long one. A few common examples, found in The Greenleaf Functions are:

—determine installed equipment
—generate random number
—general system interface
—initialize serial port
—write to serial port
—get character from serial port
—peek
—poke

If you are looking for more detail in a specific area, look for specialized libraries. You can find, for example, interrupt driven communications libraries, ISAM libraries, data entry libraries, "windows" libraries, fast video libraries, libraries that concentrate on math functions, and more. The guidelines above may help in the selection of a library for your application. The lists above may give you some ideas for things to look for in libraries. The important point is that many of the functions you need have already been written, and are easily available to you. While re-inventing them may provide a learning experience, the time and effort that experience requires are unnecessary. By building on the work of others, you are free to proceed with the development of your own applications.

## CONCLUSION

This chapter has covered the basic points of creating functions and libraries: the building blocks of modular code. Remember that many of the modules you need have already been written, and can easily be purchased and incorporated into your code. Assemble a useful collection of the types of functions you will need in writing your applications.When the appropriate functions can not be found, write them yourself, keeping them general in purpose and clearly documented so that you and others can use and reuse them.

# 7
# Modularity

*Contributors:* Larry Karnis and Jon Simkins of Softfocus
*Reviewer:* Fred Butzen of Mark Williams Company

## INTRODUCTION

C is designed for modular programming, i.e., dividing a program into a number of discrete packages called modules. The interactions among these modules are carefully controlled. A modular C program provides significant advantages over its alternative—a linear sequence of commands. Both the advantages and the methodology of modular programming are discussed in this chapter.

## What Is a Module?

Formally, a module is a syntactic unit that provides separate compilation and data encapsulation. Some languages have very precise modular architecture (e.g., Ada, Modula2, Turing). C is more relaxed in its approach to modules. A module in C is simply any single compilation unit. A module usually consists of a set of related functions and their corresponding data. In short, a module is a file of code.

## Why Use Modules?

The major advantages of modular programming in C are presented below:

1. Most real-world programs will not fit in one file. Because modules are independent files, they allow you to write larger programs.
2. Re-compiling a large file takes time. A single module, which is much smaller than an entire program, can be compiled reasonably quickly.
3. A module can isolate a single, useful set of functions, and can thus be reused in other programs.

4. A module can be written, tested, and debugged independently of the rest of the program. The debugging process is thus simplified, since it covers only one small, manageable piece of code at a time.
5. Modules provide you with more ways of scoping than would otherwise be available, and as the following sections will demonstrate, scoping helps you write readable, error-free code.

## STORAGE CLASSES

As discussed in Chapter 4, Elementary Data Types, a variable's storage class determines its lifetime and its scope: where in the program it is known. Briefly reviewing our discussion of a variable's scope from Chapter 4:

1. A variable declared with no storage class within a module can be used by any function in the program. It can be used by any function in its own module without a special declaration. Any other module must declare it **extern** in order to use it.
2. A variable declared **static** within a module, but not within a function, can only be used by functions within that module.
3. A variable declared **static** within a function can only be used by that function.
4. A variable declared with no storage class within a function (an **auto** variable) can only be used by that function, and it ceases to exist as soon as the program exits that function.
5. As mentioned in Chapter 3, Style, it's often a good idea to define all globally known variables in a single file, and declare them as **extern** in a corresponding header file. You are then guaranteed of the appropriate declarations in all modules by a single **#include** statement in each module.

Functions are also subject to storage classes. Only two storage classes apply to functions:

1. A function defined with no storage class is available to all other functions in the program. One caution applies, however. To call a non-integer function from another module, you must declare it, with its type and storage class, within the calling module. You can declare it outside of the calling function, as

   **extern char \*function();**

   for example, or within the calling function, as

   **char \*function();**

Without such a declaration, the compiler will assume that the function returns an integer.

2.  A function defined as **static** can only be called by functions defined in the same module. The **static** storage class is used to avoid name clashes in programs that have many function definitions. As we will see, it has other, even more important uses.

A common practice in C is to omit storage class declarations, relying on the compiler to select the appropriate class through context. If you follow this practice, all functions and all variables you declare outside of functions will be known throughout the program. While this is the most flexible arrangement possible, it is inconsistent with the approach of modular programming. Modules become less independent as the number of ways in which they can be affected by the rest of the program increases.

Modules in C make heavy use of the **static** storage class declaration. **Statics** are effectively hidden from the rest of the program, because they can only be affected by functions within their scope.

## AN EXAMPLE OF MODULAR DEVELOPMENT

The example used here is a simple stack. As we have seen in Chapter 5, Advanced Data Types, a stack is a data type that supports at least two operations: pushing and popping. Values are either pushed onto or popped from the top of the stack. The last value pushed will be the first value popped.

Suppose a stack is required as part of a larger project. Suppose, further, that the only values that will be stacked are positive integers. Coding quickly and without regard for modularity, a programmer might produce code structured like Figure 7-1.

The code in Figure 7-1 is poor code written in a hurry: It consists of a single source file with many function and data definitions and lots of global variables. These globals are available to all functions, not just to those that need them. Error checking takes a back seat to the task at hand.

The code in Figure 7-1 is only ready for testing when all of it has been written. The programmer's next job is to force each function to work within the entire program. Often, time is spent making sure that one function does not accidentally destroy global data that other functions depend on, or correcting such data when they are destroyed.

Because of time or other considerations, the programmer might even be tempted to skip coding some functions, and code **push()** as **stack[stk_indx++]** = **x** and **pop()** as **x = stack[--stk_indx]** whenever they are needed. While simple enough, such code is not self-documenting. Repeated in-line code is also redundant. The compiler must generate a new set of instructions every time it executes the same sequence, rather than doing it once and referring to the in-

```
/* Stack code; part of a larger program */
#define STACKSIZE 100
         .
         .
         .
/* other #defines */

int stk_indx = 0;
int stack[STACKSIZE];
/* other declarations */
         .
         .
         .
/* function definitions */

push(x)
int x;
{
    stack[stk_indx++] = x;
}

pop()
{
    return stack[--stk_indx];
}
         .
         .
         .
/* other function/data declarations */
main()
{
         .
         .
         .
}
/* even more function/data declarations */
```

**FIGURE 7-1**

structions by their function name. Since no checking is performed on the top or bottom of the stack, unusual conditions can cause the code to alter memory outside of the stack array and cause the program to "blow up" in quite mysterious ways.

Fortunately, few programmers take such a direct approach to solving a problem. Most recognize the benefits of separate compilation for larger programs and often use some of the techniques that lead to modular programming. It seems natural to pull the stack operations out of the main program and put them in their own source file. A more plausible example of the stack module is presented in Figure 7-2.

```
/* Stack module */

#define STACKSIZE 100

static int stk_indx;
static int stack[STACKSIZE];

push(x)
int x;
{
   if (stk_indx == STACKSIZE - 1)
   {
     error("stack overflow");
     return ERROR;
   }
   stack[stk_indx++] = x;
   return OK:
}

pop()
{
   int result;
   if (--stk_indx < 0)
   {
     error("stack underflow");
     return ERROR;
   }
   result = stack[stk_indx];
   stack[stk_indx] = 0;
   return result;
}

init()
{
   int i;
   stk_indx = 0;
   for (i=0; i < STACKSIZE; i++)
   {
     stack[i] = 0;
   }
}
```

FIGURE 7-2

In this case, we have gone out of our way to explicitly state the initializations required. The compiler is not relied on to do the job, and other programmers will find the starting state of the module better defined. There are other examples of defensive programming in this code. The location that held the most recently popped value is set to zero so that it can never be confused with valid data. This approach greatly speeds debugging by limiting the potential for problems.

All functions that need access to the stack data are included in this file. To avoid possible name clashes, the **stk_indx** and **stack** variables have been declared **static.** These variables are now safe from reference (or indirect reference) by functions in other modules. Debugging becomes a much simpler task. The stack module stands alone and can be tested alone. Once the stack module works, it can be put aside with some confidence.

This strategy illustrates a typical advantage of modules. They are built to package a set of related operations on a single type of data (in this case a stack). You can debug them by writing test cases that exercise all non-static functions. Once they are debugged and documented, you can put them into a "tool chest" and use them again whenever a new program needs them. Using the new module is as simple as making calls to its external functions. The inner workings of the module are of no concern. All that matters is that the module was tested and worked reliably.

The code in Figure 7-2 handles errors reasonably well. It performs enough testing to ensure that the operation being requested makes sense (no items are popped from an empty stack) and that it can do the job required (no item is pushed onto a full stack). Like most modules, it can do little about an error condition other than report it to the caller and leave the caller to handle the error in an appropriate way. A good rule of thumb is to write code that returns a success/failure status.

It is a simple task to pass the new module on, for other programmers to use. Documentation as simple as an explanation of what the code does and a short description of each externally known function in the module will suffice. Programmers can use each others' functions without having to concern themselves with the details of the code involved.

Our example is well on its way to being a useful piece of software. It still leaves room for improvement, though. A stack must be initialized via an **init()** call. With larger programs, you may find it difficult to remember the names of all the initialization functions for each module called. Even greater problems arise if the initialization routine is inadvertently called a second time. A good way around this is to have the module initialize itself, as in Figure 7-3.

In Figure 7-3, two **#defines**, **LOCAL** and **ENTRY**, are introduced. They are meant to better document the scope of functions and variables within the module. Since **LOCAL** is a synonym for **static**, anything preceded by the word

```
/* Stack module, self-initializing */

#define STACKSIZE 100
#define ENTRY
#define LOCAL static

LOCAL int stk_indx;
LOCAL int initialized = FALSE;
LOCAL int stack[STACKSIZE];

ENTRY int push(x)
int x;
{
    int result;

    result = ERROR;                    /* always assume the worst */
    if (!initialized)
    {
        init();
    }
    if (stk_indx == STACKSIZE - 1)
    {
        error("stack overflow");
    }
    else
    {
        stack[stk_indx++] = x;
        result = OK;
    }
    return result;
}

ENTRY int pop()
{
    int result;

    result = ERROR;
    if (!initialized)
    {
        init();
    }
    if (--stk_indx < 0)
    {
```

FIGURE 7-3

```
        stk_indx = 0;
        error("stack underflow");
    }
    else
    {
        result = stack[stk_indx];
        stack[stk_indx] = 0;
        result = OK;
    }
}

LOCAL int init()
{
    int i;
    if (initialized)
    {
        return;
    }
    stk_indx = 0;
    initialized = TRUE;
    for (i=0; i < STACKSIZE; i++)
    {
        stack[i] = 0;
    }
}
```

**FIGURE 7-3** (*Continued*)

**LOCAL** is known only within that module. It is applied to all non-**auto** variables in the module, and to every function that is not needed outside the module. **ENTRY** does not define anything (the C pre-processor just ignores it), but it does inform the reader that this function is a callable entry point of the module. It has another use that we will see later.

Self-initialization is accomplished through the introduction of one new variable: **initialized**. It ensures that **init()** is called only once, whenever the module is first entered. The function **init()** itself has an extra line of code that prevents it from being called a second time from within the module. This is an extra bit of defensive programming that thwarts any attempt to re-initialize the module incorrectly. The cost of the entire mechanism is not high: one **static** integer and an **if** statement in every **ENTRY** function. The benefit is that the programmer need never worry about initializing the module.

The stack module is now complete enough that it can be documented and used. However, just like the code in Figure 7-1, it could rightly be accused of being overly specialized. It currently will stack up to a maximum of 100 positive integers, and will only manage one stack. In order for our new tool to be more useful, we will remove one of these restrictions, in Figure 7-4.

```
/* Stack module, self-initializing, stacks any data type */

#define STACKSIZE 100
#define ENTRY
#define LOCAL static

struct stacktype
{
    char *value;
    int length;
};

LOCAL int stk_indx;
LOCAL int initialized = FALSE;
LOCAL stacktype stack[STACKSIZE];

extern char *malloc();
extern void free();

ENTRY int push(x, size)
char *x;
int size;
{
    int result, i;

    result = ERROR;
    if (!initialized)
    {
        init();
    }
    if (stk_indx == STACKSIZE - 1)
    {
        error("stack overflow");
    }
    else if ((stack[stk_indx].value = malloc(size)) == (char *) 0)
    {
        error("out of memory");
    }
```

FIGURE 7-4

```
    else
    {
      for (i=0; i < size; i++)
      {
          stack[stk_indx].value[i] = x[i];
      }
      stack[stk_indx].length = size;
      stk_indx++;
      result = OK;
    }
    return result;
}

ENTRY int pop(dest)
char *dest;
{
    int result;

    result = ERROR;
    if (!initialized)
    {
        init();
    }
    if (--stk_indx < 0)
    {
        stk_indx = 0;
        error("stack underflow");
    }
    else if (stack[stk_indx].value == (char *) 0)
    {
        error("illegal stack value pointer");
    }
    else
    {
        for (i=0; i < stack[stk_indx].length; i++)
        {
            dest[i] = stack[stk_indx].value[i];
        }
        free(stack[stk_indx].value);
        stack[stk_indx].value = (char *) 0;
        stack[stk_indx].length = 0;
        result = OK;
    }
    return result;
}
```

FIGURE 7-4 (Continued)

```
LOCAL void init()
{
    int i;
    stk_indx = 0;
    initialized = TRUE;
    for (i=0; i < STACKSIZE; i++)
    {
        stack[i].value = (char *) 0;
        stack[i].length = 0;
    }
}
```

**FIGURE 7-4** (*Continued*)

Various stack calls now look like

```
push(buf, sizeof(buf));
pop(nextname);
push(name, strlen(name));
pop(name);
push(&token, sizeof(struct tokentype));
pop(&token);
```

Making initialization a separate function has finally paid off. The initializations are now complex enough that it would be difficult if not impossible to do the job with C's initializers.

The stack module will now operate on any type of data. This is possible because **push()** takes a pointer to the item to be stacked and the item's size. Because the type of the item being stacked is unknown, its pointer is declared as **char \***, since character pointers are usually the least restrictive type. Since the size of the item is also unknown, the number of bytes it consumes must also be passed. C provides the **sizeof** operator to determine the item's size.

Before actually stacking an item, the **push()** function allocates room for it by calling **malloc()**. The **malloc()** function is a general-purpose storage allocation function that makes a chunk of **size** bytes available to the module. The stacked item is protected from accidental modification by the calling module, since copies of items, not originals, are pushed and popped. Finally, with **malloc()**, only the amount of storage really needed is claimed.

The stack module still has two restrictions: It only allows a maximum of 100 items to be stacked, and it only manages one stack at a time. The first restriction is fairly reasonable, and can be tailored when the module is compiled, if necessary. The second may prove to be much more of a problem. We will leave it as a task for the reader to recode the module to define:

**makestack()**: creates a new stack and returns a number that references the new stack; and

**freestack()**: deletes an unwanted stack

and to modify **push()**, **pop()**, and **init()** accordingly.

The **ENTRY** pseudo-label has another significant use besides internal documentation. It can be used to build automatically a file that contains the definitions of all functions that other modules can call. Using an editor or a pattern searching program (such as UNIX's **grep**), you can produce an entry header. For example,

    **grep "ENTRY" modname.c > modentry.h**

will extract all lines that declare an entry point within the module **modname.c** and copy them to **modentry.h**. Some simple editing will result in an entry header file that would (in the case of our stack module) look like Figure 7-5.

```
/* Entry header file for stack module */

extern int push()
extern int pop()
```

**FIGURE 7-5**

This header can be **#included** in any program that uses the stack functions.

## ERROR HANDLING MODULES

Modularity provides a useful option in error handling techniques. There is no single right way to handle error processing. In some cases it is best to return an error value to the calling function and let the calling function take any recovery action. In other situations, it is more appropriate to try to recover locally, or even to abort program execution. In general, however, it is best to centralize all error handling within an error handling module.

Creating a single error handling module allows you to make any changes in error processing philosophy within that module, without affecting the rest of the program. The error handler is passed a number that signifies the problem, for example,

**error(OUTOFMEMORY);**

In this case, it would probably be appropriate to print an informative message and cease execution.

In Figure 7-6, several good practices are illustrated.

1. Error values are specified as **#defined** constants.
2. Each module is assigned a range of error values that it can use.
3. All error values are contained within header files.

The header file in Figure 7-6 allows the maximum possible errors per module to be easily changed to suit the requirements of a developing program. In this case, the first error number will be 100, and up to 100 errors can be defined within any module.

```
/* General error value header */

#define MAXERRORS      100         /* max errors per module */
#define ERRSTART       100         /* lowest error number */

#define MODULEONE      ERRSTART
#define MODULETWO      ERRSTART + MAXERRORS
#define MODULETHREE    ERRSTART + (MAXERRORS * 2)
...
```

**FIGURE 7-6**

For each module, produce a file (perhaps called "**modname.err**") that will look something like Figure 7-7.

```
/* Error codes for module "moduleone" */

#define FIRSTERR       MODULEONE      /* explain it here */
#define SECONDERR      FIRSTERR + 1   /* explain it here */
#define THIRDERR       SECONDERR + 1  /* explain it here */
...
```

**FIGURE 7-7**

A practical example of this technique is shown in Figure 7-8.

```
/* Central error definition */

#define MAXERRORS        100      /* maximum errors per module */
#define ERRSTART         100          /* lowest error number */
#define STACKERR         ERRSTART


/* stack.err */

#define STACKOVER        STACKERR
#define STACKUNDER       STACKOVER + 1
#define NOMEMORY         STACKUNDER + 1
#define ILLEGAL          NOMEMORY + 1
...
```

FIGURE 7-8

Each module, then, begins something like the module shown in Figure 7-9.

```
/* Stack module */

#include <any compiler dependent include files>
#include "my_favorite_constants.h"          /* file with often used,
                                                non-program dependent
                                                         constants */
#include "program_specific_constants.h"      /* any defines that
                                                all modules need */
#include "program_externals.h"               /* external declarations */
#include "errornum.h"               /* include files that specify range
                                                           values */
#include "stack.err"               /* constants specific to this module */

/* local declarations */

/* function definitions */

/* end of module */
```

FIGURE 7-9

The module that handles errors needs to know the values of the error constants, as does the module that first catches the error. A central error handler leaves room for considerable creativity. The example in Figure 7-10 prints an informative message and, if the error is signaled from **MODULEONE**, terminates the program. Other actions can be taken for ranges of error values within other modules.

```
/* Error handling for "some_program" */

#include "errornum.h"
#include "stack.err"
#include "queue.err"
#include "input.err"
...                          /* a #include statement for each module */

error(value)
int value;
{
   switch(value)
   {
      case ERRORONE:
         msg = "informative message";
         break;
      case ERRORTWO:
         msg = "descriptive error message";
         break;
      case ERRORTHREE:
         msg = " ... ";
         break;
   }
   fprintf(stderr, "program_name: error %d: %s", value, msg);
   if (value > = MODULEONE && value < MODULETWO)
   {
      exit(ERROR);            /* errors from module one are terminal */
   }
   else if ( ... )
   {
      ...
   }
   else if ( ... )
   {
      ...
   }
   ...
}
```

**FIGURE 7-10**

In Figure 7-10, all constants are available to the error handling module without any repeated definitions. As a program evolves and the range of errors changes, only one include file needs to be edited. When the system is recompiled, it will continue to work.

Using this technique, you can delete an error message by removing its definition from an error include file and editing to preserve the relationship between errors. (The next error is one value greater than the previous error).

The advantages to this method of error handling are:

1. You can easily find and edit definitions.
2. There is less chance of redundancy.
3. You can easily change your manner of error handling as the program evolves.

The single greatest disadvantage is the rapid proliferation of error header files. Use of a program maintenance utility, that is, a **make** program, is almost essential.

## TOOLS

Several software tools are available to ease development and design of large modular programs.

The first is an editor that can manage several source files independently in discrete windows. For example, See, by Prologic Corporation, supports the simultaneous editing of up to 20 source files. With such an editor, you can load all pertinent files into separate editor windows, and reference them as necessary.

A string search utility (such as the aforementioned **grep**, found in UNIX) is very handy for quickly building header files and invaluable in general for tracking global variables through a large number of modules. Public domain versions of **grep** are becoming available for nearly every operating system.

Finally, a compilation manager is almost essential. As a program grows, compiling and linking become more complex. When the program is small, it is fairly simple to keep track of which modules have been edited, and ensure that they are compiled before the system is re-linked. But the chances of forgetting to compile a changed module grow as more modules are added to the program. A **make** utility, discussed in Chapter 14, will automate this process for you.

## CONCLUSION

Modularity is one of the distinguishing features of C code. Generally useful, self-contained modules make your code easier to test, debug, modify, and maintain, and allow you to reuse your own pieces of code as well as those written by others. The example presented in this chapter is a model of many important considerations in writing modular code: scoping, error checking, generality, and self-contained functionality.

# 8
# Portability

*Contributor:* Kenneth Pugh of Pugh-Killeen Associates
*Reviewer:* James F. Gimpel, Ph.D. of Gimpel Software

## INTRODUCTION

C is one of the most portable of programming languages. The compiler writer's reliance on a single reference book has created few differences between compilers. Further enhancing the portability of C, an ANSI committee is (at this writing) creating a standard for the language. This standard will cover items such as the minimum size for data types, number of significant characters in variable names, and similar issues. The basis for the standard is Kernighan and Ritchie.

## MACHINE DEPENDENCIES

A few machine-dependent operations do exist in C, however. The major areas of concern in transporting code from one machine to another are discussed below.

### Length of Data Types

The lengths of data types often vary from one machine to the next. For example, an **int** on some machines is 16 bits. On others it is 32 bits. A program developed on a "large integer" machine using large numbers will not work on the "small integer" machine. One method for overcoming this incompatibility is to use either a **typedef** or **#define** for declaring the variable, as in

**#define INTEGER int**

on the small integer machine and

**#define INTEGER long**

on the large integer machine, so that

**INTEGER i;**

will be compiled as a 32 bit integer regardless of the machine.

The **sizeof()** operator can be used to determine the size of a data type, so that you can use the appropriate declaration. For example, the code in Figure 8-1 will set the declaration to the appropriate type.

```
#if sizeof(int) = = 2
#define INTEGER long
#endif
#if sizeof(int) = = 4
#define INTEGER int
#endif
```

**FIGURE 8-1**

If an **int** is neither 2 nor 4 bytes, then **INTEGER** will be undefined and the program will not compile. You can then decide what size to use for this data type.

## ANSI Standard Data Type Lengths

C compilers that meet the new ANSI standard guarantee that data types will be able to hold at least the values shown in Table 8-1. Bytes (**char**) contain at least 8 bits. **Floats** and **doubles** have at least 6 decimal digits of precision and an exponent range from $10^{-38}$ to $10^{38}$.

**Table 8-1**

| Type | Minimum Range |
| --- | --- |
| **char** | 0 to 127 |
| **signed char** | $-127$ to $+127$ |
| **unsigned char** | 0 to 255 |
| **short int** | $-32767$ to $+32767$ |
| **unsigned short int** | 0 to 65535 |
| **int** | $-32767$ to $+32767$ |
| **unsigned int** | 0 to 65535 |
| **long int** | $-2147483647$ to $+2147483647$ |
| **unsigned long int** | 0 to 4294967295 |

## Mixing Pointers and Integers

Word length differences can cause an insidious error if you mix pointers and integers. Pointers on some machines are 32 bits, while standard integers are 16 bits. Thus for the code in Figure 8-2, the variable **pc** will not have the same value after execution.

```
int *pc;
int i;
i=pc;
pc=i;
```

**FIGURE 8-2**

This error is easily overlooked in functions that return pointers rather than integers. Since the compiler assumes that functions return integers (unless declared otherwise), code such as that shown in Figure 8-3 will, with some compilers, compile and run.*

```
int *pi;
int k;
...
pi = func(a);
k = *pi;

int *func(a)
int a;
{
    ...
}
```

**FIGURE 8-3**

When the value of the pointer returned exceeds the maximum value of an integer, however, the program will yield incorrect results. It is wise to declare explicitly all functions not returning integers in a header file that is **#included** in all source files. The value of a function that does not return a parameter is undefined, so declaring it as type **void** helps the compiler (and **lint**) check that this undefined value is never used.

Pointers to functions may have different lengths than pointers to data, even on the same machine. For example, 8088 machines have both a current segment

---

*A **lint** program applied to the source code will catch the error illustrated in Figure 8-3.

(near) function call and a non-current segment (far) function call. The former is a 2-byte pointer, while the latter is a 4-byte pointer.

## Byte Order

Computers differ in the order in which they store bytes in an integer (see Table 8-2), in their internal representation of **floats**, and in the requirements for alignment of data types in storage. Unless you try to access the individual bytes of an integer or to transfer files that contain internal representations of numbers, this normally creates no problems. Consider, for example, the code in Figure 8-4, executed on machine 1:

```
int buffer;
...
write(file,&buffer,sizeof(buffer));
```

**FIGURE 8-4**

The file is then transferred to machine 2 and read as shown in Figure 8-5.

```
int buffer;
...
read(file,&buffer,sizeof(buffer));
```

**FIGURE 8-5**

On machine 2, the value of **buffer** may be different than on machine 1. The only way to ensure that files of numeric values are transferable is to put the values into text format.

Pointers are sometimes used to access the individual bytes of an integer, as in Figure 8-6.

```
char *pc;
int *pi;
int i = 513;
pi = &i;
pc = (char *) pi;
printf("Bytes are %d and %d", *pc, *(pc+1));
```

**FIGURE 8-6**

As Table 8-2 shows, the values printed out will vary from machine to machine. To avoid this, you could code routines for each machine, as in Figure 8-7.

```
getbyte(value,byte)
/* gets a byte from an integer value */
int value;                           /* value to get byte from */
int byte;                            /* byte to get 0=lsb to 3 for msb */
/* returns value of the byte */
{
    char *pc;
    pc = (char *) value;
    return *(pc+byte);
}
```

**FIGURE 8-7**

The routine in Figure 8-7 would differ based on the order of bytes and the size of **ints**. If you cast a **char** pointer into an **int** pointer, as in Figure 8-8, the result may be an invalid pointer. This would occur on machines where an **int** has stricter alignment requirements than a **char** (see Table 8-2).

### Table 8-2 Machine Differences on Some Typical Machines

|           | Byte Ordering on **Ints** | Storage Alignment |
|-----------|---------------------------|-------------------|
| PDP-11    | LSB/MSB                   | char-byte* otherwise-even byte |
| VAX-780   | MSB/LSB                   | all-byte          |
| 8086/8088 | LSB/MSB                   | all-byte          |
| Z-80      | LSB/MSB                   | all-byte          |
| 68000     | MSB/LSB                   | char-byte otherwise-even byte |
| IBM-370   | MSB/LSB                   | int-even byte float-mod 4 byte double-mod 8 byte |

*A long int is stored in memory as
  Byte 1, Byte 0, Byte 3, Byte 2
where Byte 0 is the least significant and Byte 3 is the most significant.

```
char *pc;
int *pi;
char c = 'A';
pc = &c;
pi = (int *) pc;
printf("Two bytes are %d", *pi);
```

**FIGURE 8-8**

## Input/Output

Machines also differ in their handling of input and output. If your program simply uses standard stream I/O (as found in Kernighan and Ritchie), you are unlikely to run into portability problems.The size of disk blocks may differ in unbuffered I/O functions, but such differences can be taken care of by **#defines**.

Some operations, such as cursor positioning, are not accounted for in the standard I/O packages. Routines must be written for each machine in order to implement these operations. This topic is discussed in the "I/O Portability" section of this chapter.

# COMPILER DEPENDENCIES

Although most compilers meet the Kernighan and Ritchie (K&R) standard, some include variations and extensions that make it difficult to compile a program written for a different compiler. The major areas of difference among compilers are discussed below.

## Significant Characters

The number of significant characters in variable names and function names is a primary difference among compilers. The K&R standard states that eight characters are significant for variables and six are significant for functions. Many compilers (and the ANSI standard) have extended the number to 31 for variables and macros.

The size of function names is not typically limited by the compiler, but by the linker. To ensure that function names are portable, the first six letters of each name must be unique, without distinguishing cases (i.e., **func1()** and **Func1()** are regarded as the same name).

## Redefinition of Macro Names

Many compilers differ from the K&R standard in two major areas: redefinition of macro names and the definition and declaration of external variables. Macro names cannot be **#defined** again until they have been **#undefed**, but some compilers will not report an error in an example such as the following:

    #define NAME "ANAME"
    ...
    #define NAME "BNAME"

Portable code should read

    #define NAME "ANAME"
    ...
    #undef NAME
    #define NAME "BNAME"

The ANSI standard will require an error to be reported in the first case.

## Definition and Declaration of External Variables

The K&R standard requires only one definition of external variables, such as

    **int global;**                                 /* appearing outside any function */

If this definition appeared in another source file linked to this one, a "multiple definition of global" would be reported by the linker. This external is referenced in other source files as

    **extern int global;**

Compiler writers have taken a variety of approaches to this area, producing portability problems. One approach, for example, allows you to code the definition as **int global;** which will be implicitly converted to **extern int global;**. Under this approach, an initialization statement, such as

    **int global=5;**

will be treated as the definition of the variable. If two initialization statements appear, then a "multiple definition" error will occur.

Using the K&R standard should produce the most portable code: Declare globals only once, and use them in other files by declaring them as **extern**. To further clarify the declaration and use of globals, you can write a **globals.c** file, containing the definitions of all global variables, and an **extern.h** file, containing the **extern** declarations of all global variables. In all other source files (excluding the **globals.c** file), **#include** the **extern.h** file. All globals will then be properly declared and referenced.

## Additional Features

The current version of UNIX C, which was developed after K&R was published, contains a few additional features. They include **unsigned char**, enumeration, and the ability to assign structures and unions as a whole, pass them as arguments, and return them from functions. These capabilities will be required by the ANSI standard.

Using these constructs might prevent code from being compiled by many current compilers. The benefit of these constructs will have to be traded off against these disadvantages.

## Bit Fields

The only major construct that is not supported by many compilers is bit fields. Bit fields are used in specialized applications, and are machine dependent in both order of the bits and the maximum size of the field. (The maximum size of a bit field is the size of an **int**.) Whether or not bit fields are sign extended when expanded to integers is compiler dependent. If bit fields are required, they can be coded as either macros or **#defines**. An example is shown in Figure 8-9. The second form in Figure 8-9 would execute faster than the first (unless the compiler recognized that the implicit right shift for the bit field was not necessary). The third form would be slower, but is more general.

## Compiler Library Functions

Each compiler usually includes a library of functions. Most include the functions as listed in K&R, as well as some extensions, such as the common UNIX functions. Use of non-K&R or non-UNIX functions can almost guarantee that the code will not be portable among machines. If you use such non-standard functions, their source code should be available so that they can be compiled on the target machine. The ANSI standard has specified a number of functions that should be included with a compiler. These are mostly a combination of K&R and UNIX functions.

## Other Compiler Dependencies

C also contains a number of "implementation defined" behaviors. One is whether a **char** is treated as **signed** or **unsigned** (see Figure 8-10).

```
struct sbyte
{
    int bit0: 1;
    int bit1: 1;
    ...
};
struct sbyte byte;
    ...
if (byte.bit1) ...
```

can be replaced by:

```
#define BIT0 byte&0x01
#define BIT1 byte&0x02
    ...
char byte;

if (BIT1) ...
```

or:

```
char byte;
if (bit(byte,1)) ...
    ...
bit(abyte,abit)
/* returns the bit value of abit in abyte */
int abyte;
int abit;
    ...
```

**FIGURE 8-9**

```
char c;
c = '\377';
if (c > 0)
    ...
```

**FIGURE 8-10**

On some machines, the test in Figure 8-10 will succeed, as **c** is treated as **unsigned**. On others, it will fail, as **c** is treated as **signed** and its value (since it is implicitly converted to an **int**) will be $-127$. In order to be strictly portable, **char** variables and constants should only contain values from 0 to 127.

The sign extension on right shifts may be either logical (i.e., the sign bit value is replaced by zero) or arithmetic (i.e., the original sign bit value is preserved), depending on the machine. If the values kept in **int** data types are all positive or if an appropriate mask is applied to the result, then this behavior should not create many problems. Portable code should not assume the nature of sign extension.

Each compiler and machine may not use the same number of register variables. This should not affect program execution, except in terms of speed, as excess register variables are ignored by the compiler.

## THE ANSI STANDARD

The ANSI standard committee is adding a few things to the language which will make it more usable, but these additions may not bear fruit for a few years as compiler manufacturers incorporate them into their products. These include such things as compiler type-checking of function arguments, and syntax for declaring functions that take a variable number of arguments (such as **printf()**). The premise behind the committee's standard is that no currently existing programs should fail to be compilable under the standard, but that the standard should allow for more features than currently available.

Several areas are labeled "undetermined" by K&R, displaying "unspecified or undefined behavior," according to the ANSI committee. These areas include the order of evaluation of expressions and the order in which side effects take place. Do not assume a right to left or left to right evaluation of expressions or arguments to a function. Side effects are changes to variable values which result from calling functions, incrementing or decrementing, and assignment. For example,

```
int a;
int b = 0;
a = b + (b=1);
```

may result in **a** being set to either 1 or 2. This expression is better rewritten as either

```
b = 1;
a = b + b;
```

or

```
b = 1, a = b + b;
```

The latter is acceptable, as the comma operator is guaranteed to be evaluated from left to right.

The ANSI standard has created a new data keyword called **volatile** to eliminate a particular problem. Compilers had the option of optimizing code to eliminate certain "useless" computation. Many programmers code delay loops as

```
for (i = 0; i < DELAY; i++)
{
  ;
}
```

The optimizing compiler might recognize that the value of **i** is never used and thus would eliminate the code for this loop entirely. Making **i volatile** forces the compiler to compile this code.

## I/O PORTABILITY

C is a portable language largely because it does not contain any input or output constructs. This means that the compiler does not have to deal with the idiosyncrasies of every machine's I/O devices. These machine dependencies are taken care of by the I/O functions. The I/O areas are keyboard, screen, RS-232 port, and disk files. These areas will be discussed both in terms of control of their actions and the availability of their operations.

### Keyboard

The keyboard varies from computer to computer. The ANSI standard for character codes only allows 128 values, but keyboards such as that on the IBM PC are capable of producing over 256 values. A program that is going to be portable to other machines should not take advantage of this wide range of keyboard values. Using more than 255 values may change the meaning of **getchar()**, for example. In the case of one compiler on the IBM PC, **getchar()** returns values from 1 to 255 for some keys. For other keys, it needs to be called twice—first returning a 0 and the next time a value from 1 to 255.

### Screen

The screen display has a number of features which vary widely from machine to machine. (Screen display is meant to include not only displays that are integral to the computer, such as on most personal computers, but also terminals that are attached via an RS-232 cable to a computer.) First are the commands that the display accepts to perform operations such as positioning the cursor.

Some screen displays use an escape sequence to position the cursor. Most of these use the ANSI standard escape sequences. Others require that direct commands be given to the screen driver. The differences in cursor control can be minimized by creating a cursor routine for each machine with a standard parameter interface.

The ANSI standard for terminal control specifies over a hundred different operations. These include everything from clearing the screen to turning on and off highlighted video. Not all terminals support all operations. Selecting a necessary subset of the operations and providing routines for each screen display to perform each operation will simplify transporting screen code.

A second difference is the number of colors or character attributes that can be displayed in text mode. Most all screen displays support some form of reverse video. Others have numerous attributes, such as underlining, dim, and blinking. Avoid describing screens as having certain attributes (such as color) unless you are certain that those attributes will exist on all target computers. Using **#defines** to determine the actual values of attributes will ease the transition between machines, as shown in Figure 8-11.

```
#define HIGHLIGHT      3
#define NORMAL         5
#define UNDERLINED     7

...
setattri(HIGHLIGHT);
```

**FIGURE 8-11**

On a particular machine, **setattri()** might either set a variable or send a particular sequence to turn on highlighting. If underlining were not available, then **#define UNDERLINED 3** would simply highlight all previously underlined characters.

Another difference is the ability to display graphics (i.e., raster graphics). Machines that have graphic capability also vary with the number of colors available and the resolution of the screen. The GKS (Graphic Kernel Standard) set of routines will aid in overcoming the screen dependencies. The PORT PACKAGE contains an equivalent set of routines for personal computers that do not have the memory required for the GKS routines. Both sets of these graphic routines contain features such as plotting points, changing point color, and drawing lines.

Both of these packages work by using "virtual commands"—commands that are not dependent on the particular resolution or characteristics of a display. For example, instead of describing a point as numbers that represent the actual pixel position, a point is described either as percentage offsets of full-screen widths or as pixel numbers on a high-resolution screen (see Figure 8-12).

| | |
|---|---|
| **struct point xy = {50,100};** | /* actual pixel for a point in the center of a 100 by 200 screen */ |
| **struct point xy = {.5,.5};** | /* percentage offset for the same point */ |
| **struct point xy = {16384,16384};** | /* pixel numbers for a "virtual" 32768 by 32768 screen */ |

**FIGURE 8-12**

## RS-232 Port

The RS-232 port differs widely among computers. Some computers support it as a standard device which can be accessed via **fgetc()** and **fputc()**. On others, custom drivers must be written. The method of setting characteristics (such as baud rate and parity) differs from computer to computer. On a few, these may be set by operating system commands. With others, the hardware must be sent the command directly. In those instances that the hardware must be accessed, each hardware I/O circuit has different configurations for things such as testing for character received. In addition, some computers do not support interrupts, so that creating received character buffers is almost impossible. This forces the program to check the port continuously for characters received (polling).

## Disk Files

Although disk files that are handled through the standard I/O routines are fairly similar, slight variations still exist. The determination of the end of file (EOF) varies on some machines. On text files, an ASCII EOF (value 26 - control Z) is used to signify the end of file. On binary files, the end of file is determined from the size of the file. The K&R standard call does not differentiate between binary and text files.

Each compiler manufacturer has determined his own extension to the I/O to handle this difference. A few add a global variable that must be set to BINARY or TEXT. Any subsequent calls to **fopen()** open the file in that manner. Others extend the second parameter of **fopen()**. For example,

"r" open file for read only in text mode
"rb" open file for read only in binary mode

One way to avoid this problem is to create a set of routines that call **fopen()**, as shown in Figure 8-13.

```
fbinopen(name,mode)
/* opens file in binary mode */
char *name;                                    /* file to open */
char *mode;                                     /* mode */
    ...

ftxtopen(name,mode)
/* opens file in text mode */
char *name;                                    /* file to open */
char *mode;                                     /* mode */
    ...
```

**FIGURE 8-13**

One other aspect of non-portability occurs in the **seek()** function. If you try to perform the equivalent of random access (or relative record access), you can use **seek()** to position the file at a particular record. But some systems differentiate between sequential files and relative files. A **seek()** on a sequential file to a position before the current one will result in the file being rewound and the file read up to that point. A **seek()** on a relative file will simply go to that position directly. Thus you might want to create further routines that access files in both sequential and relative modes. The PORT PACKAGE includes a set of random access functions that perform the record seeking for relative records in a machine-independent manner.

## CODING AND DOCUMENTING MACHINE DEPENDENCIES

There are two approaches to writing code that will vary from machine to machine. The first is to use conditional compilation, as in Figure 8-14.

```
#ifdef IBMPC
/* code for IBMPC */
    ...
#endif
#ifdef AT_T
/* code for AT_T */
    ...
#endif
    ...
```

**FIGURE 8-14**

On the first line of the code, or on the command line that invokes the compiler, the appropriate macro would be defined.

The other approach is to create a separate library with the machine-dependent functions for each one. To create a program for a new machine, you would create a new library. This method has several advantages over conditional compilation:

1. The code is not cluttered with multiple **#ifdefs**.
2. Adding another machine does not require that the higher level code be changed or re-compiled.
3. The library can be tested stand-alone to ensure that it works properly.

In either case, a separate header file can be used to set machine-dependent options, as in Figure 8-15.

```
/* in IBMPC.H */
#define LONG long

/* In IBM370.H */
#define LONG int
```

**FIGURE 8-15**

## CONCLUSION

C is noted and often chosen for its portability. Its non-portable aspects are thus important to the programmer who intends to write portable C code. Most of these aspects have been discussed in this chapter, including constructs to avoid and coding schemes to ensure portability. The ANSI standard, under development at this writing, promises to address many of the current discrepancies among compilers and machines, removing many of the obstacles to portability and enhancing the usefulness of the language.

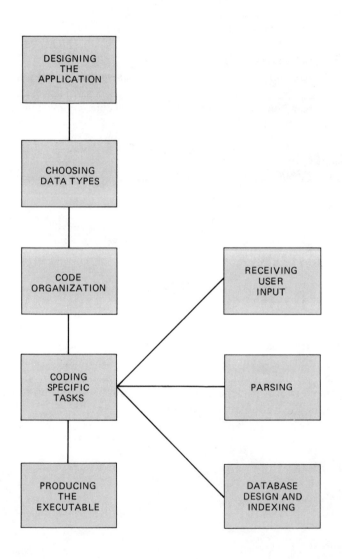

# Section D

# CODING SPECIFIC TASKS

As you begin writing code, you have already divided the application into smaller, specific tasks. You can now concentrate your efforts on the individual tasks and not the application as a whole. This is the essence of modular programming. The careful planning stages you have already gone through ensure that you can safely complete one task at a time, and later fit them together to form the application.

The number and variety of tasks necessary for your application are beyond the scope of this or any book. This section presents a discussion of the algorithms and implementations of a few very common tasks: receiving user input, parsing, and indexing.

# 9
# Receiving User Input

*Contributors:* Mark A. Clarkson of Concept Software Design
Dominic Galliano of Omnisoft Associates
Robert H. Jones IV of Amber Systems, Inc.
Robert M. Murton of O.E.S. Systems
*Reviewer:* Rick Pendzick of Strawberry Software, Inc.

## INTRODUCTION

Briefly reviewing our discussion in Chapter 2, Designing the User Interface, the user's interaction with a program consists of giving commands (non-transparent interactions) and manipulating data (transparent interactions). The former, implemented well, makes the program seem powerful and easy to use. The latter, when implemented at all, passes the apparent control to the user, making him or her feel in command of the program's processes. Both types of interactions are necessary in most programs.

Our discussion of the user interface continues in this chapter, with implementation as the key issue. Various methods have been developed for receiving both transparent and non-transparent user input. This chapter discusses several, presenting some of their advantages and disadvantages, and discusses their implementation in C. Sophisticated tools to aid in this implementation, particularly on the IBM PC, are also discussed.

## RECEIVING USER COMMANDS

In current applications, we find three methods of receiving command (i.e. non-transparent) input from the user: menus, command lines, and embedded commands.

## Menus

A menu is a list of choices available to the user at a given point in the program. Through some mechanism, the user selects one or more of these choices. There are many ways to design a menu. Menus can fill the screen, display on the top of the screen or across the bottom, or appear as needed in windows covering portions of the screen. Menus can be displayed vertically or horizontally, and can be nested to provide several levels of choices. Menus that fill the screen are usually only used at the beginning of a program, or between major program sections. In the midst of program operation, you will likely find it best not to cover all the data on the screen in order to elicit a command from the user.

Perhaps more important than the shape and size of the menu is the method of selecting an option. The user can select items by pointing to them with a cursor or mouse, by typing in a corresponding number or letter, or by typing one or more function keys.

**Pointing.**   A pointing device, such as a mouse or cursor, is ideally suited to menu selection. The menu lists options, either horizontally or vertically, and either constantly or only when needed. The user points to a particular option by moving the mouse or cursor. The pointed-at option is highlighted, either in bold, a special color, or reverse video. (Blinking is generally considered too annoying). Lotus 1-2-3, for example, uses a horizontal, one-line menu. The line directly beneath the menu explains the currently pointed-at option in slightly greater detail. The user can select the current option with the Enter key, or directly (without pointing) by typing the first letter of the option. Pointing is intuitive, and takes little time to master. The user need not remember anything except how to move the pointing device and how to select an option—operations that are consistent for the entire menu system.

**Numbered/Lettered Choices.**   Many programmers avoid introducing the user to the reasonably new concept of a pointing device. Instead, the user selects options by typing a corresponding number or letter. This approach is simple, easy to learn, and generally sufficient for small menus. With larger menus, the amount of text the user must read and the amount of time your program will take to display that text are both large enough to be drawbacks. And if your menu is constantly displayed, you will need some way of distinguishing the numbers and letters that represent a menu selection from the numbers and letters used in data manipulation.

**Function Keys.**   Function keys are likely choices for recording user commands, since they are unambiguously reserved for command input and can't be confused with text. A program might, for example, implement a list of commands the user can select by function key. The program displays the menu as a single line across the bottom of the screen—a very convenient shorthand for frequently used commands. Since the command associated with any particular function key is user-definable, this particular style can prove very useful for some applications.

The trouble with function keys lies in complexity. As we stated in Chapter 2, the power of non-transparent interactions is simplicity: insofar as they are simple, they are easy to learn and use. Most people would not intuitively guess that <F3> means "move left one word," and unless they use the program very frequently, they will forget which meanings are attached to which function keys.

Some solve this problem by constantly displaying the single-line menu on the screen. The user can thus refer to it when he or she needs reminding. This method is reasonable as long as the user doesn't have to refer to the menu too often. If the commands are often-used ones, the user is less likely to need reminding, and more likely to be satisfied with function keys for command input.

Some menus use modified function keys, i.e., function keys in conjunction with the <Ctrl>, <Alt>, <Shift>, or <Esc> keys. Rarely is such complexity justified. If your menu provides enough choices to require modified function keys, it likely provides too many command sequences for the user to remember.

Conventions in user interface design will make function keys more intuitive to the user. Many programs use the <F1> function key for on-screen Help. Maintaining this convention will make it easier for the user with experience in other such programs to remember how to use yours. Within your own program, maintain any conventions on function keys: if the "mode" of program operation changes, or the program involves several sections, keep the meanings of function keys at least similar, if not identical.

**Processing Menu Input.** Menu input is easily processed via C's **switch** statement. For small menus, a simple case for each legal option (number, letter, or option returned by the pointing device) is sufficient. Nested **case** statements can handle slightly more complicated menu systems. Figure 9-1 shows code to examine the character just typed and to pass control to the appropriate routine.

In Figure 9-1, we pass all screen navigation keys to one routine (**navigate()**), process the <Esc> and <F1> keys in line, and pass any other keys to the input processor function (**doinput()**). One substantial problem with the routine in Figure 9-1 is that the **doinput()** function has no information about the effects of the **navigate()** function, and vice versa. A simple enhancement, shown in Figure 9-2, provides this information.

```
main()
{
    int c;
    int done = FALSE;
    while (!done)
    {
        c = getch();
        switch(c)
        {
            case UP:
            case DOWN:
            case LEFT:
            case RIGHT:
            case HOME:
            case END:
            case PAGEUP:
            case PAGEDOWN:
                navigate(c);
                break;

            case ESC:
                done = TRUE;
                break;

            case F1:
                do_help();
                break;

            default:
                doinput(c);
                break;
        }
    }
}
```

**FIGURE 9-1**

```
int state = 0;

state = navigate(c,state);

state = doinput(c,state);
```

**FIGURE 9-2**

By passing the current state to each function and letting each function update the state, the code in Figure 9-2 allows the two functions to interact without the use of **global** variables. (**Globals** could accomplish the same effect, but would not be as readable nor as maintainable).

The approach taken in Figures 9-1 and 9-2 is sufficient for programs with only a few command choices, but does not easily expand to handle more complex cases. Most powerful menu-driven programs implement a set of tables which define various states in which the program can exist, and which function will be called for each type of input. A sample of such a table is shown in Figure 9-3.

```
struct state
{
    char value;                              /* character value */
    int (*funct)();                          /* function to be called */
};

struct state_list
{
    struct state *states;                    /* pointer to list of states */
    int size;                                /* number of states in list */
    int (*d_fault)();                        /* default function */
};

struct state state0[] =
{
    { 0x0a, do_line_feed     },
    { 0x20, do_space         },
    { 0x0d, do_carriage_ret  },
        ...
};
```

FIGURE 9-3

The first **struct** in Figure 9-3 defines a function to be called if the corresponding key is found. The second **struct** defines a list of states, along with a default function that will be called if the character isn't found in the list. The last **struct** is an example of an array of state **structs**.

This type of structure allows you to implement a simple core routine that processes keys and dispatches them to the appropriate function for the current state list. To change the behavior of the program, you merely need to add a new state list. Figure 9-4 shows a state list to implement a menu with the choices Print, Delete, Select, Help, and Quit. The example includes a function that will dispatch to the appropriate function, given an input character and state list.

```
#define COUNT(array) (sizeof(array) / sizeof(*(array)))

extern int do_print();
extern int do_delete();
extern int do_select();
extern int do_help();
extern int do_quit();
extern int bad_choice();

struct state menu[] =
{
    { 'P', do_print  },
    { 'D', do_delete },
    { 'S', do_select },
    { 'H', do_help   },
    { 'Q', do_quit   }
};

struct state_list menulist =
{
    menu;                         /* pointer to list of states */
    COUNT(menu);                  /* number of states in list */
    bad_choice;                   /* default function */
};

/* Dispatch to the selected function if the input character is found in the
   state table. */

do_cmd(ch, sm)
char ch;
struct state_list *sm;
{
    int i = 0;
    struct state *s;

/* Search the state machine for an entry which matches the specified
   character */

    while(i < sm->size)
    {
        s = &sm->states[i++];
        if(ch == s->value)
        {
```

FIGURE 9-4

/* We have found a state machine entry which matches the specified
character. If there is a function defined for this state, then call it. Note
that the absence of a function turns this character into a NOP. */

```
        if (s- >funct)
        {
            (*s- >funct)(ch);
        }
        return;
    }
}
```

/* The specified character was not explicitly defined in this state
machine, so if there is a default function, call it. */

```
    if (sm- >d_fault)
    {
        (*sm- >d_fault)(ch);
    }
}
```

**FIGURE 9-4** (Continued)

## Command Lines

Some very successful programs take their command input as text on a command
line—a portion of the screen reserved for the user to type commands. In using
command lines, you must allow for some basic editing—backspace, delete—
and you'll need to verify the input, since the user has an infinite potential for
errors.

Command line input, which must be error-checked, verified for legality, and
interpreted, requires the use of a parsing mechanism. Parsing, the process of
breaking down a string into its basic components for interpretation, is the subject of the next chapter.

Although the command line is a somewhat archaic approach, it contains some
important benefits. Commands can be read from either the keyboard or a disk
file, and the user can enter complex commands (i.e. commands with parameters) more easily than with a menu. While command driven systems are more
difficult to learn, sophisticated users tend to prefer them to menus—perhaps
because of speed, or perhaps because they feel more in control and less "cod-
dled" by the application.

## Embedded Commands

For many applications, you must allow the user to enter commands without opening a menu or a command line. An editor, for example, would not be very easy to use if you had to navigate through a series of menus just to delete a line of text.

Embedded commands are surrounded by data, so they must be recognized as commands and not data. Often, function keys, the <Ctrl> key, and/or the <Alt> key are used to distinguish embedded commands from the data that surrounds them. (The user would give such a command, for example, by holding the <Ctrl> key while pressing another key). Applications that use embedded commands, like applications using command lines, need a parsing mechanism to receive and interpret those commands.

## RECEIVING DATA MANIPULATION

The two most common forms for receiving the user's transparent interactions are templates and free-form screens.

## Templates

A template is a screen that contains fields: areas in which the user can enter input. Typically, the user navigates among the fields, entering and editing any data on the screen. The program receives the input after the user has signified that the entire screen is complete. The input information passed to the program, then, must include not only the data itself, but the field in which each piece of data was entered.

Receiving user input in discrete fields allows you to simplify your error-checking while reducing the user's chances for making an error. You can restrict the legal characters for each field, based on the type of data that should be entered there. For example, in a field reserved for a date, the user would only be allowed to type digits, slashes, and/or dashes.

## Free-Form Screens

A free-form screen allows the user to enter data anywhere on the screen. Word processors, for example, use free-form screens for text input. A free-form screen can be considered one field. Your program needs to intercept and interpret cursor movement keys, and echo characters typed to the screen. You can either pass the input data to your program as the user enters it, or once the screen is complete. You will likely need embedded commands for non-transparent input pertaining to a free-form screen, for example, to delete a line of input. Again, a parsing mechanism is necessary to find and interpret these embedded commands.

Free-form screens such as those used in word processors are somewhat more difficult to implement, since they typically feature word-wrap and scrolling.

## SCREEN MANAGEMENT TOOLS

Implementing the mechanisms for receiving user input is frequently as much as half of the total coding effort, and sometimes even more. Constructing the necessary hardware-specific low-level functions to manage the types of screens discussed in this chapter would be a significant task. Many different parts of your program are likely to affect the screen, but should not destroy the data written to the screen by any other part of the program. For example, a general purpose help facility should not be restricted to its own reserved portion of the screen, nor should it have to consider the current state of the screen every time it's invoked. Ideally, it should just display its help information, wait for an "end help" signal from the user, then erase its display, leaving the screen exactly as it was before help was invoked.

You can greatly simplify the screen management necessary to implement many of the techniques described in this chapter by using commercial tools such as Lattice Windows, Panel, Omniscreen, the Hammer Library, and many others. These tools allow you to interact with the screen much more easily than by writing your own low-level screen management routines.

### The Hammer Library

The Hammer library includes a utility that allows you to easily create horizontal, multi-level menus similar to those used by Lotus 1-2-3. It also includes routines to create and implement fields, either singly or grouped in templates, and an extensive library of various screen management functions.

### Lattice Windows

Lattice Windows allows you to create "virtual" screens of any size up to 255 rows or columns, and to write to each of these screens as if it were a separate file. Lattice Windows keeps track of which screens are "opened" (i.e., displayed) and which screens are on top of others. It allows you to put any of several types of borders around a window, and to change the type of border, the size and location of the screen window, the relative priority of one screen to another, the text written into the window border, and many other characteristics, quickly and easily. Figures 9-5 and 9-6 show a simple program that uses

Lattice Windows to create a small menu screen, a free form text input screen, and a help screen.

```
main ()
{
    int menu_scr;
    int free_scr;
    int ret;
    unsigned key;
    vinitmem(10000, 0);                    /* Initialize with 10K of screen
                                                           buffer space */

/* Create menu screen with 2 rows and 80 columns and free form screen
   with 23 rows and 80 columns. */

    if ((ret = vnewscr(&menu_scr,2,80)) ||
        (ret = vnewscr(&free_scr,23,80)))
    {
        printf("Couldn't create screen...\n");
        exit(1);
    }

/* Write text into menu screen */

    vwriteat(menu_scr, 0, 0, "Press <ESC> to quit");
    vwriteat(menu_scr, 1, 0, "Press F1 for help");

/* open the menu and free form screens */

    vwindopn(menu_scr);
    vwindloc(free_scr, 2, 0);
    vwindopn(free_scr);

    while(1)
    {
        key = getks();                     /* see Fig. 9-7; works like getch() */
        if (key == ESC)

        {
            break;
        }
        if (key == F1)
```

**FIGURE 9-5**

```
        {
            do_help(key);
        }
        else
        {
            vputchr(free_scr, key);
        }
    }

    /* quit and exit the program */

        vbyebye();
}
```

FIGURE 9-5 *(Continued)*

In Figure 9-5, the call to **vinitmem()** sets up a 10,000 byte buffer pool for use by the window management routines. (The size of this pool must be at least 10,000 bytes, but can be as large as 64K). The calls to **vnewscr()** create screens and return the screen's assigned number in the function's first argument. This "screen number" is just like a file handle, in that it is all you need to know to manage the screen. The **vwriteat()** function writes a string at the specified row and column on the specified screen. The **vwindloc()** function specifies the screen's position on the physical display. The **vwindopn()** function displays the window. The function library included with Lattice Windows contains close to 100 low-level screen management routines.

The code to display the help screen, shown in Figure 9-6, is equally simple.

Lattice Windows is not a highly portable package, however. It is written entirely in 8086 Assembly language, for optimal performance under the IBM PC environment.

Using Lattice Windows, it is very easy to create menu screens, free form screens, and command input screens. You can also use the package to create template screens, but numerous other packages specific to template creation are available.

## Panel

Panel is one such template management tool. It includes a library of functions and a set of utility programs to create and maintain screens. The functions allow you to present a template screen (a "panel"), to let the user fill in the screen's fields, and to retrieve and update the data in the template. Panel also allows you

```
do_help(key)
unsigned key;
{
    extern char *help_text[];
    int scr;

/* create help screen */

    vnewscr(&scr, 5, 40);

/* put the screen on row 10, column 20 */

    vwindloc(scr, 10, 20);

/* Write help text into the screen */

    vwrite(scr, help_text[key]);

/* wait until user presses any key */

    key = getkey();

/* close and surrender the help screen */

    vsurnder(scr);
}
```

**FIGURE 9-6**

to supply your own code to validate or otherwise process data in particular fields or in the template as a whole.

Panel is written almost entirely in C, and is thus highly portable to environments other than the IBM PC. There is a version of Panel which uses Lattice Windows for its screen presentation. This interface allows you to create templates which occupy only a portion of the physical screen, and allows you to use Lattice Windows for other portions of your program without conflicting with Panel.

## Omniscreen

Omniscreen is another template management tool, specific to the IBM PC environment. Its interactive screen formatting utility allows you to specify fields with restrictions on allowed input, use graphics characters and video attributes, and test your screens outside of your application. It also includes a set of functions that allow your application to display, manipulate, and retrieve user input from these screens.

## THE IBM PC KEYBOARD

The IBM PC keyboard is somewhat different from traditional keyboards. Most keyboards simply return an ASCII value in the range of 1 to 127 or 1 to 255 for any key pressed. Special keys, such as HOME, UP, DOWN, LEFT, RIGHT, etc., and all of the function keys and modified functions keys, do not have ASCII representations.

To address this problem, IBM has assigned each key a unique value which depends on its physical location on the keyboard. Since there are 83 keys on the standard keyboard, the key values have been assigned accordingly. The < ESC > key has a value (called a "scan code") of 1; the key to the right of the < ESC > key is 2; and so on. These values are listed in the technical reference manual for the IBM PC. Particular combinations of the < Shift >, < Alt > and < Ctrl > keys with other keys have been assigned values in the range 84 to 255.

A further problem involves the way that the **getch()** function works. With some compilers, the **getch()** function calls a DOS function that reads a single character without echo—unless that character is a Ctrl/C. Thus C's standard input functions may produce unwanted results on the IBM PC: your program may echo unwanted characters, or abort execution. If you are faced with this situation, you will have to decide between portability and optimal performance.

If you choose, in such a situation, to optimize your program's performance for the IBM PC environment, you might consider writing your own keyboard input routine like that shown in Figure 9-7.

```
unsigned saveks = 0;

/* Save a key - this function corresponds to ungetch */

ungetks(key_scan)
unsigned key_scan;
{
    saveks = key_scan;
}

/* get a keystroke and its scan code */
```

**FIGURE 9-7**

```
unsigned getks()
{
    unsigned key_scan;
    union REGS regs;                  /* defined in Lattice "dos.h" file */

    if (saveks)
    {
        key_scan = saveks;
        saveks = 0;
        return (key_scan);
    }

/* get character from console using BIOS function 16 */

    regs.h.ah = 0;
    int86(0x16, &regs, &regs);
    return ((unsigned) regs.x.ax);
}
```

**FIGURE 9-7** *(Continued)*

The function **getks()** in Figure 9-7 will return the scan code in the high byte and the key value in the low byte. If the low byte is zero, then the key is one of the non-ASCII keys (UP, DOWN, F1, etc.). Otherwise, the key is a standard ASCII key equal to the value of the low byte. This is the **getks()** function used earlier, in Figure 9-5.

## CONCLUSION

In our discussion of the implementation of the user interface, we have maintained the divisions first described in Chapter 2, "Designing the User Interface": the user is either giving commands to the program, or manipulating data.

The three most often used methods for receiving user commands are menus, command lines, and embedded commands. Menus are easily implemented via **switch** statements; commercial tools are available to simplify their display on screen. Command lines and embedded commands are also reasonably straightforward to implement, requiring a parsing algorithm to find and interpret the commands and a **switch** statement to act on them. (Parsing is the subject of the next chapter). More complex sets of commands are best implemented by recording the state of the program, which allows functions to "communicate" with each other.

In manipulating data, the user is generally presented either with a template of discrete fields, or a free-form screen. Because of the low-level screen management functions necessary to implement either of these techniques, the programmer is best served by one or more of the many screen management tools available. Such tools simplify the creation and manipulation of screens, and the retrieval of user input from them.

# 10

# Parsing

*Contributors:* Michael E. Duffy and Walt Bilofsky of The Software
Toolworks
*Reviewer:* Fred Butzen of Mark Williams Company


## INTRODUCTION

To parse something is to break it into its component parts. In its most common
usage, parsing refers to sentences: The elementary school tree diagrams drawn
of the subjects, predicates, nouns, and verbs in English sentences were parsing
diagrams. In the more specialized world of computer science, the term is usually applied to an input string, which must be broken down into its elementary
parts (called tokens) in order to be interpreted by the rest of the system. Compilers, assemblers, and interpreters all parse code in order to translate it into
object code (or immediately executed instructions). Translators and "pretty
printer" routines both parse code before manipulating it.

Most relevant to our discussions, a text editor (contained in many programming applications) must parse input strings to determine their legality and their
meanings. Every program that accepts input can be thought of as a parser,
because the program must make sense of its input before acting upon it. We
will explore this type of parsing in this chapter: the type of parsing that virtually
every application will involve.


## ELEMENTS OF A PARSING ALGORITHM

To parse any input, you must know three things:

1. What are the basic components of the input? If you are parsing an English
   sentence, the basic components are words. If you are parsing C, the basic

components, or "tokens",* are identifiers, keywords, constants of various types, operators, and white space.
2. What are the rules for putting basic components together? For example, in English, we create a "noun phrase" with the rule

A < noun phrase > may consist of an < article > followed by a < noun >.

The implicit assumption is that we also know the rules that determine which things are proper articles and nouns.

The items enclosed in angle brackets (< >) are called "non-terminal symbols." As we combine terminal symbols according to rules, we create these new symbols. Non-terminal symbols represent constructs created, according to rules, from terminal symbols and/or other non-terminal symbols.
3. What does the input represent? When we read English, we know that words must ultimately build a sentence; that is the "goal" of the parser. This goal is our ultimate non-terminal.

Taking a bottom-up approach, we construct our task as follows: Given the rules we have for building non-terminal symbols out of terminals and other non-terminals, can we reach the non-terminal that is our goal from the terminals we must parse?

Alternately, we can take a top-down approach, asking: With the rules at our disposal, can we break our goal non-terminal into the sequence of terminals that we must parse?

## AN EXAMPLE: PARSING AN ENGLISH SENTENCE

As an example, we will use a bottom-up and then a top-down approach to parse the same simple English sentence. To keep the example simple, we will limit our legal sentences as follows:

1. A < sentence > consists of a < subject > followed by a < predicate >.
2. A < subject > is either:
   a. a PRONOUN or
   b. an ARTICLE followed by a NOUN.

---

*Tokens are also referred to as "terminal symbols," because they are the atomic units of meaning. You can't break them down any further (e.g. into individual characters) without losing that meaning. These terminal symbols are our basic components, whose meaning can be represented unambiguously. (For example, COLON would be a terminal symbol, clearly represented as ":".)

3. A <predicate> is either:
   a. a VERB or
   b. a VERB followed by a PRONOUN or
   c. a VERB followed by an ARTICLE followed by a NOUN.

Restating Rules 3b and 3c (which include our definition of a <subject>),

3. A <predicate> is either.
   a. a VERB or
   b. a VERB followed by a <subject>.

Those terms printed in capital letters in the rules above are tokens: those items that we assume we can recognize unambiguously.

## Bottom-Up

Using a bottom-up approach, we first look at our sample sentence:

We like the dogs

and identify each of its words as a particular token:

We = PRONOUN
like = VERB
the = ARTICLE
dogs = NOUN

—Using Rule 2a (a <subject> is a PRONOUN), we identify "We" as a <subject>.
—Using Rule 2b (a <subject> is an ARTICLE followed by a NOUN), we identify "the dogs" as a <subject>.
—Using Rule 3b (a <predicate> is a VERB followed by a <subject>), we identify "like the dogs" as a <predicate>.

Our sentence now consists of a <subject> ("We") followed by a <predicate> ("like the dogs"), which qualifies, by our Rule 1, as a <sentence>.

## Top-Down

Approaching the task from a top-down perspective, we first look at our goal non-terminal, <sentence>, which we have defined by Rule 1 as a <subject> followed by a <predicate>.

—By Rule 2a, a <subject> may consist of a PRONOUN.
—By Rule 3b, a <predicate> may consist of a VERB followed by a <subject>.

—By Rule 2b, a <subject> may consist of an ARTICLE followed by a NOUN.

Putting all these rules together, our <sentence> may thus consist of

PRONOUN VERB ARTICLE NOUN.
Our sample, "We like the dogs," also consists of
PRONOUN VERB ARTICLE NOUN,
and is thus a legal <sentence>.

Using our rules, we have broken down <sentence> into the specific tokens present in our sample string. Notice that, in this implementation of the top-down approach, we have chosen the one path that will lead us to our sample string. There are, of course, several others paths that would lead to different combinations of tokens, but would not match our sample string. In actual implementation, we would have to break <sentence> down into each of its possible combinations of tokens, then compare each legal combination of tokens to our sample string.

## GENERALIZED PARSING

With only three pieces of information (tokens, rules for combining them into non-terminal symbols, and a goal) we can write a parser for any input. You can think of these three items as defining a specific input language. These three items are sometimes called the "grammar" for a language.

Although computer scientists have developed a significant amount of parsing theory, most of it has centered around the problem of automatically creating a parser for a given input language. Programs that do this are called "parser generators" or "compiler-compilers." One such program is called YACC (Yet Another Compiler Compiler) and was originally developed for the UNIX operating system. Austin Code Works has developed a YACC for the PC-DOS operating system. YACC is a very useful tool for generating programs that must parse complex inputs (e.g., queries to database management programs).

## A DETAILED EXAMPLE: PARSING AN MS-DOS FILE SPECIFICATION

Most problems you are likely to encounter will not require a program like YACC. The remainder of this chapter illustrates some useful techniques for parsing an input, using the problem of parsing a valid MS-DOS file specification as an example. For the interested reader, a short bibliography is provided at the end of the chapter.

We begin by writing down the rules for a "file specification," which will be our goal non-terminal. This is a useful approach, because it forces you to think about the structure of the input stream and to identify the terminals and rules.

## Generating Rules

We use a notation known as Backus-Naur Form, or BNF. BNF notation specifies rules for creating non-terminals from tokens and other non-terminals using the same logic we employed in parsing the simple sentence, above. The only difference is that BNF notation uses symbols to represent the relationships.

Rule FS1:   < file-spec > : = < drive > < firstpath > < file >
Rule FS2:   < file-spec > : = < device >

Rule FS1 says that a file specification ("< file-spec >"), is made up of a drive specification ("< drive >"), a pathname (Version 2.0 of MS-DOS and later), and a filename. (The reason for the symbol < firstpath >, as opposed to < path >, will become clear when we create the rules for pathnames.) Rule FS2 says that another way of making up a file specification is to use one of the reserved device names, such as "PRN."

Each of the elements that create a < file-spec > must also be defined. Every time we write down a new non-terminal symbol, we have to specify the rules for generating it. A drive specification is made up of a single alphabetic character, followed by a colon.

Rule D1:   < drive > : = ALPHA COLON
Rule D2:   < drive > : = < empty >

Rule E:   < empty >       : =

Rule D2 simply says that there may be no drive specification. We define the "empty" non-terminal to help out.

The next set of rules, for a pathname, illustrates that a rule can be recursive (i.e., refer to itself), as long as there is some way to end the recursion. (In this case, the fact that the path name may be empty will eventually end the recursion.)

< path >   : = SLASH < path >
< path >   : = < file > SLASH < path >
< path >   : = < empty >

The recursive rule (< path > : = SLASH < path >) allows for a pathname with more than one directory specification, for example, \dir1\dir2\filename. As specified, however, the rule also allows for a file specification such as c:\\\\\\filename, which DOS does not. Our general problem is typical: The rule should only be applied once. We can enforce this limitation by breaking the rule into two:

Rule FP1:   <firstpath> : = SLASH <path>
Rule FP2:   <firstpath> : = <path>

Rule P1:   <path> : = <file> SLASH <path>
Rule P2:   <path> : = <empty>

The recursion is thus limited to <path>s, which must always have a <file> between SLASHes. The <firstpath> cannot have more than one SLASH before a <file>.

We define <file>:

Rule F1:   <file> : = <word> <ext>
Rule F2:   <file> : = PERIOD
Rule F3:   <file> : = PERIOD PERIOD

Finally, defining <ext> and <word>,

Rule EX1:   <ext> : = PERIOD <word>
Rule EX2:   <ext> : = PERIOD
Rule EX3:   <ext> : = <empty>

Rule W1:   <word> : = LCHAR <word>
Rule W2:   <word> : = LCHAR

where LCHAR is a token, representing any legal character (which we can unambiguously identify). All our tokens, then, are

LCHAR   a legal character
PERIOD   a period
SLASH   a backslash
ALPHA   the characters A, B, C, and D (legal drives)
COLON   a colon

## Applying Rules to a String

For example, suppose we have the sample string

\X\Y\Z\ABC.DAT

In terms of tokens, this string is:

SLASH LCHAR SLASH LCHAR SLASH LCHAR SLASH LCHAR
LCHAR LCHAR PERIOD LCHAR LCHAR LCHAR

We will determine if the sample string is a legal file specification. Since we can use the string itself for reference in choosing which rules to apply, we will use a top-down approach and attempt to rewrite the string using our rules. Since our input begins with a backslash character, we will use Rule FS1.

| RULE | | \X\Y\Z\ABC.DAT = |
|------|---|------------------|
| FS1 | < file-spec > : = < drive > < firstpath > < file > | < drive > < firstpath > < file > |

\X\Y\Z\ABC.DAT = < file-spec > = < drive > < firstpath > < file >

Since our string does not begin with an ALPHA, we will use Rule D2:

| D2 | < drive > : = < empty > | < empty > < firstpath > < file > = < firstpath > < file > |
|----|-------------------------|------------------------------------------------------------|

\X\Y\Z\ABC.DAT = < firstpath > < file >

Rule FP1 specifies a < firstpath > that begins with SLASH, as does our string.

| FP1 | < firstpath > : = SLASH < path > | SLASH < path > < file > |
|-----|----------------------------------|--------------------------|

\X\Y\Z\ABC.DAT = SLASH < path > < file >

The unidentified part of our string (everything following the initial SLASH) begins with a character, so we use Rule P1.

| P1 | < path > : = < file > SLASH < path > | SLASH < file > SLASH < path > < file > |
|----|--------------------------------------|----------------------------------------|

\X\Y\Z\ABC.DAT = SLASH < file > SLASH < path > < file >

We now have a < file > sandwiched between the first two SLASHes, indicating that "X" is a < file >. Because "X" is a LCHAR (which are combined to form < word > s), we use Rule F1.

| F1 | < file > : = < word > < ext > | SLASH < word > < ext > SLASH < path > < file > |
|----|-------------------------------|------------------------------------------------|

\X\Y\Z\ABC.DAT = SLASH < word > < ext > SLASH < path > < file >

We can then use rules for creating < word > s and < ext > s to identify "X" as a LCHAR.

| W2 | \<word\> := LCHAR | SLASH LCHAR\<ext\>SLASH<br>\<path\> \<file\> |
|---|---|---|
| EX3 | \<ext\> := \<empty\> | SLASH LCHAR\<empty\>SLASH<br>\<path\> \<file\><br>=SLASH LCHAR SLASH\<path\><br>\<file\> |

\X\Y\Z\ABC.DAT = SLASH LCHAR SLASH \<path\> \<file\>


Moving on to the remaining undefined parts of our string:

| P1 | \<path\> := \<file\>SLASH<br>\<path\> | SLASH LCHAR SLASH\<file\><br>SLASH\<path\> \<file\> |
|---|---|---|

\X\Y\Z\ABC.DAT = SLASH LCHAR SLASH \<file\> SLASH \<path\> \<file\>


Again, \<file\> is sandwiched between two SLASHes, indicating a course of action in identifying "Y" as a LCHAR similar to the one we used in identifying "X" as a LCHAR:

| F1 | \<file\> := \<word\> \<ext\> | SLASH LCHAR SLASH\<word\><br>\<ext\>SLASH\<path\> \<file\> |
|---|---|---|
| W2 | \<word\> := LCHAR | SLASH LCHAR SLASH LCHAR<br>\<ext\>SLASH\<path\> \<file\> |
| EX3 | \<ext\> := \<empty\> | SLASH LCHAR SLASH LCHAR<br>\<empty\>SLASH\<path\> \<file\><br>=SLASH LCHAR SLASH LCHAR<br>SLASH\<path\> \<file\> |

\X\Y\Z\ABC.DAT = SLASH LCHAR SLASH LCHAR SLASH \<path\> \<file\>


The unidentified portion of the string begins with a character, so we use Rule P1.

| P1 | \<path\> := \<file\>SLASH<br>\<path\> | SLASH LCHAR SLASH LCHAR<br>SLASH\<file\>SLASH\<path\><br>\<file\> |
|---|---|---|


Again, \<file\> is left between two SLASHes, so we use the following rules to isolate "Z" as a LCHAR:

| F1 | \<file\> := \<word\> \<ext\> | SLASH LCHAR SLASH LCHAR SLASH\<word\>\<ext\>SLASH \<path\>\<file\> |
|---|---|---|
| W2 | \<word\> := LCHAR | SLASH LCHAR SLASH LCHAR SLASH LCHAR\<ext\>SLASH \<path\>\<file\> |
| EX3 | \<ext\> := \<empty\> | SLASH LCHAR SLASH LCHAR SLASH LCHAR\<empty\>SLASH \<path\>\<file\> =SLASH LCHAR SLASH LCHAR SLASH LCHAR SLASH \<path\> \<file\> |

\X\Y\Z\ABC.DAT = SLASH LCHAR SLASH LCHAR SLASH LCHAR SLASH \<path\> \<file\>

The unidentified portion of our string, "ABC.DAT," contains no SLASH, so the only applicable rule is Rule P2.

| P2 | \<path\> := \<empty\> | SLASH LCHAR SLASH LCHAR SLASH LCHAR SLASH \<empty\> \<file\> =SLASH LCHAR SLASH LCHAR SLASH LCHAR SLASH\<file\> |
|---|---|---|

\X\Y\Z\ABC.DAT = SLASH LCHAR SLASH LCHAR SLASH LCHAR SLASH \<file\>

We use Rule F1 to rewrite the unidentified part of the string.

| F1 | \<file\> := \<word\> \<ext\> | SLASH LCHAR SLASH LCHAR SLASH LCHAR SLASH\<word\> \<ext\> |
|---|---|---|

\X\Y\Z\ABC.DAT = SLASH LCHAR SLASH LCHAR SLASH LCHAR SLASH \<word\> \<ext\>

Since a period appears in our string, we will use Rule EX1 (which contains a period) to rewrite the string.

| EX1 | \<ext\> := PERIOD \<word\> | SLASH LCHAR SLASH LCHAR SLASH LCHAR SLASH\<word\> PERIOD\<word\> |
|---|---|---|

\X\Y\Z\ABC.DAT = SLASH LCHAR SLASH LCHAR SLASH LCHAR SLASH \<word\> PERIOD \<word\>

To break the <word>s into LCHARs, we will use Rules W1 and W2.

| W1 | <word> := LCHAR<word> | SLASH LCHAR SLASH LCHAR SLASH LCHAR SLASH LCHAR <word>PERIOD<word> |
|----|----|----|
| W1 | <word> := LCHAR<word> | SLASH LCHAR SLASH LCHAR SLASH LCHAR SLASH LCHAR LCHAR <word>PERIOD<word> |
| W2 | <word> := LCHAR | SLASH LCHAR SLASH LCHAR SLASH LCHAR SLASH LCHAR LCHAR LCHAR PERIOD<word> |

\X\Y\Z\ABC.DAT = SLASH LCHAR SLASH LCHAR SLASH LCHAR SLASH LCHAR LCHAR LCHAR PERIOD <word>

We use the same process on the second <word>.

| W1 | <word> := LCHAR<word> | SLASH LCHAR SLASH LCHAR SLASH LCHAR SLASH LCHAR LCHAR LCHAR PERIOD LCHAR <word> |
|----|----|----|
| W1 | <word> := LCHAR<word> | SLASH LCHAR SLASH LCHAR SLASH LCHAR SLASH LCHAR LCHAR LCHAR PERIOD LCHAR LCHAR<word> |
| W2 | <word> := LCHAR | SLASH LCHAR SLASH LCHAR SLASH LCHAR SLASH LCHAR LCHAR LCHAR PERIOD LCHAR LCHAR LCHAR |

Our final representation is, indeed, the same series of tokens that we first used to represent our string. We have parsed the entire string \X\Y\Z\ABC.DAT to find that it is a <file-spec>. Had we encountered any false conclusions on the way (unresolvable by recourse to any of our rules) we would conclude that the string was not a <file-spec>.

For clarification, we repeat the above parsing process in consolidated form in Table 10-1.

## Implementation

With our rules and tokens thus established, and our logic sketched out, we present the code to parse for a legal file specification, in Figure 10-1. Once we

## Table 10-1

| RULE | | STRING |
|---|---|---|
| | | \X\Y\Z\ABC.DAT |
| FS1 | < file-spec > := < drive > < firstpath > < file > | < drive > < firstpath > < file > |
| D2 | < drive > := < empty > | < firstpath > < file > |
| FP1 | < firstpath > := SLASH < path > | SLASH < path > < file > |
| P1 | < path > := < file > SLASH < path > | SLASH < file > SLASH < path > < file > |
| F1 | < file > := < word > < ext > | SLASH < word > < ext > SLASH < path > < file > |
| W2 | < word > := LCHAR | SLASH LCHAR < ext > SLASH < path > < file > |
| EX3 | < ext > := < empty > | SLASH LCHAR SLASH < path > < file > |
| P1 | < path > := < file > SLASH < path > | SLASH LCHAR SLASH < file > SLASH < path > < file > |
| F1 | < file > := < word > < ext > | SLASH LCHAR SLASH < word > < ext > SLASH < path > < file > |
| W2 | < word > := LCHAR | SLASH LCHAR SLASH LCHAR < ext > SLASH < path > < file > |
| EX3 | < ext > := < empty > | SLASH LCHAR SLASH LCHAR SLASH < path > < file > |
| P1 | < path > := < file > SLASH < path > | SLASH LCHAR SLASH LCHAR SLASH < file > SLASH < path > < file > |
| F1 | < file > := < word > < ext > | SLASH LCHAR SLASH LCHAR SLASH < word > < ext > SLASH < path > < file > |
| W2 | < word > := LCHAR | SLASH LCHAR SLASH LCHAR SLASH LCHAR < ext > SLASH < path > < file > |
| EX3 | < ext > := < empty > | SLASH LCHAR SLASH LCHAR SLASH LCHAR SLASH < path > < file > |

## Table 10-1  (Continued)

| RULE | | STRING |
|---|---|---|
| | | \X\Y\Z\ABC.DAT |
| P2 | < path > : = < empty > | SLASH LCHAR SLASH LCHAR SLASH LCHAR SLASH < file > |
| F1 | < file > : = < word > < ext > | SLASH LCHAR SLASH LCHAR SLASH LCHAR SLASH < word > < ext > |
| EX1 | < ext > : = PERIOD < word > | SLASH LCHAR SLASH LCHAR SLASH LCHAR SLASH < word > PERIOD < word > |
| W1 | < word > : = LCHAR < word > | SLASH LCHAR SLASH LCHAR SLASH LCHAR SLASH LCHAR < word > PERIOD < word > |
| W1 | < word > : = LCHAR < word > | SLASH LCHAR SLASH LCHAR SLASH LCHAR SLASH LCHAR LCHAR < word > PERIOD < word > |
| W2 | < word > : = LCHAR | SLASH LCHAR SLASH LCHAR SLASH LCHAR SLASH LCHAR LCHAR LCHAR PERIOD < word > |
| W1 | < word > : = LCHAR < word > | SLASH LCHAR SLASH LCHAR SLASH LCHAR SLASH LCHAR LCHAR LCHAR PERIOD LCHAR < word > |
| W1 | < word > : = LCHAR < word > | SLASH LCHAR SLASH LCHAR SLASH LCHAR SLASH LCHAR LCHAR LCHAR PERIOD LCHAR LCHAR < word > |
| W2 | < word > : = LCHAR | SLASH LCHAR SLASH LCHAR SLASH LCHAR SLASH LCHAR LCHAR LCHAR PERIOD LCHAR LCHAR LCHAR |

have written the rules down clearly, it is a very straightforward translation. Generally, each rule translates into a C function. The comments are intended to refer back to the rules we have derived above. (This program was compiled using both Toolworks C (MS-DOS), as well as UNIX System III (PC/IX).)

```
/*
** External references
*/

#ifdef TOOLWORKS
#include <stdio.h>

extern int      isalpha();      /* true functions under Toolworks C */
extern int      isalnum();
#else
#include <ctype.h>              /* for is?????() macros */
#endif

extern char *strchr();
extern int strncmp();

/*
** Forward references
*/

static char *device();
static char *drive();
static char *ext();
static char *file();
static int      lchar();
static char *firstpath();
static char *path();
static char *word();

/*
** char *valid(filespec)
** char *filespec;
**
** If filespec points to a string that represents a valid MS-DOS
** file specification, returns pointer to next unparsed
** character. Otherwise, returns (char *) 0 (the null pointer).
*/

char *valid(filespec)
char *filespec;
{
    char *p;
#ifdef DEBUG
    printf("valid(\"%s\")\n", filespec);
#endif
```

FIGURE 10-1

```
/*
**     < filespec > : = < device >
*/

    if ((p = device(filespec)) != (char *) 0)
    {
     return p;
    }
    else

/*
**     < filespec > : = < drive-spec >  < firstpath >  < file >
*/

    {
     if ((p = drive(filespec)) = = (char *) 0)
     {
      return (char *) 0;
     }
     else if ((p = firstpath(p)) = = (char *) 0)
     {
      return (char *) 0;
     }
     else
     {
      return file(p);
     }
    }
}
static char *device(p)
char *p;
{
#ifdef DEBUG
 printf("device(\"%s\")\n", p);
#endif
 return (char *) 0;                                    /* just a stub for now */
}

static char *drive(p)
char *p;
{
#ifdef DEBUG
 printf("drive(\"%s\")\n", p);
#endif
```

FIGURE 10-1 (Continued)

```
/*
**      <drive> := ALPHA COLON
*/

    if (isalpha(*p) && (*(p + 1) == ':'))
      {
        return p + 2;
      }
else

/*
**      <drive> := <empty>
*/

      {
        return p;
      }
}

static char *firstpath(p)
char *p;
{
#ifdef DEBUG
  printf("firstpath(\"%s\")\n", p);
#endif

/*
**      <firstpath> := SLASH <path>
*/

    if (*p == '\\')
      {
        return path(++p);
      }
    else

/*
**      <firstpath> := <path>
*/
      {
        return path(p);
      }
}

static char *path(p)
```

FIGURE 10-1 (*Continued*)

```
char *p;
{
    char *p2;

/*
**    <path> := <file> SLASH <path>
*/

    if ((p2 = file(p)) != (char *) 0 && *p2 == '\\')
    {
        return path(++p2);
    }
    else

/*
**    <path> := <empty>
*/

    {
        return p;
    }
}

static char *file(p)
char *p;
{
    char *p2;
#ifdef DEBUG
 printf("file(\"%s\")\n", p);
#endif

/*
**    <file> := PERIOD PERIOD
*/

    if (strncmp(p, "..", 2) == 0)
    {
        return p + 2;
    }
    else

/*
**    <file> := PERIOD
*/

    {
```

FIGURE 10-1 (Continued)

```
        if (strncmp(p, ".", 1) = = 0)
        {
          return p + 1;
        }
    }
    else

/*
**    <file> := <word8> <ext>
*/

    {
      p2 = word(p);

      if ((p2 - p) < 1 || (p2 - p) > 8)          /* 0 < len < = 8 */
      {
        return (char *) 0;
      }
      else
      {
        return ext(p2);
      }
    }
  }
}

static char *word(p)
char *p;
{
#ifdef DEBUG
 printf("word(\"%s\")\n", p);
#endif
    while (char(*p+ +))
    {
        ;
    }
    return --p;
}

static char *ext(p)
char *p;
{
    char *p2;
#ifdef DEBUG
 printf("ext(\"%s\")\n", p);
#endif
```

FIGURE 10-1 (Continued)

```
/*
**    <ext> := <empty>
*/

    if (*p != '.')
    {
        return p;
    }

/*
**    <ext> := PERIOD <word3>
**    <ext> := PERIOD
*/

    else
    {
        p2 = word(++p);

        if ((p2 - p) <= 3)                    /* length of word is 0 to 3 chars */
        {
            return p2;
        }
        else
        {
            return (char *) 0;
        }
    }
}

static int lchar(c)
int c;
{
                                              /* < > and ¦ not allowed */
    static char others[] = "$&#@!%'()-{}_^~' ";

/*
**    One small caution: if c is '\0', it will be found by
**    strchr() at the end of the others[] array. So we have to
**    check that it's not.
*/

    return isalnum(c) ¦¦ (c != '\0' && strchr(others, c) !=
                    (char *) 0);

}
```

FIGURE 10-1 (Continued)

```
#ifdef MAIN

/*
** A small test program for valid(). For example,
**
**     A> validate A:\X\Y\Z\FOO.BAR
*/

main(argc, argv)
int argc;
char *argv[];
{
    char *p;

    if (argc > 1)
    {
      if ((p = valid(argv[1])) = = (char *) 0 )
      {
        puts("INVALID (bad parse)");
      }
      else

/*
** Make sure that we consumed the entire string in parsing it.
*/
      {
        if (*p != '\0')
        {
          printf("INVALID (didn't consume \"%s\")\n", p);
        }
        else
        {
          puts("VALID");
        }
      }
    }
}

#endif
```

**FIGURE 10-1** *(Continued)*

The terminal LCHAR is assumed to represent one of the legal characters for a filename. The rules for a <word> say that a <word> consists of one or more legal characters. Notice that we do not specify that a legal extension is a maximum of three characters, or that filenames are limited to eight characters.

We could have done so as part of the grammar, by defining

<file> := <word8> <ext>

<ext> := PERIOD <word3>
<ext> := PERIOD
<ext> := <empty>

<word3>          := LCHAR
<word3>          := LCHAR LCHAR
<word3>          := LCHAR LCHAR LCHAR

and similarly for <word8>, but you can see that it significantly complicates the grammar. Instead, we simply check, within the code, to make sure that the word was the right length for the rule being used.

Using the code in Figure 10-1, if you turn on the debugging **printf()** statements, you can see how the **firstpath()** function is called recursively. This method of parsing is called "recursive-descent," a top-down parsing strategy. It works well as long as none of the rules cause a recursive loop. In general, top-down parsing is easier to do; most bottom-up strategies require a program like YACC to be of any use. The trade-off is that top-down approaches tend to be somewhat less efficient. Unless parsing occupies a large part of your application's execution time, you will probably find top-down approaches adequate.

We do not have enough room here to cover all the aspects of parsing which an advanced C programmer should know. The basic rules, though, are clear: Figure out what the terminals of the input language are, and the rules for grouping them together. Write simple functions to recognize the terminals (like **word()** in the example), and functions to implement the rules. Use comments to relate the code you are writing to the rules (this makes it a lot easier to figure out where things are going wrong). Add debugging code that can be turned off (but not removed) once the "last" bug is out.

## CONCLUSION

This chapter has logically sketched and implemented a top-down scheme for parsing simple user input. This technique, and similar ones, will often provide all the translation your program's input will need. Parsing, however, goes far beyond the treatment received in this chapter. Below is a sample exercise in implementing the technique described above, and a list of further reading on parsing techniques.

## Sample Exercise

Using the method employed in this chapter, write a program that recognizes the following grammar:

```
<expression> : = <expression> PLUS <term>
<term>       : = <term> TIMES <factor>
<term>       : = <factor>
<factor>     : = LEFT_PAREN <expression> RIGHT_PAREN
<factor>     : = <number>
<number>     : = DIGIT <number>
<number>     : = DIGIT
```

This grammar describes simple arithmetic operations, using the addition (PLUS) and multiplication (TIMES) operators. Good luck!

## Additional Reading

If you encounter a more complex parsing problem, you will probably need to learn something about finite-state machines, pushdown machines, and context-sensitive grammars (the grammars above are both context free). Although both of these books are intended for those who want to understand how to parse computer languages, they are interesting reading for anyone faced with a complex parsing task.

1. Aho and Ullman, *Principles of Compiler Design,* Addison-Wesley, 1977.
2. Lewis, Rosenkrantz, and Stearns, *Compiler Design Theory,* Addison-Wesley, 1976.
   A reasonable introductory text, with more emphasis on LL grammars and top-down techniques. Implements a BASIC compiler as an example. More applied than Aho and Ullman, particularly with regard to finite-state machines and pushdown machines.

# 11

# Database Design and Indexing

*Contributors:* Tim Farlow of Strawberry Software, Inc.
David Graham and Peter Brooks of
PHACT Associates, Ltd.
*Reviewers:* Jon Simkins and Larry Karnis of Softfocus

## INTRODUCTION

Applications involving large amounts of similar data—database applications—require reasonably sophisticated data manipulation techniques. Several standard techniques have been developed to address this need. This chapter introduces the essential concepts of database design and indexing, and explains a few of the more popular techniques for manipulating data. The chapter also provides code examples you can use in implementing simple databases. At the end of the chapter, references are given for more advanced treatments of database design and indexing.

## General Principles

For our purposes, we define a database as a two-part entity. The first part is a collection of data records. The second part, useful in large collections of data, is an index to the data records, enabling you to access the records easily.

Each data record is analogous to a **struct**, in that it is a collection of data in a predefined format. For example, in a database of employee information, each record contains the name, social security number, address, salary, and the like, for a single employee. The database is the collection of such records for every employee.

Each record to be stored in a database needs to be identified uniquely, so that user operations like retrieval and modification can be performed on a single record. The identifier is called a **key**, and is usually a part of the data record.

In our employee database example, the social security number has a unique value for each employee, and can thus serve as a key.

The data type we will use for such an employee record is shown in Figure 11-1.

```
/* Record Data Type */

struct REC
{
    char ssno[10];                          /* social security # */
    char fname[15];
    char lname[20];
    char address[25];
    char city[15];
    char state[3];
    char zip[6];
    char hirdate[10];
    float salary;
};
```

**FIGURE 11-1**

Given the record defined in Figure 11-1, we define a corresponding **index**: a method of accessing a record via its key. Generally, such a method is based on the following scheme: The key is read from each record. As the data record is written to the data file, its address within the data file is saved. This address is stored along with the key. The structure containing the record's key and address provides all the information necessary to find the record. We will refer to this structure, defined in Figure 11-2, as an **element**.

```
/* Element Data Type */

struct ELSTRUCT
{
    char key[SIZE];                                     /* key */
    long data_adr;          /* file offset, in data file, of data record */
};

typedef struct ELSTRUCT EL;
```

**FIGURE 11-2**

The elements corresponding to each data record will be stored together to comprise the index. Thus we have defined the two parts of our database: the actual data and the set of elements, known as the index. These parts can be stored in the same file or in separate files. Commonly, the index is kept sorted by key.

## DATA AND INDEX STORAGE

In the UNIX system, portions of a file that do not contain data take up no data space. (These unused bytes are read as null bytes.) On UNIX, then, an indexed database can exist in one file: the index stored in locations 0 through N, and the data stored in locations $N+1$ through M. Since any unused bytes take up no extra space, a database with fewer than N elements can be efficiently stored, and still has room to grow to up to N elements.

On non-UNIX systems, such as MS-DOS, files must be contiguous: Unused portions do take up data space. Storing both the index and the data in one file is thus an inefficient scheme. On such a system, the data and the index should be stored in separate files. This method provides an added advantage: You can have multiple index files, each containing a different key into the common data file. For the remainder of this chapter, we will assume that the index and data are stored in separate files.

## DATA RECORD MANIPULATION

Most of this chapter discusses various schemes for handling the index file. Assuming that the address of a particular record has been determined from the index file, only six functions are necessary to handle the data file. These functions are:

**open_data()**: opens a data file
**put_data()**: adds a record to the data file
**get_data()**: retrieves a record from the data file
**close_data()**: closes a data file
**delete_data()**: deletes a record from the data file
**update_data()**: replaces information in an existing record

In fact, only the first five are necessary, since **update_data()** can be replaced by **delete_data()** (for the old record) and **put_data()** (for its replacement). The single function **update_data()**, however, is more efficient. The code to perform these functions is presented at the end of this chapter.

## INDEXING TECHNIQUES

We will discuss five common ways to organize the index portion of the database. These are:

1. As an unsorted linear array.
2. As a sorted linear array.
3. As a linked list.
4. As a hash table.
5. As a B-tree.

Each indexing method handles the tasks listed below somewhat differently: Some are more efficient at one task than another. You, as the designer, will need to weigh these trade-offs for each application, depending on how your particular database will be used.

## General Efficiency Concerns

In discussing indexing schemes, we will consider the ability to accomplish the following tasks:

Insert a new key
Delete a key
Search for a key
Sort the index
Minimize the amount of RAM used

Depending on how your database will be used, some of these tasks will be more important than others. Search time, for example, is an important consideration in databases that will be searched often. Sort time is only important for indices that are not presorted, or for indices you will resort based on a different criterion. No single indexing scheme is clearly better than the rest; the technique you choose depends on many factors specific to your application.

*Note:* Throughout this chapter, we will assume that the index file is small enough to be read into memory as a whole. If this is not the case, you have two options: You can create and read into memory an index to the index, or you can read only a part of the index into memory at a time. In either case, the techniques below assume that the index has already been read into memory, and are thus applicable to either a partial index or a double index.

## Linear Arrays

A linear array is the simplest of indexing schemes. The elements are stored as an array in memory. We will discuss two ways in which a linear array can be searched: a linear search or a binary search. We divide our discussion of linear arrays into unsorted (those that will use a linear search) and sorted (those that will use a binary search).

## Unsorted Linear Arrays

*Deletion.*   We discuss deletion of an element from an unsorted linear array first, since your choice of a deletion method will dictate your choice of an insertion method. Two standard methods are available for deleting elements from an unsorted linear array. You can:

1. Remove the element from the array and shift the positions of all elements following it.
2. Mark the element's position as unfilled, later to be replaced by a new element. This method makes both deletion and insertion more efficient. To further simplify insertion, you can maintain a linked list of all unfilled positions as you delete elements.

The function in Figure 11-3 marks an array space as unused by replacing the key portion of the element with a null string. It returns the address of the corresponding record in the data file, making it easier for you to delete the record itself. The function assumes that the elements are stored in an array called **elements**. The **elements** array can store up to **MAXELS** elements, and currently contains **numels** elements.

```
/* Unsorted Linear Array Delete Function */

long delete(elements,el_index)
EL elements[];
int el_index;              /* index of element to delete fm. elements[] */
{
    elements[el_index].key[0] = '\0';
    return(elements[el_index].data_adr);
}
```

**FIGURE 11-3**

*Insertion.*   Analogous to the methods for deleting an element from an unsorted array, two methods are available for inserting an element into such an array.

1. Corresponding to the deletion method numbered ''1'' above, you can add each new element to the end of the array.
2. If you marked unfilled positions as available, you can insert the new element at the first unfilled position. This method requires a search for an unfilled position, unless your delete function also maintains a linked list of unfilled positions.

The function in Figure 11-4 searches for an unused space in the array, and inserts a new element there. It assumes that unused spaces are occupied by elements with a null string as the key. Like the delete function in Figure 11-3, it assumes that the elements have been read into the array **elements**.

```
/* Unsorted Linear Array Insert Function */

int add(elements, new_el)
EL elements[];
EL *new_el;
{
    int i;

    for(i = 0; i < numels; ++i)
    {
        if(elements[i].key[0] == '\0')
        {
            strcpy(elements[i].key, new_el->key);
            elements[i].data_adr = new_el->data_adr;
            return(NOERROR);
        }
    }
    if (numels++ < MAXELS)
    {
        strcpy(elements[i].key, new_el->key);
        elements[i].data_adr = new_el->data_adr;
        return(NOERROR);
    }
    printf("No room.\n");
    return(ERROR);

}
```

**FIGURE 11-4**

*Searching.* An unsorted array must be searched from beginning to end for a match. Such a search is very simple to implement, but slow for large arrays. The search time for any specific element is, on average, proportional to the number of elements. The code to perform a search of an unsorted linear array is presented in Figure 11-5.

The function in Figure 11-5 returns a pointer to the element that matches. The address part of this structure can be used to access the actual data record.

```
/* Unsorted Linear Array Search Code */

EL *search(elements, target)
char *target;              /* key of the record to be searched for */
EL elements[];
{
    int i;

    for (i = 0; i < numels; ++i)
    {
        if (strcmp(target, elements[i].key) == 0)
        {
            return(&elements[i]);
        }
    }
    return((EL *)NULL);                        /* not found */
}
```

**FIGURE 11-5**

*Sorting.* Several standard methods have been devised for sorting an array (bubble, insertion, selection, etc.). We present below the code for performing a **quicksort** of an array. A quicksort divides an array into two arrays: one containing values higher than some median, and another containing values lower than that median. The two arrays are recursively sorted, then rejoined. To sort the entire array, call **qsort(elements, 0, numels-1)**. This particular algorithm is, as its name suggests, one of the most efficient.

The **qsort()** function in Figure 11-6 calls two functions for which code is not provided: **val()** and **swap()**. The **val()** function converts the key to a long value, making the calculation of a median easier. It is similar to the standard library function **atoi()**, which converts an ASCII string to an integer value. The **swap()** function exchanges the array positions of the two elements whose indices are parameters of the function.

*Size.* The size of the code to implement a linear array is small. The array itself must be large enough to hold all the elements. More important, the array must be large enough to accommodate any elements added at run time. If you expect the user to add many records to your database, you may find a linear array too rigid a memory structure.

**Sorted Linear Arrays.** A slightly more sophisticated method of finding an element in a linear array is the binary search. In order to implement an array

```
qsort(elements, low, high)
EL elements[];
int low;                         /* indices to the portions of the array */
int high;                        /* currently being sorted */
{
  int divider;                   /* array location at which to split array */
  int median;
  int i;

  if(low > = high)               /* 1 element - it's sorted */
  {
    return;
  }
  if(low = = high − 1)           /* only 2 elements - easy to sort */
  {
    if(val(&elements[low]) > val(&elements[high]))
    {
      swap(elements, low, high);
    }
    return;
  }

  /* choose a median */

  median = (val(&elements[low]) + val(&elements[high])) / 2;

  divider = low;
  for(i=low; i < = high; i++)     /* split the array */
  {
    if(val(&elements[i]) < median)
    {
      swap(elements, i, divider++);
    }
  }
  qsort(elements, low, divider-1);    /* sort the lower array */
  qsort(elements, divider, high);     /* sort the upper array */
}
```

FIGURE 11-6

that will use a binary search, you must maintain the array in sorted order. Insertion and deletion functions, therefore, are designed accordingly.

*Searching.*   The name "binary" derives from the way in which a sorted array is searched. The search begins in the middle and eliminates half the array elements as either too high or too low. The next element checked is in the middle of the remaining half, half of which is then eliminated as either too high or too low. This process continues until either the element is found, or the array can be divided no further (i.e., the element is not in the array). This elimination process is possible because the array is sorted, guaranteeing that if the checked element is too high, all elements following it are also too high.

The following example will clarify the process. All array elements are ordered numerically by key, which for the sake of simplicity will be a two-digit number. The sample array is depicted in Figure 11-7.

12 16 19 22 23 25 26 29 33 37 41 42 45 48 56 72 73 76 80

**FIGURE 11-7**

To search for the number 25, we begin in the middle of the array, that is, we compare 25 with 37. Since 37 is too high, we can eliminate the upper half of the array. We are left with Figure 11-8.

12 16 19 22 23 25 26 29 33

**FIGURE 11-8**

Again, we begin our search in the middle, comparing 25 with 23. Since 23 is too low, we eliminate the lower half of the array, yielding Figure 11-9.

25 26 29 33

**FIGURE 11-9**

We begin in the middle, which, because integers are truncated, is 26. Since 26 is too high, we eliminate the upper portion of the array, and are left with the correct element: 25.

A binary search makes finding an element easier and faster. The average search time per element is proportional to log base 2 of the number of elements in the array. The code to perform a binary search of a sorted array is presented in Figure 11-10. To start the search, call **search(key, &location)**.

*Insertion.* Inserting an element in a sorted array requires two steps. The program must first search for the nearest element within the array, then reposition other array elements to create space for the new element. The implementation in Figure 11-11 uses the search function from Figure 11-10 to find the element closest to but lower than the new element, then increments the position of each element following it in the array and inserts the new element. Insertion time is, on average, proportional to the number of elements in the array plus log base 2 of the number of elements.

```
/* Sorted Array Search Code */

/* returns NOERROR if found, ERROR otherwise */

int search(keytomatch,location)
char *keytomatch;                    /* key of target element */
int *location;             /* location of found element, or last examined
                                              if not found */
{
    int current;              /* element to check against keytomatch */
    int high = numels;                /* highest element left to try */
    int low = 0;                       /* lowest element left to try */

    if (strcmp(elements[high].key,keytomatch) == 0)
    {
        *location = high;
        return(NOERROR);
    }
    while (low < high)
    {
        current = (high - low)/2 + low;       /* check in the middle */
        result = strcmp(elements[current].key,keytomatch);
        if (result == 0)                     /* it matches - success! */
        {
            *location = current;
            return(NOERROR);
        }
        if (result > 0)         /* the correct key is somewhere lower */
        {
            high = current;
        }
        else                   /* the correct key is somewhere higher */
        {
            low = current;
        }
    }
    *location = current;                                /* not found */
    return(ERROR);
}
```

**FIGURE 11-10**

```
/* Sorted Array Insert Function */

add(elements, new_el)                /* assumes new_el isn't in index */
EL elements[];
EL *new_el;
{
    int storeat;                /* array location in which to insert new_el */
    EL *p, *trial;
    EL lowmove;                    /* lowest element to re-position */
    if (search(new_el- >key,&storeat) = = NOERROR)
    {
        return(ERROR);                        /* it's already there!! */
    }
    trial = &elements[storeat];

    for (p = &elements[numels-1]; p > trial; --p)            /* shift */
    {
        strcpy(p- >key, (p-1)- >key);
        p- >data_adr = (p-1)- >data_adr;
    }

    /* insert element */

    strcpy(trial- >key, new_el- >key);
    trial- >data_adr = new_el- >data_adr;
    highest+ +;
    return(NOERROR);
}
```

**FIGURE 11-11**

*Deletion.*   In deleting an element from a sorted array, the program must again reposition other array elements. The implementation in Figure 11-12 decrements the position of each array element following the deleted element. Deletion time is, on average, proportional to the number of elements in the array.

## Linked Lists

Linked lists, described in Chapter 5, provide another indexing method. In the implementation in Chapter 5, we assumed a small enough collection of data that the use of keys and index files separate from data files was unnecessary.

Only small modifications to that code are necessary to use a linked list to organize keys in an index, however. We use, as our element, a hybrid of the element structure used elsewhere in this chapter, and the link structure used in Chapter 5. The structure we will use is shown in Figure 11-13.

```
/* Sorted Array Delete Function */

void delete(elements, target)
EL elements[];
EL *target;
{
    EL *p;

    for (p = target; p < highest; ++p)
    {
        strcpy(p->key, (p+1)->key);
        p->data_adr = (p+1)->data_adr;
    }
    --numels;
}
```

**FIGURE 11-12**

```
struct ELSTRUCT
{
    struct ELSTRUCT *previous;      /* pointer to previous element */
    char key[SIZE];                 /* key */
    long data_adr;                  /* byte offset of the data record */
    struct ELSTRUCT *next;          /* pointer to next element */
};

typedef struct ELSTRUCT EL;
```

**FIGURE 11-13**

You can manipulate the elements in a linked list through functions nearly identical to the **find_link()**, **insert_link()**, and **delete_link()** functions shown in Chapter 5. The modifications necessary to those functions to render them useful with our element structure **EL** are as follows:

1. Replace Chapter 5's references to the structure **link_type** with references to **EL**.
2. In the **insert_link()** function, instead of merely inserting the variable string, insert both **key** and **data_adr**.

**Disk Access.** When writing a linked list to disk, you can include the **next** and **previous** pointers in the **EL** structure. This uses a good deal of disk memory unnecessarily, however. Instead, remove those parts of the structure and simply write the elements to disk in order. When next you access the linked list, you can read it from disk in order, inserting the **next** and **previous** pointers as you read each element.

**Searching, Insertion, and Deletion.**  The average search time per element in a linked list is proportional to the number of elements. Insertion and deletion, because they are performed via a search followed by a simple insert or delete operation, are also proportional to the number of elements.

**Size.**  The linked list functions shown in Chapter 5 all use calls to **malloc()** and **free()** for memory management. The size of the linked list is thus kept at a minimum, with no overhead for anticipated elements.

## Hashed Indices

In many databases, finding an element quickly is of utmost importance. In the indexing schemes discussed so far, searching for an element involves comparing it to several elements in the index—with some schemes, to an average of half the number of elements in the index. An optimal search would somehow yield a unique value for every element, which would immediately indicate its position within the index. **Hashing** provides just such a search.

In an ideal hashed index, some **hash function** assigns a unique value to each element. The **hash table** records the one-to-one correspondence between the hash value and the address of the element.

In most actual hashed indices, **collisions** will occur; that is, some elements will have the same hash value. The hash table is thus an array of pointers to storage structures. Such a storage structure, whatever its form, is generally referred to as a **bucket** or a **bin**. Each bucket contains all elements with the corresponding hash value. To find an element in an index containing N elements and B buckets, your program hashes the element, reads the hash table to find the bucket, then searches the bucket to find the element.

The illustration in Figure 11-14 will clarify the workings of a hashed index.

Although collisions often make the ideal hashed index impossible, a good hashed index satisfies the following two criteria:

1. Elements are distributed reasonably evenly among the buckets.
2. The hash function is simple, that is, quickly executed. The time required to determine the hash value is thus negligible.

With the above two criteria satisfied, your program's search for an element is reduced from a search through the total number of elements to a search through the number of elements with a particular hash value. If elements are fairly evenly distributed, then, this represents a search through the number of elements divided by the number of buckets—a significant advantage over any other indexing method.

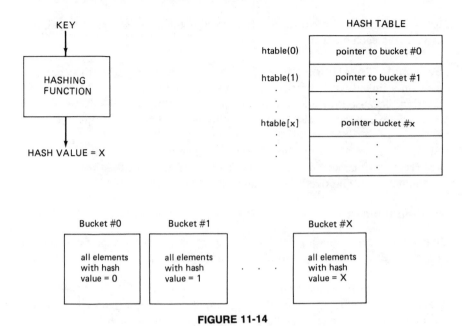

**FIGURE 11-14**

Typically, buckets are implemented as linked lists. In such an implementation, with N elements evenly distributed among B buckets, search time is proportional to log base 2 of (N/B). (The time to determine the appropriate hash value is arbitrarily small.) If the number of buckets is equal to or greater than the number of elements, the average search time is negligible.

The design and implementation of hashing schemes are discussed in detail in many other texts (e.g., Sedgewick, Robert, *Algorithms*, Addison-Wesley Publishing Co., 1983. Wirth, Niklaus, *Algorithms + Data Structures = Programs*, Prentice-Hall, 1976. Knuth, Donald, *The Art of Computer Programming*, *Volume 3: Sorting & Searching*, Addison-Wesley Publishing Co., 1973). The major issues, however, are as follows:

1. How will collisions be handled, that is, how will buckets be implemented?

We recommend a linked list implementation. For most applications, linked lists maintain advantages in search time without unnecessarily complicating code.

2. How large should the hash table be?

We recommend the smaller of:

    a. the amount of memory you can afford
    b. the number of items in your database plus about 15%.

3. How should the hashing function operate?

The optimal hashing function, given the input appropriate to your database, will produce the most evenly distributed results. The design of hashing functions can be very mathematical, and is treated in the texts referenced above. We provide one example below.

As an example, we implement a hashed index with linked lists as buckets. The hashing function performs some simple arithmetic operations on the ASCII values of the characters in the key. The necessary data types and hashing function are shown in Figure 11-15.

```
/* Data Types */
#define HTABSIZE 100                    /* size of hash table */

struct EL                               /* linked list element */
{
    struct EL *next;
    char key[SIZE];
    long data_adr;
};

EL *htable[HTABSIZE];         /* hash table - array of linked lists */

/* Hashing Function */

short hashf(key)
char *key;
{
    int result = 0;
    int i;

    /* sum the square of the ASCII values in the key */

    for (i = 0; key[i]; i + +)
    {
        result + = key[i] * key[i];
    }
    if (result < 0)                     /* overflow precaution */
    {
        result = -result;
    }
    return(result % HTABSIZE);          /* keep value within table */
}
```

**FIGURE 11-15**

**Insertion and Deletion.**  Insertion and deletion of elements in a hashed index involve two steps:

1. Hash the element and consult the hash table to find the correct bucket.
2. Use the algorithm appropriate to the bucket's data type to insert/delete the element.

Considerations of time and complexity in insertion and deletion are thus specific to the bucket implementation you choose.

The insert and delete functions for buckets implemented as linked lists are shown in Figure 11-16.

```
/* Hash Table Insert Function */

int add(key, address)
char *key;                          /* the key to the record */
long address;                       /* disk address of the record */
{
    struct EL *p, *newlink, *getlink();
    int bin;

    bin = hashf(key);
    newlink = getlink(key, address);    /* malloc new element */
    if (newlink == NULL)                /* malloc error */
    {
      return(ERROR);
    }
    p = htable[bin];                    /* get head of linked list */
    newlink->next = p;          /* insert link at head of linked list */
    htable[bin] = newlink;
    return(NOERROR);
}

/* Hash Table Delete Function */

int delete(key)
char *key;                          /* key of element to be deleted */
{
    int bin;
    struct EL *p, *old;
    bin = hashf(key);                   /* get hash table index */
    p = htable[bin];                    /* get head of linked list */
    if (!strcmp(key,p->key))            /* it's the first one */
```

**FIGURE 11-16**

```
    {
       htable[bin] = p->next;                    /* delete head */
       freelink(p);                              /* free memory */
       return(NOERROR);
    }
    for (;p->next != NULL; p = p->next)
    {
       if (!strcmp(key,p->next->key))            /* we found it! */
       {
          old = p->next;
          p->next = p->next->next;
          freelink(old);
          return(NOERROR);
       }
    }
    return(ERROR);
}

struct EL *getlink(key,d_adr)
char *key;
long d_adr;
{
    struct EL *retval;
    char *malloc();

    retval = (struct EL *)malloc(sizeof(struct EL));
    if (retval == NULL)
    {
       return (NULL);
    }
    strcpy(retval->key,key);
    retval->data_adr = d_adr;
    retval->next = NULL;
    return(retval);
}

freelink(link)
struct EL *link;
{
    free((char *)link);
}
```

FIGURE 11-16 (Continued)

**Searching.**  The hash table search function for buckets implemented as linked lists is shown in Figure 11-17.

```
/* Hash Table Search Function */

struct EL *search(key)
char *key;
{
    int bin;
    struct EL *p;

    bin = hashf(key);                          /* get hash value */
    p = htable[bin];                           /* get head of linked list */
    for (; p != NULL; p = p- >next)
    {
        if (!strcmp(p- >key,key)
        {
            return(p);
        }
    }
    return(NULL);
}
```

**FIGURE 11-17**

**Sorting.**  Because the hash function assigns random values (in order to distribute elements evenly among buckets), sorting elements can be a difficult task. If you will need to sort a hashed index of elements, consider cross-indexing by key. You can then search based on hash values, and sort based on key. If you do use more than one index, remember to perform insertions and deletions on all indices.

**Size.**  Hashing optimizes search time at the expense of memory efficiency. Aside from the structures necessary to implement the buckets, a hashed index must also keep the table of pointers to buckets—the hash table—in memory. You may therefore have to compromise on the ideal number of buckets in order to limit the amount of memory used. Again, the trade-off depends on your particular application.

## B-Trees

Trees, as first discussed in Chapter 5, are hierarchical orderings of items. In indexing, each node of the tree is an index to a lower node. The lowest nodes are known as **leaves**; the highest node is known as the **root**. For our purposes, each node will store the element itself, since the element consists only of the key and the file offset of the corresponding data record. (In other indexing schemes, memory is saved by storing the elements only in the leaves. Other nodes simply hold pointers, and use keys as reference points.) A simple illustration, shown in Figure 11-18, will clarify our definition.

As illustrated in Figure 11-18, a balanced tree, or **B-tree**, is a tree with the following properties:

1. The root is either a leaf, or has at least two children.
2. Both a minimum and a maximum number of children per node are predetermined. (The root and the leaves are exempt from the minimum, but not the maximum.)
3. Each path from the root to a leaf has the same length.

Because of the above properties, a B-tree has a guaranteed worst search time. B-trees are very useful in situations where memory efficiency is important, since only the highest-level (and thus smallest) index need be kept in memory.

**Searching.** Searching through a B-tree is relatively simple, and can easily be traced in the diagram in Figure 11-18. Each node is searched linearly for the target element. If the target is not found, the element closest to it is found. If the closest element is higher than the target, the pointer immediately preceding the element is followed. If the closest element is lower than the target, the pointer immediately after it is followed.

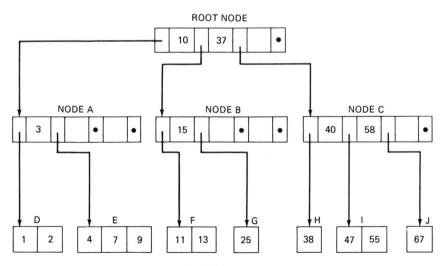

**FIGURE 11-18**

To clarify this process, we trace the algorithm for finding the number 25 in the B-tree illustrated in Figure 11-18.

1. The root node is searched linearly for 25.
2. The number 25 is not found, so the closest number, 37, is identified.
3. Since 37 is higher than 25, the pointer preceding the number 37 is followed to the node labeled B.
4. The node B is searched for 25. The target is again not found, but the closest (and only) number, 15, is identified, instead.
5. Since 15 is lower than 25, the pointer after 15 is followed, to the leaf node labeled G.
6. The leaf node is searched, and its only element, 25, is found to match the target.

Note that our tree contains a total of 18 elements, but only 4 were searched before we found our target (the two elements in the root node, the single element in node B, and the single element in the leaf node G).

**Insertion.** Because a B-tree must remain balanced, insertion and deletion are complex procedures. To insert a new element, the program first locates the leaf in which the element should appear. If the leaf is not full, the element is inserted there. As a leaf node becomes full, insertion causes the tree to grow backward: A node splits into two nodes, and inserts a new parent into the level above it. If the parent node is full, the parent node splits into two nodes, and inserts a new "grandparent" in the node above. We return to the B-tree illustrated in Figure 11-18, and trace the algorithm for inserting the number 8.

1. We first search the tree for the appropriate leaf: Scanning the root node, we find 10 to be the closest number.
2. Because 10 is too high, we follow the pointer preceding 10 to the node labeled A.
3. Scanning A, we find 3 to be the closest number.
4. Because 3 is too low, we follow the pointer after 3 to the node labeled E.
5. We search E to confirm the fact that 8 does not yet exist in the tree.
6. The number 8 should be inserted in E, but E is full. We must therefore split E into two nodes: E' and E''.
7. E' will contain 4 and 7; E'' will contain 9.
8. The new element, 8, will be inserted into the parent node, A.
9. Since A is not yet full, our task is complete, and the tree appears as shown in Figure 11-19.

**Deletion.** Deleting an element from a B-tree is simple, unless that deletion leaves a node with fewer than the minimum number of children. As a node

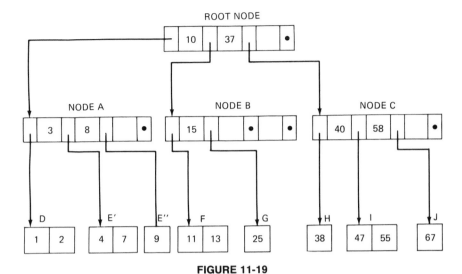

**FIGURE 11-19**

reaches its minimum, deletion requires a modification of the node's parent. In essence, the tree shrinks backward. Again, we return to the B-tree illustrated in Figure 11-18, and trace the algorithm for deleting the number 25.

1.  The tree is searched, yielding the location of 25 in leaf G.
2.  Deleting 25 leaves node B with only one child—fewer than the minimum of two. Therefore, node B must be combined with one of its siblings. We choose to combine it with its left sibling. (Combinations are done always to the left or always to the right.)
3.  In order to combine two nodes, we must demote the separating element in the node above them. The node above A and B is the root node; the element separating them is 10. We merge A and B by moving the element 10 into the resulting node, between the original nodes A and B. The resulting tree is shown in Figure 11-20.

**Size.**    B-trees are ideally suited to environments where all the keys cannot be kept in memory. Instead of storing the entire index in memory, you can store only the root, reading and writing individual nodes to and from disk as necessary.

**Sorting.**    B-trees are also useful in databases that must be sorted, since elements are stored in sorted order. (Looking again at Figure 11-18, reading all elements from left to right produces a list sorted by key.)

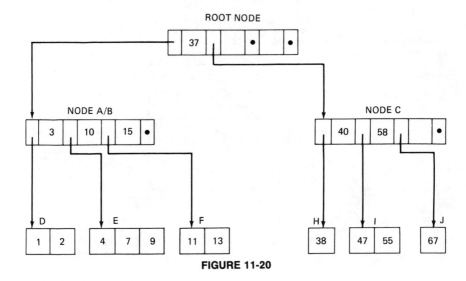

**FIGURE 11-20**

**Tools.** As you will note from the discussion above, B-trees provide substantial advantages as an indexing method, but are complex to implement. The C programmer is best served by one of the many B-tree packages commercially available, such as PHACT-dbrm from PHACT Associates, Softfocus B-Trees from Softfocus, and others. (See the Appendix for more information.)

### Summary Table of Speeds

The table in Figure 11-21 summarizes the speed and size statistics for each of the five indexing methods discussed in this chapter. All values are given for the average case, and values are relative rather than absolute. For example, speed values refer to the number of repetitions of a block of code. Actual speeds and sizes will be proportional to the values given.

In Figure 11-21, the figures quoted for deletion speed do not include the search for the appropriate element that must precede any deletion. Insertion times, on the other hand, do include any necessary searches for empty spaces, closest elements, and the like, since these speeds differ depending on the type of insertion performed.

Two insertion and deletion speeds are given for unsorted linear arrays. These values correspond to the two different methods discussed within this chapter for inserting and deleting elements. The figures in the upper portions of the grid represent speeds for marking unused array spaces as empty and inserting new elements in empty spaces; the figures in the lower portions represent speeds for inserting elements at the end of the array, and repositioning elements after deletion.

| | SEARCH | INSERT | DELETE | QUICK SORT | SIZE |
|---|---|---|---|---|---|
| UNSORTED LINEAR ARRAY | $\frac{N}{2}$ | $\frac{N}{X+1}$ / 1 | 1 / $\frac{N}{2}$ | $N \log_2 N$ | N + space for inserted elements |
| SORTED LINEAR ARRAY | $\log_2 N$ | $\log_2 N + \frac{N}{2}$ | $\frac{N}{2}$ | — | N + space for inserted elements |
| LINKED LIST | $\frac{N}{2}$ | $\frac{N}{2} + 1$ | 1 | — | N (dynamic allocation) |
| HASHED INDEX (for bucket size app. 1; no. of buckets app. N) | 1 | 1 | 1 | $N + N \log_2 N$ | N |
| B-TREE | $\log_2 N$ | $2 + \log_{m/2}[N/B]$ | $2 + \log_{m/2}[N/B]$ | — | N + code space* |

*B-trees can use less memory than this figure indicates, since all nodes need not reside in RAM at one time.

**FIGURE 11-21**

KEY:

N = Total number of elements in index
X = Total number of empty elements in index
m = Maximum number of children per node
B = Average number of elements per leaf

## DATA MANIPULATION FUNCTIONS

As mentioned at the outset of this chapter, indexing schemes provide your program with the offset of the data record within the data file. The functions illustrated in Figure 11-22 will then suffice to manipulate the records themselves.

```
/***********************************************************/
/* open_data( ): opens a data file                         */
/***********************************************************/

int open_data(name)                    /* open for reading and writing */
char *name;
{

/* Open for reading and writing (in untranslated [binary] mode) */
      /*       == "rb+"                    */

    if((data_file = fopen(name, "rb+")) == NULL)
    {
      return(ERROR);
    }
      return(NOERROR);
}


/***********************************************************/
/* put_data( ): adds a record to the data file             */
/* uses find_free( ) to find the first available hole in data */
/***********************************************************/

/* complex version: simple deletion can be used */

long put_data(rec)
REC *rec;
{
    long ret_adr;
    long find_free( );

    if((ret_adr = find_free(data_file)) == ERROR)
    {
      fprintf(stderr, "Cannot find free space\n");
      return((long)ERROR);
    }
```

**FIGURE 11-22**

```
        if(fseek(data_file, ret_adr, F_START) != 0)
        {
            fprintf(stderr, "Cannot seek to free space\n");
            return((long)ERROR);
        }

        if(fwrite((char *)rec, sizeof(REC), 1, data_file) != 1)
        {
            fprintf(stderr, "Cannot write record to datafile\n");
            fprintf(stderr, "Error = %d\n", ferror(data_file));
            return((long)ERROR);
        }

        return(ret_adr);
}

long find_free(fp)

FILE *fp;
{
    REC rec;
    long ftell( );
    int bcnt;

    if(fseek(fp, 0L, F_START) != 0)
    {                                          /* rewind to beginning of file */
        fprintf(stderr, "Cannot rewind datafile\n");
        return((long)ERROR);
    }
    while((bcnt = fread((char *)&rec, 1, sizeof(REC), fp )) == sizeof(REC))
    {
        if( rec.ssno[0] == '\0' )                        /* if empty, */
        {                                                /* go to start of entry */
        if(fseek(fp, -1L * sizeof(REC), F_CURPOS) != 0)
        {
            fprintf(stderr, "Cannot seek to start of empty record\n");
            return((long)ERROR);
        }
        break;
        }
    }
    /* if no entries found, current file-pointer will be at
       end of entries */
```

FIGURE 11-22 (Continued)

```
        return(ftell(fp));                        /* return current file position */
}


/****************************************************************/
/* get_data( ): retrieves a record from the data file          */
/****************************************************************/

REC *get_data(adr, rec)
long adr;
REC *rec;
{
    if(fseek(data_file, adr, F_START) != 0)
    {
        return(NULL);
    }

    if(fread((char *)rec, sizeof(REC), 1, data_file) != 1)
    {
        return(NULL);
    }

    return(rec);
}


/****************************************************************/
/* close_data( ): closes a data file                           */
/****************************************************************/

int close_data( )
{
    if(fclose(data_file) != 0)
    {
        fprintf(stderr, "Cannot close datafile!\n");
        return(ERROR);
    }

    if (fclose(indx_file) != 0)
    {
        fprintf(stderr, "Cannot close index file!\n");
        return(ERROR);
    }

    return(NOERROR);
}
```

FIGURE 11-22 (Continued)

```
/***********************************************************/
/* delete_data( ): deletes a record from the data file    */
/***********************************************************/

int delete_data(adr)
long adr;
{
   REC record;

   setmem((char *)&record, sizeof(REC), 0);
   if(fseek(data_file, adr, F_START) != 0)
   {
     fprintf(stderr, "Cannot seek in datafile\n");
     return(ERROR);
   }

   if(fwrite((char *)&record, sizeof(REC), 1, data_file) != 1)
   {
     fprintf(stderr, "Cannot update record in datafile.\n");
     return(ERROR);
   }

   return(NOERROR);
}

/***********************************************************/
/* update_data( ): replaces an existing record with new data  */
/***********************************************************/

REC *update_data(adr, rec)
long adr;
REC *rec;
{

   if(fseek(data_file, adr, F_START) != 0)
   {
     return(NULL);
   }

   if(fwrite((char *)rec, sizeof(REC), 1, data_file) != 1)
   {
     return(NULL);
   }

   return(rec);
}
```

**FIGURE 11-22** *(Continued)*

## MAINTAINING DATA INTEGRITY

In implementing any database of reasonably important information, you must address the question of data integrity: In the event of some destruction of the index file, or a system crash, how easily are your data recovered? While complex schemes for maintaining data integrity have been developed, a general, simple rule of thumb is to flush all buffers (i.e., update the data on disk) after every write operation. For more information on data integrity, see the texts referenced below.

## CONCLUSION

This chapter has provided a brief overview of several important concepts in database design and indexing. We have defined a database, introduced the concept of an index, illustrated several methods for arranging the index, and discussed the relative advantages of these methods. More advanced treatments of database design and indexing can be found in texts such as the following:

Aho, Alfred V., Hopcroft, John E., and Ullman, Jeffrey D., *Data Structures and Algorithms*, Addison-Wesley Publishing Co., 1983.

Kernighan, Brian W. and Ritchie, Dennis M., *The C Programming Language*, Prentice-Hall, Inc., 1978.

Knuth, Donald, *The Art of Computer Programming, Volume 3: Sorting & Searching*, Addison-Wesley Publishing Co., 1973.

Ullman, Jeffrey D., *Principles of Database Systems (2nd Edition)*, Computer Science Press, 1982.

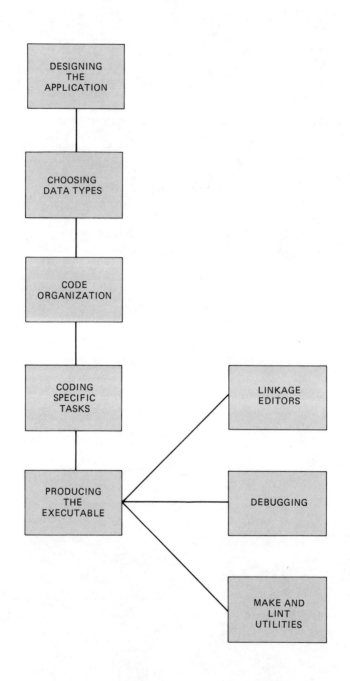

# Section E
# PRODUCING THE EXECUTABLE

Your task is hardly finished once you have written all the source code for an application. The trivial actions of compiling, linking, debugging, and testing small programs become major features of the development cycle for professional applications. Because these activities are major features, commercial utilities have been produced to facilitate the process of creating an efficient, bug-free executable from source code.

The chapters in this section discuss linking, overlaying to conserve memory, debugging, testing, and revising code.

# 12
# Linkage Editors

*Contributor:* Dave Hirschman of Phoenix Software Associates, Ltd.
and Phoenix Computer Products Corporation
*Reviewer:* John Hutchinson of Solution Systems and The
Programmer's Shop

## INTRODUCTION

In most cases, a C program must be processed with a linkage editor before it can be executed. A linkage editor assembles all the pieces necessary to create an executable file, such as compiled object modules, applicable modules in included libraries, and referenced functions from the compiler's library. This chapter is a discussion of why linkage editors evolved, what they do, and how you can use them on microcomputers to increase the utility of your software. As a detailed example, the operation of Plink86 (a commercial linkage editor for the IBM PC and compatibles) is described.

Today, virtually all language compilers produce an intermediate form of the program called an ''object file,'' which is not executable. Furthermore, most languages (including C) are ''modular'': the source code for a typical program is divided into several files that are compiled separately. The linkage editor reads the intermediate object files and links them together into an executable file.

Unlike the C language, linkage editors are not the subject of any popular books or of national standards for desig.ı and operation. This is because object file formats and linkage editors are typically very different from one operating environment to another. They are involved with the basic addressing mechanisms of the particular processor being used. Linkers are therefore a highly nonportable aspect of software development.

Academia, in properly attempting to provide generally useful knowledge, tends to bypass linkers. Computer systems provided for programming homework assignments generally do not use them. If a linker is used, its operation is usually hidden from the students, so they may concentrate on the languages and algorithms being taught. The most one usually finds in compiler language textbooks is a brief chapter about what linkage editors are and some commands used for a linker on a particular machine.

Programmers must cope with linkage editors when they leave the educational environment and begin to write software for industrial and business environments. For simple programs, all the programmer needs to do is tell the linker the names of the object files making up the program. As the limitations of the machine are reached, however, more sophisticated techniques must be used to obtain a practical system. In particular, sharing of a block of memory among different blocks of code may be necessary to create a program that will fit into available memory. Such capability, known as ''overlaying,'' is provided by the linkage editor.

## WHY HAVE LINKAGE EDITORS?

Many older mainframe computers had no linkage editors. On these machines a programmer would write a program as a monolithic chunk of code contained in a single source file. The compiler would translate the source program into machine code ready for execution on the target machine. This approach immediately runs into problems when a program consists of more than one module.

On the earliest machines, ''modular programming'' was achieved by combining the various source files making up the program at compilation time. A popular way to do this was to create a ''master'' file which caused the compiler to read the required source files via a source ''include'' facility. If C programs were written this way, for example, and a program consisted of three modules, a master file containing the following statements might be used:

```
#include "SOURCE1.C"
#include "SOURCE2.C"
#include "SOURCE3.C"
```

Master files like this would be given to the compiler, which would then compile all three source modules. If a programmer wanted to fix a bug in **SOURCE3.C**, the other two modules would be re-compiled, as well. This did not matter a great deal on mainframe machines that were fast enough that re-compiling a large source program was not objectionable. As programs became larger and mini- and microcomputers became popular, however, people realized that the strategy of combining program modules on a source level was not going to work very well.

The problem would be even worse on microcomputers than on minicomputers. The tiny memories of the first microcomputers could hardly hold the compiler and the operating system, let alone the enormous symbol tables that the compilation of a complete program might require.

A more important objection to the concept of combining program modules at the source level is that it becomes awkward for the language compiler to provide standard functions. In C, for example, most compilers provide standard functions like **read()**, **write()**, **printf()**, and so on. These functions are often called the ''run-time support'' functions, because they are needed as the program executes.

The only way to include run-time support functions as part of a program, if modules are to be combined on the source level, is to supply source code for them and **#include** them at compile time. However, a programmer would not want to **#include** the **fprintf()** function, for example, if that function were not called by any program modules. This would waste memory space. The compiler author could provide a separate file for each and every run-time support function, but then the program author would have a difficult time determining which functions were actually needed in the program, and would be constantly writing and rewriting **#include** statements.

Many run-time support functions are ''invisible'' to the programmer. Calls to these functions are generated by the compiler, and they generally support operations that are not provided by the computer processor the program will execute on. For example, the Intel 8086 processor does not have an instruction to multiply 32-bit integers, so C compilers on these machines use calls to ''hidden'' functions in order to provide a multiplication operator for long integer variables.

Determining which ''hidden functions'' are needed would be even more difficult than getting the correct standard functions included in the program. Some early non-linkable compilers offered source libraries and mechanisms for performing automatic inclusions of the right routines. Most run-time support routines, however, must be written in assembly language, in order to access low-level features of the operating system and hardware. Another approach to the problem of modularization was clearly needed: one which would allow modules written in different languages to be combined, and which would offer some automatic mechanisms for selecting run-time support modules.

## OBJECT FILES

The modular programming problem was solved by providing for the separate compilation of each module into an intermediate file called the ''object'' file. Object files contain the machine code generated for the high-level language statements, plus information used by the linker to put the program together. By the time high-level, modular languages like C were developed, linkage editors were coming into common use; by the time microcomputers became available, linkage editors were familiar technology. To modify a program, only the source modules that change need to be re-compiled. The linker can combine object files much more quickly than a compiler can translate them into machine code, thereby shortening the software development cycle.

Object files are typically organized into records of the following kinds:

1. Module Identification Record. This record assigns a name to the module. On machines where several different object file formats are used, the linker may use this record to determine which format was used in the file it is reading.

2. Segment Records. Typically, a module's code and data are divided into separate blocks called "segments." This allows the linker to put code and data into different memory locations (if necessary). The segment record will tell the linkage editor how much memory space the segment will require. Other items that may be included are: a name for the segment, an indication of what type the segment is (code, data, common block), and required alignment.

3. External Symbol Records. These records list the names of functions and variables that the module wants to reference within other modules. Whenever the C **extern** statement is used, the compiler generates an external symbol record.

4. Public Symbol Records. These records list the names and addresses of symbols that the module is making available to other modules in the program. If you define a variable or function in C that is not local (inside a function definition) and do not put the **static** keyword in front, the C compiler will create a public symbol record for it.

5. Code and Data Records. These records define the contents of the program segments. The compiler places the machine code generated for the module source statements, as well as the values needed to initialize data areas, in these records.

6. Address "Fix Up" Records. The code and data records typically contain empty slots where the linkage editor will insert the addresses of external symbols. If an external C function is called, for instance, the compiler will place the machine code for the call instruction into a code and data record, but will leave zeros within the address portion of the instruction. When the linker reads the "fix up" record, it places the proper address in the hole left by the compiler.

7. Module End Record. This record tells the linker that the end of the module has been reached. Often these records are also used to define a starting address for the program. In a C program, for instance, the compiler might place the address of symbol **main** here, because that is where C programs begin executing.

To create an executable program, the linkage editor reads the object files and decides where in memory each segment of each module will be loaded. Public symbols are defined by the compiler as offsets from a particular segment. Therefore, the final address of each public symbol is known once the segment addresses have been chosen. The linkage editor can then perform "fix up" operations to handle all references made to external symbols.

Plink86 includes a utility program to print Intel format object files in a readable form. Figure 12-1 shows what the object file generated by the Lattice C compiler for the "Hello, world" program looks like.

```
main()
{
    printf ("Hello, world.\n");
}


Dump of HELLO.OBJ

 0  THEADR "HELLO"
27  SEGDEF 1: "PROG", Class "PROG", PUBLIC MOD1 Len=E
31  SEGDEF 2: "DATA", Class "DATA", PUBLIC MOD2 Len=F
42  GRPDEF 1: "PGROUP"
    SI = 1
49  GRPDEF 2: "DGROUP"
    SI = 2
50  PUBDEF GroupIx=1 SegIx=1
    "MAIN" Offset=0 TypeIX=1
6C  EXTDEF
    1: "PRINTF"
78  LEDATA SegIX=1 Offset=0
    55 8B EC B8 00 00 50 E8   00 00 8B E5 5D C3        U.....P. ....].
8D  FIXUPP
    FIX @8 Mode=Self LOC=Offset  = > FRAME=GI(2) TARGET=SI(2)
96  FIXUPP
    FIX @8 Mode=Self LOC=Offset  = > FRAME=EI(1) TARGET=EI(1)
9F  LEDATA SegIX=2 Offset=0
    48 65 6C 6C 6F 2C 20 77   6F 72 6C 64 2E 0A 00    Hello, world...
B5  MODEND
```

**FIGURE 12-1**

The THEADR record at address 0 is the module identification record, and the SEGDEF records following it define the module segments. The GRPDEF records are arcane records involved with Intel 8086 addressing mechanisms. At address 50 a PUBDEF record makes symbol **main** a public.

The LEDATA record at address 78 contains the 8086 machine language that the Lattice compiler generates for this module. You can see a "hole" at offset 4 within this record where the linker will insert the address of the "Hello, world" message defined in the LEDATA record at 9F. This is done by the FIXUPP record at 8D. Similarly, a hole at offset 8 is left to hold the address of the **printf()** function. This address is inserted when the FIXUPP record at 96 is encountered. The external reference is defined by the EXTDEF record at 6C. Finally, the MODEND record terminates the object module.

## OBJECT LIBRARIES

The use of object files and linkage editors was a great boost to modular programming. Very quickly, programmers realized that linkage editors could be made to perform other useful services.

As discussed elsewhere in this book, good C programmers find that after writing several programs, various useful functions can be adapted for use in future programs. New programs are written more quickly if many of the problems have already been solved in other programs.

Instead of telling the linkage editor the names of all the useful object modules you want to add to your program, you can collect them in an "object library." The linkage editor can perform a library search on this file, and include only those modules containing functions that are called from elsewhere in the program. You can have a huge library containing many routines that will never all be used in the same program, and rely on the linker to pick out the required routines. If a library routine is selected and it calls another routine in the same library, the linker will include the second routine, as well.

Some object libraries are merely a concatenation of the object files they contain. The linker scans through these sequentially, looking for modules that contain needed functions. Other libraries have a table containing all of the public symbols defined within the library and a pointer to the module defining each one. This is called an "indexed library," and results in faster library searching by the linkage editor.

Because of the usefulness of libraries, special programs called "object librarians" have been developed for manipulating them. These programs typically have commands for combining object modules into a library, adding and deleting individual modules to or from a library, and so on. If an indexed library is being used, the librarian updates it after changing the library contents.

Every C compiler comes with a library containing the standard C functions like **printf()**, **strcmp()**, and so on. In fact, an important measure of compatibility for C compilers is how well the run time library functions adhere to the standard. You will see ads for compilers claiming something like "full implementation of UNIX version 5." For the most part, this claim refers to the run-time library. Magazine reviews of C compilers often discuss the implementation of the standard functions and point out which compilers offer the fastest **read()** and **write()** routines, for example.

The typical C run-time library has many other functions in addition to the standards. These might do things like access obscure hardware or operating system functions. Usually, the C library routines are not written in C at all, but are written in assembly language in order to accomplish tasks impossible in C and to achieve better performance.

Many software packages in the form of libraries are available in the 8086/ IBM PC marketplace, designed for use within C programs. You simply buy one and have the linker search it for you, along with the standard C library. Packages are available for higher math functions, statistics, graphics, data-bases, data entry, and others.

## INDUSTRY OBJECT FORMATS

On 8-bit microcomputers based on the Intel 8080 and Zilog Z80 microproces-sors, the Digital Research CP/M operating system is a standard, but many dif-ferent object file formats are used.The leading format is that used by Microsoft, as well as many other companies selling compilers in this marketplace. Digital Research offers compilers that use a variation of the Microsoft format. Many of these come with their own linkage editors, and can not be linked with the Microsoft linker. Whitesmith, BDS, Technical Design Labs, and other com-panies all use their own object formats and linkage editors  Plink-II, Phoenix Software's 8-bit linker, handles many of these formats, but not all.

In the 16-bit, Intel 8086 processor, IBM PC marketplace, the object file for-mat problem is not as severe as it was in the 8-bit, CP/M marketplace. Intel Corporation has published a manual describing the object format they use, and Microsoft and many other companies have followed suit.*

Some companies, like Computer Innovations and Mark Williams, originally used their own object formats for their C compilers and provided their own linkage editors. Computer Innovations dropped their own format, however, and converted to the Intel/Microsoft format. Mark Williams now offers a version of their C compiler which generates output in the standard format.

Why have compiler manufacturers gravitated toward a standard object format in the 8086/IBM PC marketplace but not in the 8080/CP/M marketplace? In the 8-bit environment, Microsoft Corporation did not dominate the language marketplace as completely as it did when the 16-bit machines first came out. Furthermore, the IBM PC quickly created a hardware and software standard

---

*Microsoft designed their own format for library files. They use a "scatter table" design which allows the linkage editor to look up symbol names more quickly than if the sequential Intel table were used.

which other manufacturers have been forced to adopt. The Microsoft linkage editor is shipped with each IBM PC as part of the standard utility program package and is documented in the DOS manual.

Another probable reason for the existence of a de-facto object format standard is that the Intel 8086 addressing mechanisms are considerably more complicated than those found on the 8-bit machines, and this makes the design of object file formats more difficult. The Intel manual on the subject is about 100 pages long! This is certainly one of the most complicated object formats ever created, and probably contains more flexibility than is actually needed. The object format used by Microsoft for 8080/CP/M machines is documented in about four pages. Perhaps people realized that re-inventing the wheel in the case would be too costly. The Intel format was well documented before the compiler marketplace really began to develop, and it was natural to use it.

## PROGRAM OVERLAYS

Computer memories have tended to fall into two categories. Some are fast, but have the disadvantage of being small, expensive, and volatile (e.g., semi-conductor memories). Other types of memory are slower, but are larger, cheaper, and permanent (e.g., disk drives). As yet, no technology available can create the ideal fast, large, and inexpensive memory.

Because of this design constraint, virtually all modern computers combine one or more types of memory in the hope of gaining the advantages of each. This is done by providing (at least) a two-tier memory system. A large, inexpensive "secondary" memory provides adequate permanent storage at reasonable cost. To achieve acceptable execution speed, programs and the data they require are loaded into a fast "primary" memory where the processor can operate on them at high speed. For example, most small business computers have a primary memory made up of integrated circuits (called "RAM" for "random access memory") and a secondary memory made up of floppy and/or hard disk drives. We tend to accept this state of affairs as natural, but it is important to realize that it is actually an arbitrary arrangement made necessary by current hardware technology.

The size of the primary memory is typically much smaller than the secondary memory. This design is necessary to hold down the total cost of the computer system. Some microcomputers may seem to have more RAM storage than disk storage, especially if the system's secondary memory is made up of only a single floppy drive. Since diskettes can be changed when necessary, however, the effective size of the secondary memory is much larger than the actual drive capacity.

Many large computer systems now provide a feature called "virtual memory." In these systems, programmers do not have to worry about swapping programs and data back and forth between the secondary and primary memories. The operating system and hardware combine to create a "virtual address space" for the executing program—it appears to the program as if there were only one fast, large memory. If the program attempts to access something not in primary memory, the program is temporarily suspended until the required code or data is loaded from the secondary memory. Computer designers have expended a great deal of effort to ensure that this process is rapid enough to produce a practical system.

Microcomputers, however, do not yet have this feature, although they may some day if they continue to follow the evolutionary track of larger machines. The microcomputer programmer is therefore faced with the problem of fitting everything into the primary memory at the right time. For sophisticated programs, a software engineer can easily spend more time fighting memory management problems than working directly on the application.

Software solutions to the memory management problem can be divided into two types: those that help manage data, and those that help manage code. A database package can handle the former, for instance.

Some interpretive languages provide some memory management help for program code. (An interpreter is a software system that executes the program directly, as opposed to a compiler, which translates the program into machine language.) For example, many BASIC interpreters allow one program to "chain" to another one. The new program is loaded into primary memory on top of the old one, and execution continues. Clearly, this is an inflexible scheme. Some fancier interpreters provide for the loading of individual procedures automatically from disk as the executing program requires them. This feature is not too difficult to implement, because the interpreter has full control over the execution of the program and can easily catch references to objects not in primary memory. Interpreters also provide other valuable features such as interactive program editing and better debugging facilities. Unfortunately, performance is always a crucial issue for microcomputer software authors, and interpreted programs typically run 10 or more times slower than non-interpreted programs. This forces most system designers to avoid using interpreters and use compilers instead. Virtually all C language packages are compilers.

Linkage editors can help handle the memory management problem for compiled programs on systems that do not provide a virtual memory capability. They typically offer automatic or semi-automatic methods for swapping various components of the program in and out of primary memory as required during execution. These components are called overlays. Since portions of the code share the same memory locations, the total primary memory requirement of the program can be greatly reduced.

## PLINK86

Plink86 is Phoenix Software's linkage editor for the 8086/IBM PC marketplace. It is the only other general-purpose linkage editor available for these machines besides that offered by Microsoft and IBM. In addition to handling the Micro-soft languages, it can read object files generated by most of the available C compilers, including Lattice C, Computer Innovations C86, Mark Williams C, and Wizard C.

Everyone purchasing an IBM PC receives the "LINK" program (which is really the Microsoft linker) as part of the DOS package. This linker is adequate if your program is not too large. If you want to develop a large program (about 300K or larger), you may find Plink86 to be an essential tool. Plink86 can also be used to port programs from minicomputers and mainframes to the IBM PC, when these programs are so large that they would not execute on the IBM PC without Plink86's overlay capabilities.

Plink86 overlays are sections of the program that you set up to use the same memory area. When overlays are requested, an overlay loader module is auto-matically included in the program. The loader reads the overlays from disk into memory automatically, as required by the executing program. Since portions of the program share the same memory space as the program runs, memory needs are lessened. The disadvantage is that the program runs more slowly, due to the extra time needed to load the overlays from disk.

There are several versions of the Plink86 overlay loader. Some print debug-ging messages as the program executes. This can help you isolate bugs in your overlay structure.

Plink86 offers a block structured overlay description language that you use to define the overlay structure of your program. Organize the overlay structure to minimize the number of times overlays have to be loaded. If a program loop that is executed 100,000 times has to switch from one overlay to another each time, and it takes 0.05 seconds to load an overlay, the program will run for almost 3 hours! In other words, set up overlays containing isolated functional areas that will execute to completion and then will not be returned to for a long time.

The division of the program into overlays sometimes conflicts with guidelines for dividing programs into modules. Each module should contain and isolate all the information necessary to manipulate a data structure. Do not base module design on the execution order of tasks. Major modules representing tasks such as "general ledger," "accounts payable," and "inventory," however, lend themselves well to an overlay structure, since the program stays in each of these subsystems for a significant amount of time. If your modules happen to conform to this kind of structure, your program is likely to benefit from the use of an overlay linker.

## An Example: Using Program Overlays

As an example, we will consider a simple program and design an overlay struc-ture for it. Our program will be a bulletin board that can answer calls, accept a user ID and password, and allow the user to transfer files to and from the bulletin board's disk area and list the files it contains. The program should also be able to handle two different kinds of communications protocols: XMODEM and KERMIT. The program will consist of the following modules:

1. **MAIN.C:**              main module of program, including common routines.
2. **PASSWORD.C:**   handles password checking.
3. **LOGON.C:**         handles user ID and log-on operation.
4. **FILEIO.C:**          handles disk file operations.
    4.1 **TRANSFER.C:**   handles upload and download operations.
    4.2 **DIR.C:**             does directory listing for remote terminal.
5. **XMODEM.C:**      handles XMODEM format messages.
6. **KERMIT.C:**       handles KERMIT format messages.
7. **MODEM.ASM:**   assembler routines to manipulate the modem.

Only one of the message-formatting modules will be needed at a time, suggesting that they should share an overlay area. At any given time, a user is either logging on or manipulating disk files, suggesting another logical division of the program. Within the area of disk file handling are two possibilities: transferring files and performing disk directory listings. The overlay structure for this program would be generated with the Plink86 input illustrated in Figure 12-2. (The input lines have been numbered for later discussion).

```
 1:  OUTPUT  BULLETIN.EXE
 2:  FILE        MAIN.OBJ, MODEM.OBJ
 3:  LIBRARY C.LIB
 4:  BEGIN
 5:        SECTION FILE LOGON, PASSWORD
 6:        SECTION FILE FILEIO
 7:        BEGIN
 8:              SECTION FILE TRANSFER
 9:              SECTION FILE DIR
10:        END
11:  END
12:  BEGIN
13:        SECTION FILE XMODEM
14:        SECTION FILE KERMIT
15:  END
16:  VERBOSE
```

**FIGURE 12-2**

Figure 12-3 shows a picture, or "memory map," of the overlay structure that would be generated. Low memory addresses are at the bottom of the figure.

Where two overlays appear side by side, they occupy the same memory locations. Only one of them can be in memory at a time.

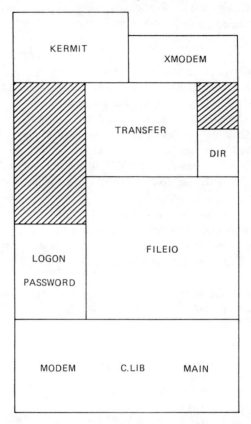

**FIGURE 12-3**

The shaded areas represent memory space that is not used when the overlay underneath it is in memory. The area at the bottom of the figure containing **MAIN**, **MODEM**, and **C.LIB** is permanently resident in memory: It shares its memory space with no other parts of the program. This is called the "ROOT," since the overlay structure can be viewed as a tree, with the overlays as branches.

Now we examine the input commands that generated this structure. Line 1 (**OUTPUT BULLETIN.EXE**) gives the name of the program to be linked. On MS DOS and PC DOS operating systems, executable files have a ".EXE" appended to an eight-character file name. On line 2 (**FILE MAIN.OBJ, MODEM.OBJ**), the object files making up the main portion of the program are given to the linker via the "FILE" command. In the MS DOS/PC DOS environment, object files have an eight-character name followed by ".OBJ".

Plink86 assumes ''.OBJ'' for object files as a default, so the extension is omitted from the remaining object files.

On line 3 (**LIBRARY C.LIB**), Plink86 is given the name of the C run-time support library. The definition of the overlay structure follows. Since C.LIB is searched before this, all of the modules selected from it will go into the ROOT.

Line 4 (**BEGIN**) begins the first overlay area with the **BEGIN** statement. The overlay area ends with the corresponding **END** statement. On line 5 (**SECTION FILE LOGON, PASSWORD**), the first overlay in this area is created with the **SECTION** statement, and two object modules are placed within it via the **FILE** statement. Line 6 (**SECTION FILE FILEIO**) creates another overlay within the same area. Since the PASSWORD and LOGON modules are never needed while the file handling module is executing, these modules are set up to share the same memory space.

On line 7 (**BEGIN**), a ''nested'' overlay area is defined. The TRANSFER and DIR overlays are needed only when the FILEIO overlay is active, so these overlays are placed in an area that is subsidiary to the file I/O overlay.

On line 12 (**BEGIN**) a new, independent overlay area is created to hold the two message-formatting modules. One of these modules will always be in memory, regardless of processes in the other overlay area. The presence of one message-formatting module is necessary in this program because both the logon process and the file-handling routines will need to send messages over the communications line. Only one of the two message-formatting modules is used at a time, however, so they share the same memory space in the overlay area.

Line 16 (**VERBOSE**) instructs the linker to print progress messages during the linkage process.

Once you set up a command file like the preceding sample, you can re-link the program at any time, with no added effort.

In most cases, data areas can not be overlaid along with code areas, because of the design of the Intel 8086 processor family. Most compilers use a single 64K memory area for data segments. This allows the code generator to assume that the DS (data segment) register will be set to the front of this area, and to use the simple 16-bit offset instructions for accessing it.

If the data areas were mixed in with the code areas in the overlays, it would be impossible for the lowest data area in memory to be within 64K of the end of the highest data area in memory. Therefore, the 16-bit addressing scheme commonly used would not work. Some of the new compilers, however, can generate a private data segment for each program module. Whenever any function within the module is called, the function ''setup'' code prepares the DS register for accessing the module's data area. With one of these compilers, data areas can be overlaid with a linkage editor.

Because data can sometimes be overlaid with code segments, Plink86 forces you to define a static overlay structure. It could load overlays into any available spots in memory and redirect function calls itself, but overlaid data areas would be impossible to find. Code areas can be loaded anywhere only because Plink86 inserts the "overlay vectors" into the flow of program execution. This can not be done for data references, without some help from the hardware (e.g., an interrupt whenever a non-resident data area is accessed, and some virtual address modes instead of the absolute addresses used by today's microprocessors) and a private data segment for each module provided by the language compiler.

Plink86 offers considerable flexibility in defining the organization of the program overlays on disk. You can tell it to place all overlays in the same ".EXE" file that contains the main program, or you can have some overlays placed into one or more separate files.

The disadvantage in having overlays in separate files is that you can easily link the wrong versions of the files. If you link a new version of the program and are not careful to delete the old overlay files, you may run into problems. You may need to store overlays in separate files, however, if the program is too large to fit on a floppy diskette as a single file.

Plink86 requires no changes to the program source files in order to use overlays. Suppose, for example, that your program has a call to a function called **MoveCursor()** that accepts x and y coordinates. The function must be invoked as

**MoveCursor (X,Y);**

regardless of whether this function is in an overlay or not. To do this, Plink86 replaces the target address of the call instruction that the C compiler generates for this function call. The address indicates a small piece of code called an "overlay vector." Plink86 creates one of these for each public symbol in each overlay. The vector passes the number of the overlay containing that public symbol to the overlay loader. The overlay loader then reads the overlay from disk into memory (assuming it is not already there). Next, the overlay vector jumps to the true address of the public symbol.

This mechanism makes the overlay process "transparent" to the source program. Some other linkage editors would require the programmer to call explicitly the overlay loader before calling the **MoveCursor( )** function.

## CONCLUSION

This chapter has discussed the historical evolution of linkage editors, and their place in the creation of applications. Linkage editors facilitate modular programming by allowing the system to find and include only those modules needed for each executable. Perhaps most useful to the programmer, many linkage editors provide overlay features that help solve some of the memory management problems posed by microcomputers. This chapter has also discussed the efficient use of such overlay features, particularly in terms of Plink86, a popular overlaying linkage editor for the PC-DOS operating system.

# 13
# Debugging

*Contributor:* Christopher J. Williams of Purart, Inc.
*Reviewer:* David Gore Graham of PHACT Associates

## DESIGNING AND IMPLEMENTING TO REDUCE DEBUGGING

### The Phases of Program Development

When developing an application, the goal is usually to produce a working program in the shortest possible time. This time can broadly be divided into three phases:

—design
—coding
—debugging and testing

In the three sections to follow, the trade-offs among time spent on each phase are considered.

**Design.**   You can design programs to "protect" them from internal problems. Functions can check that they are passed valid arguments and that returned values are within legal bounds. For example, a function that calculates the square root of its input parameter can check that the input parameter is non-negative and that the result is non-negative. Programs written in this manner tend to be larger and slower than other programs, but are very resilient. Such a program can often announce a programming error and continue to run (even with incorrect results). Another advantage to this technique is that additions to the program are less likely to cause large-scale disruption.

The resilient functions described above should return an error message, even if they can correct the problem, so that the initial bug can be found and corrected. This style of programming requires a significant time investment in designing the routines so that correct input and output behavior can be determined. For this style to be most effective, the checking and correction code should not be tacked on as an after thought; it should be an integral part of the behavior of the program. For some software that absolutely must work, this style of programming is almost essential. For most applications, this technique might be usefully applied to critical areas if not to the whole program.

At the other end of the self-checking extreme, you can design functions that work correctly only when passed the correct parameters. The rest of the program is assumed to pass correct parameters any time it calls a function. This usually produces the shortest, fastest program, but the program resembles a house of cards: Each piece must perform exactly as expected, or large-scale havoc results.

**Coding.** Sometimes, a programmer codes hastily under the illusion that the program will be completed more quickly. This is usually not so, since time saved coding is easily lost in debugging a poorly written application. In particular, spend time in coding to save time in debugging in the following areas:

1. If you write empty or partial functions so that the program will link and can be partially tested, define all the data structures and values that these functions will use when communicating with the rest of the program.
2. Insert calls to a checking function for any conditions that should ''never happen,'' for example, if a function argument should never be negative, or if a string should always have a certain length. These calls to checking functions can be removed once the debug phase is completed. In the mean time, checking functions can point to problems before they cause subtler errors further along in the program.

**Debugging and Testing.** Ideally, debugging time should be zero. Time cannot be accurately allocated for debugging, since by its nature it is dealing with the unexpected. What you can establish is a relationship between time spent on the previous phases of the program and time spent making it work correctly. Simply stated, the more time spent designing and implementing, the less time spent debugging. This relationship is often not a direct trade-off in time: A problem introduced by avoiding an extra hour in coding can take many hours to find in debugging.

### "Tricky" Coding Practices

Everyone has pet techniques they are attached to, either because they save a byte of code or are just "elegant." Since C has an almost infinite variety of ways to code even fairly simple expressions, some consistency should be established and adhered to. One of the best criteria to use when choosing how to form a statement is: Does the code describe the intended operation? For example, if the intent is to clear a single bit in a word, the fragment

**word &= ~4;**

expresses the intent more clearly than

**word &= 0XFFFB;**

The second version also presumes, not always correctly, that **word** is a 16-bit quantity.

There are a number of constructs that can present trouble, some of them obviously dangerous, others less obvious. For example:

1. Relying on side effects:
   ```
   char *p;
   p[3] = *p++;
   ```
   In this case, you cannot predict (without intimate knowledge of your compiler) whether **p** will be incremented before or after it is used to generate the pointer **p[3]**. Different compilers evaluate it differently.

2. Relying on the order of data allocation in memory:
   ```
   func1()
   {
       char a[10], b[10], *p;
       p = &a[10];
       .
       .
       .
   }
   ```
   Here, does **p** point to the first element of array **b**? As in the previous example, it depends on the compiler being used. Auto allocations are not guaranteed to have any relationship to each other. This problem can also occur using static allocations when letting a pointer to data "run into" another area. Some compilers allocate static data contiguously while others start all allocations on word boundaries, leaving "holes" in the data.

## Transportability

One of the great advantages of C is that well written code is highly transportable between different operating systems and hardware environments. The key phrase here is "well written."

The largest source of errors in writing transportable code is making assumptions about the sizes of data and pointers. Many programmers assume that integers and pointers have the same size: 16 bits. This can cause problems when pointers have been stored in integers and vice versa. Some compilers do not complain about these assignments, making locating the problem even harder. A variation of this problem is assuming that a given data type has a certain size, for example, presuming that **int** has a size of 16 bits. For example,

```
int i;
i & = 0XFFFE;
```

This will make **i** into an even number, but erroneously truncate the high bits if integers are 32-bit quantities. A more subtle source of errors occurs when memory buffers are written to files. Some machines store the low byte of a word at the lower memory address, while other machines store the high byte first. If a buffer of words is written to a file and then read back a byte at a time, the bytes may not be in the expected order.

## THE TOOLS OF THE TRADE

### Software Debuggers

A software debugger is a program that allows you to examine the contents of memory and the state of the processor as a program executes. A debugger also allows you to stop the program at specified places to examine the memory and processor states. These places in the program are called breakpoints. Most debuggers allow you to specify a number of separate breakpoints.

**Assembler Code Debugging.** Most debuggers work at the machine instruction level, allowing individual instructions to be executed and the results examined. This type of debugger allows you to examine and change the precise current state of the processor. To use these debuggers on C code, some understanding of how the C source code translates into machine instructions is required. You should also understand the format of the stack frame where function arguments are stored, in order to examine function arguments and automatic variables.

With a good understanding of assembler code, you can find some bugs by examining the machine code generated by the compiler. The machine code makes it easy to determine if something is being treated as a byte when it should be a word, or if the precedence of operator evaluation is causing an error.

**High-Level Language Debugging.** A high-level debugger allows you to trace program execution at the C statement level, which is convenient if you have no familiarity with the underlying machine language. A high-level debugger is usually closely married to a particular compiler environment, however, which can limit its usefulness when debugging portions of a program not written using C.

Some assembler code debuggers allow display of source code line numbers and the corresponding line from the source file. This can be used effectively as a high-level capability, especially when coupled with commands that execute machine instructions until the next source line is encountered.

## Hardware Debuggers

A hardware debugger is usually a board that plugs into the system bus of a computer and has a ''piggyback'' socket that is plugged into the processor socket on the mother board. The processor is in turn plugged into the piggyback socket. This allows all memory and I/O accesses to be examined.

A hardware debugger is good for answering such questions as:

1. What part of the program is erroneously accessing a memory location?
2. Is a routine ever being called with a value of 3 in the accumulator?

There are some software debuggers, such as Pfix86-Plus, which provide these hardware debugger capabilities, but many others do not. For day-to-day debugging, a hardware debugger is probably only slightly more useful than a software one. However, for some very obscure problems, such as memory locations being changed sporadically and some problems related to interrupt handling, they are a powerful tool.

A hardware debugger can not tell you that your hardware is malfunctioning. That would have to be deduced from the observed behavior of the program.

## In Circuit Emulators (ICEs)

An in-circuit emulator replaces the processor chip in a microcomputer. The ICE is based on the same chip that it is emulating, but it has special circuitry that allows some access to internal states of the processor. You can use this special circuitry to examine individual processor clock cycles, where the best you can do without an ICE is examine individual instruction cycles.

An ICE is very useful when debugging the firmware for a new piece of hardware. When the hardware cannot be absolutely relied upon, an ICE is often the only way of tracking down malfunctions.

ICEs are usually very expensive. They are almost essential, however, for the early phases of development of microcomputer hardware. With some of the newer processors such as the Intel 80286 which exhibit a high degree of prefetch activity on the bus, they are virtually essential to decoding bus activity.

### When to Use Which Tool

Very few problems cannot be found with the most primitive debugging tools, given an unlimited supply of time and patience. The important thing to know is when money (in the form of more sophisticated tools) should be traded for time invested in the project. Since it is not the norm for programs to function flawlessly when first written, an ongoing amount of time spent debugging is a safe bet for most programmers. Without precise and detailed knowledge of how C statements are interpreted, careful tracing of code logic and stratgegically placed **printf()** statements may be the most useful debugging tools. Software debuggers are invaluable in isolating program malfunctions (showing you where to perform the tracing of code logic and where to place **printf()** statements), and finding values of registers and variables that have obviously gone awry. Other commercial debuggers—hardware, software, or ICE—are necessary if your code deals with hardware.

## WHERE TO START WHEN IT DOES NOT WORK

### The Psychology of Debugging

When writing a program, the programmer is essentially recording a mental model of a sequence of processing steps. The process of debugging has two major subcategories based on this idea:

—Finding how the implementation does not match the mental model
—Finding defects in the mental model

It is generally assumed that the design phase has produced an accurate algorithm. The first place to look for bugs is in the implementation of the algorithm. The implementation is not only the most frequent source of error, but examining it is a good stepping stone to finding problems in the algorithm itself.

One of the easiest ways to waste time tracking down a problem is to assume that some component of a program is functioning correctly. While you should test all modules as exhaustively as possible before running the entire program, no part of a program should ever be considered flawless.

If a section of code appears to be working as expected, yet does not produce the desired results as part of the whole program, it is usually time to start considering whether the design of the section is consistent with the rest of the program.

### Isolating a Malfunction

In many situations, a wealth of information can be obtained from strategically placed **printf()** statements. Particularly if a large complicated data structure is to be dumped, for example, a program sequence to display expected values is often far quicker than stepping through linked lists using a debugger.

For example, to check if a string compare routine is failing due to a bug in the routine or due to invalid passed parameters, insert **printf()** statements as shown in Figure 13-1.

```
cmpstr(s1,s2)
char *s1, *s2;
{
    char returncode;
    printf("string1 = %s string2 = %s\n", s1, s2);
    .
    .
    printf("return value = %d\n", returncode);
}
```

**FIGURE 13-1**

For more complex analysis, you can use the **fprintf()** function to print your debugging statements to a file. Storing your debugging statements in a file allows you to examine them more carefully than statements printed to and scrolled off of the screen.

You can also build debugging commands into a program so that inquiries of the internal state can be made when the program is running. These commands can be removed once the program works, or left in as an aid in problem diagnosis. The easiest way to accomplish this is through conditional compilation, for example,

```
#ifdef DEBUG
    debug_function();
#endif
```

You may find it useful to code checks for special "debugging keys" that turn debugging flags on and off. You can type these debugging keys at run time, and a simple **if** statement before each debugging function will conditionally print only the debugging statements corresponding to the flags you have turned on. Such "conditional execution" accomplishes essentially the same purpose as conditional compilation, but does not require you to re-compile the program in order to turn debugging statements on and off. Choose unique keys or key sequences for your debugging keys, so as not to confuse them with program input at run time.

When a program malfunctions, it has usually performed some sequence of steps correctly, and then something has gone astray. The goal is to narrow down the part of the program where things start to go wrong. Even once you have isolated the area where the error appears, it is possible that the actual malfunction occurred earlier in the program, but did not manifest itself until later. This requires stepping back and finding the source of this previous problem, which may in turn be caused by a previous problem, and so on.

If the source of the malfunction is not easily located, software debuggers facilitate the "divide and conquer" technique. Check the state of the program at a place where things are known to have gone wrong. Having verified that something is amiss, restart the program but stop it somewhat before the place that it malfunctioned. Examine the program state, variables, data structures, and so on, and determine if the program is functioning correctly. If all is well so far, stop the program somewhere between where things appear to be correct and where things have gone wrong. This binary search technique can quickly narrow down the routine that is causing things to go astray.

## Correcting a Malfunction

Having discovered a problem in a program, you must then decide how to fix it. Many bugs can be fixed with a "local" change that deals with a specific occurrence of a problem. However, it is always worthwhile to consider whether a problem is merely a local situation or a single instance of a more pervasive problem. Consider Figure 13-2.

```
out = percent(in1, in2);
        •
        •
        •
out = percent(in1, in3);
        •
        •
percent(in1, in2)
{
    return(in1 * 100 / in2);
}
```

**FIGURE 13-2**

The **percent()** function in Figure 13-2 cannot handle a second operand of 0. The problem can be fixed quickly by changing the code as shown in Figure 13-3. This leaves a problem lurking that can recur later, since **percent()** is used elsewhere with different arguments. With a little more effort, the "final" fix shown in Figure 13-4 can be made.

The difference between the local patch and the real fix is usually a matter of the amount of time spent considering the nature of the bug and whether it in-

```
if (in2 != 0)
{
   out = percent(in1, in2);
}
else
{
  out = 0;
}

         .
         .
out = percent(in1, in3);
         .

         .
percent(in1, in2)
{
   return(in1 * 100 / in2);
}
```

**FIGURE 13-3**

```
out = percent(in1, in2);
         .
         .
out = percent(in1, in3);
         .

         .
percent(in1, in2)
{
   if (in2 != 0)
   {
        return(in1 * 100 / in2);
   }
   return(0);
}
```

**FIGURE 13-4**

teracts with other parts of the program. If care is not taken to fix problems at their source, even a well-organized program can become messy after a series of local patches have been made.

Use this local patch technique to try out an assumption, or if the problem clearly has no overall implications. Perform a major rewrite if the problem is the ''tip of the iceberg'' or is in an area of a program which affects other modules.

## TESTING

Programs are written to serve many purposes. Some are utilities to be used once and then never used again. Others are programs written for repeated personal use. On a grander scale, there are commercial products that will be used by people who will not have access to the author. Each of these major categories requries a different approach to debugging.

### Throwaway Programs

Since a throwaway program does not have to stand the rigors of use in many different scenarios, a lot of checking can be dispensed with. If the nature of the program is such that a visual inspection of the output data will make it clear whether or not it is functioning correctly, then proceed no further. For example, a program to turn all lowercase letters to uppercase letters needs little checking for correct behavior beyond looking at the output file. However, a throwaway program to calculate a polynomial checksum must somehow be checked. One way to do this is with a process analogous to mathematical induction, where the general behavior can be discerned from a few simple test cases. While this is probably not satisfactory for a durable program, a throwaway program can often get by with this type of testing.

### Personal Utilities

Although it is tempting to assume that a few bugs are acceptable in a personal utility, you can waste significant time trusting an unreliable program. You can forget those bugs and limitations, too, by using the program months after you first wrote and used it. Remove all but the most innocuous of bugs in any utility you will use often before declaring it complete.

### Commercial Products

Making sure that a program is ready for market is a completely different scale of task than the previous two mentioned. When a program is released, the reputation of the implementors and their company is affected by how a product fares. It is always tempting to rush a product out the door so as to be the first to market, but it is very easy for a program to get a bad reputation with a premature release which it can never quite overcome, even when future, improved versions are available.

Test a product not only with all conceivable combinations of valid input data, but with error cases, as well. One school of thought says that a program should be tested first with no input data, to see that this most elementary error is handled correctly. Tests should then progress from one piece of erroneous data through a realistic scenario. This philosophy is an attempt to see that all error paths are exercised.

Test your application, as well, under all target hardware configurations.

## Testing with Valid Input Data

Always create tests with data that is "just legal." For example, if a program should handle a range of input values from 1 to 99, then test the program with both 1 and 99 as input values. Some of the most common programming bugs are "fencepost" bugs, where something is counted one too many or one too few times.

Once a program is working, a number of test cases of input data and expected results can be compiled. These test cases can be used when the program is revised to make sure that it is still behaving correctly. These test cases should contain the test data created as part of the initial testing, since this data will often have been generated to examine a specific malfunction that should never recur.

## Testing with Invalid Input Data

Never expect a certain class of invalid data to be the only possible invalid input, even if those data are produced by another program that supposedly has known behavior.

Creating test cases for invalid input data has some things in common with creating valid input data tests. Always create test data that is "just invalid." For example, if input values from 1 to 9 are allowed, make sure that 0 and 10 are handled correctly as errors.

A useful source of test cases is examples that exposed problems in earlier releases of the software. These are good both for checking that the problem has stayed fixed and with variations to check related areas where there might be problems.

## RELEASING A PRODUCT

There are usually three phases to releasing a commercial product:

—Alpha release
—Beta release
—Final release to market

While there are no established criteria for considering a program ready for a particular phase of release, by examining the purpose of each release phase, criteria can be developed which are suitable for each situation.

## Alpha Release

This is the first release that is used by people outside the person or team implementing the product. When deciding when to make the alpha release, consider the following:

1. Does it do enough of what it is supposed to do for testers to want to use it?
2. Is it so buggy that testers will put it aside after one attempt at using it?
3. Will testers be interested in the next version if they waste a lot of time on the initial one?
4. Is time running out and any testing is better than none at all?

The best alpha testing environment is usually another team working in close association with the project team. This ensures quick reporting of problems and also allows a greater degree of "hand-holding" during the phase when the product is least reliable. It also avoids public embarrassment if the release is premature or serious problems are encountered.

## Beta Release

A product should only be moved to beta release when the alpha testers can find nothing wrong with any of the product's advertised capabilities. Beta test should not be considered as an extended alpha release where acknowledged problems will be "fixed later."

## TYPES OF BUGS

This section shows examples of classes of bugs. Some are general programming errors while others are specific to programming in C.

The examples labeled as C errors are some of the most common traps found when programming in C. By studying these examples, you will find them more easily avoided in programming.

1. Fencepost errors:                    ** GENERAL ERROR **

```
for (n = 1; n < 10; n++)
{
    .
    .
}
```

which should be

```
for (n = 1; n< = 10; n+ +)
{
   .
   .
}
```

2. Side-effect errors:                    ** GENERAL ERROR **

```
while (--n)
{
   .
   .
}
```

If **n** is not reset, the next call to the function will execute the **while** loop 65,000 times. The code should read

```
if (n)
{
   while (--n)
   {
      .
      .
   }
}
```

3. Not checking for empty input:          ** GENERAL ERROR **

This function assumes that the string always contains one or more characters:

```
stringlen(s)
char *s;
{
   int n = 0;
   do
      n+ +;
   while (*+ +s);
   return(n);
}
```

The following revised version can handle 0 length strings:

```
stringlen(s)
char *s;
{
    int n = 0;
    while (*s++)
    {
        n++;
    }
    return(n);
}
```

This example also illustrates the general problem of using a **do...while**—the test in the **while** is not performed until after the first iteration of the **do** loop. These loops are almost always safer if coded as **while...** loops. **Do...while** loops should only be used when some statement must be executed at least once.

4. Assuming it will fit:                              ** GENERAL ERROR **

This error is very confusing because the buffer overflow corrupts the stack.

```
char readnum()
{
    char buf[10], *p = buf;
    do
        read(0, p, 1);
    while (*p++ != '\n');
    .
    .
}
```

There is no reason in this routine to expect the **read()** from the standard input to terminate before buffer **buf** is full. Subsequent characters would corrupt the stack frame of the procedure.

5. Missing parameters                                 ** C ERROR **

C is quite susceptible to errors of not passing the correct number of parameters to a function. These problems can be very hard to find, since the routine may work in some circumstances (when provided with the correct number of arguments) and fail in other cases (when too few are supplied). If an argument is not supplied, a nonsense value is usually read from higher in the calling stack frame. Thus the routine may work even when called with too few arguments, if the value in the stack frame happens to be reasonable. For example,

.
.
```
moveblob(fromptr, toptr); /* missing length argument */
```
.
.
```
moveblob(from, to, length)
char *from, *to;
{
    while (len--)
    {
        *to++ = *from++;
    }
}
```

6. Sign extension bugs                                    ** C ERROR **

The standard definition of C leaves it to the compiler writer to determine whether characters are treated as signed or unsigned. This can create subtle problems when working in different environments that treat characters differently. For example, in

```
char i;
if (i < 0)
{
    .
    .
}
```

the **if** expression will never be executed on a machine that considers characters to be unsigned.

7. Relying on the order of bits in bitfields:              ** C ERROR **

The order in which bits are assigned to a machine word for bitfields is implementation dependent. This can be dangerous if bitfields are used to break apart data from an external source or when reading or writing with I/O device control registers. For example,

```
struct diskstat
{
    unsigned ready :1;
    unsigned error :1;
    unsigned intro :1;
} diskstat, *readfrom();
```

```
if (readfrom(DSPORT) - > ready)
{
    .
    .
}
```

Here, if **readfrom()** reads from an external I/O location, **diskstat** should describe the bits in the disk status register. However, without knowing whether the first bit of a bitfield is the highest or lowest in a word, the **diskstat** structure cannot be defined correctly. In situations like this, it is better to avoid a problem by using the **and** operator:

**#define STATBIT 0X80**

```
if (readfrom(DSPORT) & STATBIT)
{
    .
    .
}
```

8. Misuse of auto variables:                                    ** C ERROR **

```
convert()
{
    int i;
    .
    .
    return(&i);
}
```

The address of an automatic variable is being returned. This points into the stack frame of the function **convert()**, but by the time it is used, **convert()** has returned, and therefore the contents of its stack frame are no longer valid.

9. Wrong-sized function parameters:                             ** C ERROR **

If a function parameter is supplied which is too large or too small, all subsequent arguments will be misread by the called routine. For example, calling the library routine **lseek()**

```
lseek(filefd, 2, 1);
```

to seek 2 bytes past the current position will fail because the second argument to **lseek()** must be a **long**, not an **int**. This should be written as

**lseek(filefd, 2L, 1);**

10. Undefined function return value:                 ** C ERROR **

If a function does not explicitly supply a return value using the **return** key-word, an indeterminate value is returned. This can cause problems when a specific value is returned from within a function body, but no value is returned if the end of the function is reached. For example,

```
/* return pointer to first instance of c in s */
strpos(s, c)
char *s, c;
{
    while (*s)
    if (*s++ == c)
    {
        return(s - 1);
    }
}
```

Here, if the character **c** is not found in the string **s**, the **while** loop ends, but no specific value is returned. A **return(0)** should be placed before the terminating } of the function.

11. Old-style assignment operators:                  ** C ERROR **

The earlier definition for the C language had ambiguous syntax for some assignment operators:

**a=-2;**

could be either **a = -2; or a =- 2;**

The current definition of the language circumvents this problem by changing the definition of the assignment operators. Some compilers do not warn when an ambiguous construct is used, resulting in unintended code being generated. You can clarify this ambiguity most easily by surrounding all assignment operators with white space.

12. Confusion of = and ==:                      ** C ERROR **

One of the most annoying sources of bugs to beginners and experienced programmers alike is the way C uses = and ==. Even when these operators are understood, it is all too easy to make a typographical error that substitutes one for the other. In some cases, the resulting expression is invalid and causes a compiler error, whereas in other cases the resulting statement is still valid but has undesired results. For example,

```
if (a = 0)
{
    .
    .
}
```

is a valid statement that assigns 0 to **a** and never executes the statements controlled by the **if**. It should have been written as

```
if (a == 0)
{
    .
    .
}
```

13. Using a variable before it is initialized:                    ** C ERROR **

In C, if automatic variables are not initialized, they contain "garbage" from the stack frame. For example,

```
scanit()
{
    int i;
    while (i < 10)
    {
        .
        .
        i++;
    }
}
```

will have unpredictable results since **i** is not set to 0 each time the function is invoked.

14. Code that does nothing:                              ** C ERROR **

It is possible to have a well-formed statement in C that does not do anything useful. This is usually a typographical error, for example,

**x + y;**

which should have been

**x = y;**

15. Operator precedence confusion:                    ** C ERROR **

Since C has a large number of operators, it is easy to confuse which ones bind more tightly. For example,

**a = 5 + 3 << 2;**

loads **a** with the value 32 since the + binds more tightly than the <<. This example shows what is probably the most counter-intuitive precedence of all the C operators. In any case involving operators of questionable precedence, it is better to use copious parentheses than to make an erroneous assumption.

16. Misuse of **break** keyword:                    ** C ERROR **

The **break** keyword can only exit from one level of **while, for, do,** or **switch** statements. For example,

```
while (a > 0)
{
   .
   .
   for (...)
   {
      break;
   }
}
```

If the desired effect was for the **break** statement to cause execution to continue at the bottom of the **while** statement, this code fragment will not work. Since the **break** keyword occurred inside a **for** statement, execution will continue after the **for** statement.

17. Invalid pointer arithmetic:                    ** C ERROR **

For example,

**long \*lp;**
**lp + = sizeof(long);**

This does not cause **lp** to point to the next element in the list of **longs**. Instead, it causes **lp** to point to the fourth element past the current one (if **longs** are 4 bytes in length). When adding or subtracting a constant with a pointer, the constant is scaled by the size of the item that is pointed to. For example, to point to the third **long** past the current one, use

**long \*lp;**
**lp + = 3;**

18.  Mis-scoped variables:                              ** C ERROR **

For example,

**func1()**
**{**
**    int i;**
**    for (i = 0; i < 10; i+ +)**
**    {**
**        int i;**

            .

            .

**        printf("loop count = %d\n", i);**
**    }**
**}**

In this function, the reuse of **i** inside the for loop supercedes the **i** declared just inside the function definition. In this case, a different name for the second **i** should be chosen. This problem often arises because most programmers use a small repertoire of variable names for things like local loop counters. When declaring new auto variables inside compound statements, take special care to make sure that they do not unintentionally conflict with other autos.

19.  Macro side-effects:                                ** C ERROR **

For example,

**#define abs(a) < 0 ? (-a) : (a)**

```
int i, *p;
i = abs(*p++);
```

In this case, **p** will be incremented twice, since the macro uses it twice in the expansion. This type of error is difficult to find because looking at the code does not reveal the hidden expansion of the macro. When defining macros, it is often a good idea to distinguish them from ordinary function calls, perhaps by making them uppercase.

20. Floating null statements:                                                    ** C ERROR **

Inadvertent semicolons are accepted as null statements. In the example below, the statements inside the **for** loop will only be executed once:

```
for (i = 0; i < LIMIT; i++);
{
    ...
}
```

## RUN-TIME PROGRAM STRUCTURE

In order to debug programs written in C most effectively, you should have some knowledge of the structure of the running program. The structure of the program and the format of stack frames and other internal data structures vary with each compiler. The following examples are similar to those used by the Lattice C compiler with the small memory model.

### Program Memory Organization

The program is divided into four sections that correspond to the four types of memory allocation provided by the C programming language. These sections are illustrated in Figure 13-5.

**Functions.**   This memory contains the machine instructions that make up the executable functions in the program.

**Data.**   This memory contains the static data allocated outside of function bodies.

**Stack.**   This memory contains the return addresses to functions' callers and the automatic data for each function invocation.

**Heap.** This memory is not directly supported by the C language. Instead, most compilers have a run-time library that supports dynamic memory allocation for data not explicitly defined in a program. Library routines allow pieces of this data to be claimed and released as needed.

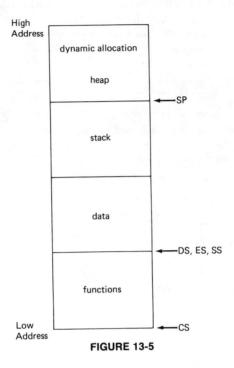

**FIGURE 13-5**

While the organization of these sections may change with different implementations, the four groups remain since they reflect features of the C language itself.

## Function Calling Stack Organization

The stack, illustrated in Figure 13-6, is used to store return addresses, register values, and arguments when one function calls another.

The arguments are pushed onto the stack first, and then the function is called. The called function then saves the caller's frame pointer (usually the BP register), and then leaves enough space on the stack for all the auto variables in the function.

While the organization of the data on the stack may change with different implementations, these four areas must be present since they reflect features of the C language function calling methods.

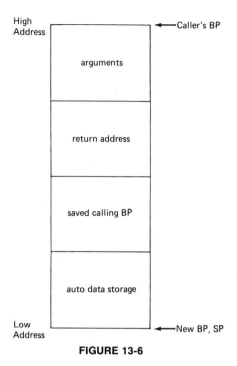

High Address — Caller's BP

arguments

return address

saved calling BP

auto data storage

Low Address — New BP, SP

**FIGURE 13-6**

When using a debugger, knowledge of the stack format for procedure calling allows procedure arguments to be examined, and calling routine addresses to be determined.

## CONCLUSION

The process of debugging can be nearly as individual as each application. Some standard procedures and warnings, however, have been discussed in this chapter. You can plan to avoid bugs from the beginning of the coding cycle by avoiding dangerous constructs. Once the code has been compiled and problems have been detected, **printf()** statements and software and hardware debuggers can all be useful in isolating the problems for solution. Finally, this chapter has listed many of the most common programming errors, both in C and in general. Knowing which common errors to look for can also reduce your debugging time significantly.

# 14

# Make and Lint Utilities

*Contributors:* Donald K. Kinzer of Polytron Corporation
Robert B. Jervis of Wizard Systems Software,
Inc.
*Reviewer:* Dave Hirschman of Phoenix Software Associates, Ltd.
and Phoenix Computer Products Corporation

## MAKE UTILITIES

### Introduction

In any substantial application, you will create files (called **target** files) that are dependent on other files. The creation of libraries is one example. A document composed of several text files is another example. Compiling is, perhaps, the most familiar example: A final executable file is composed of several object files linked together, which are in turn compiled from source files and header files. The link line that composes the executable file may contain libraries, which are in turn composed of several object modules. In all, the final executable may depend on many other files. Should you modify one or more of those files, you have two choices in updating your executable:

1. Re-compile and re-link the entire structure
2. Remember which files depend on which other files, trace the structure, and selectively re-compile and re-link only those files that are affected.

Method 2 is obviously faster, but determining which files were affected is often difficult. And should you neglect to re-compile a modified file, confusing bugs are likely to develop. A MAKE utility automates the process for you.

MAKE is a program originally developed on the UNIX system, and subsequently developed for a variety of other hosts. The basic concept of MAKE is that of dependency. An object file is said to be dependent on its corresponding source file, and any files that it directly includes. An included file is said to be dependent on any files that it, in turn, includes. In general, given a translator (such as a librarian) that processes one or more input files to generate one or more output files, each output file is said to be dependent on the input files processed to create it.

In order to use a MAKE utility, you will write a **makefile** which outlines the file dependency structure and the steps necessary to create the output file(s) from the input file(s). Once the **makefile** has been created, you simply invoke the MAKE utility after modifying any files. The MAKE utility compares the time/date stamps to determine which files need updating, then performs the minimum required re-compiling, re-linking, and any other steps necessary to update the final executable file.

## An Example

Consider the following example. To generate one executable file called **test**, you have created three source files, **input.c**, **process.c**, and **output.c**, and two include files, **keys.h** and **codes.h**. All three source files include **codes.h**, but only **input.c** includes **keys.h**. The three object files (**input.obj**, **process.obj**, and **output.obj**) resulting from compilation are linked to build the executable file, **test**. These relationships are summarized in Figure 14-1.

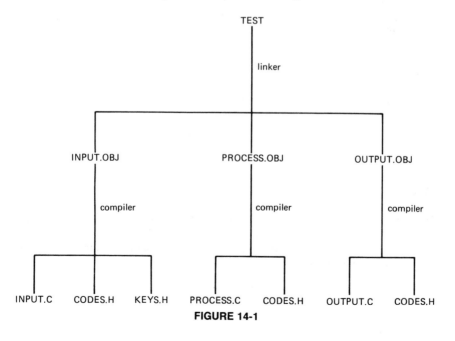

**FIGURE 14-1**

Encoded in a **makefile**, the dependencies and processes illustrated in Figure 14-1 are as shown in Figure 14-2.

```
test : input.obj process.obj output.obj
    link input.obj process.obj output.obj

input.obj : input.c codes.h keys.h
    cc input.c

process.obj : process.c codes.h
    cc process.c

output.obj : output.c codes.h
    cc output.c
```

**FIGURE 14-2**

For each **target** file (file to be generated), the **makefile** contains two lines. The first of these lines is the **dependency line**, for example,

**test : input.obj process.obj output.obj**

The **dependency line** consists of the **target** file (**test**), whose name begins in the first column, followed by a colon, followed by the names of all the files on which it directly depends: those necessary to create it (**input.obj**, **process.obj**, and **output.obj**).

The second line is the **operation line**, for example,

**link input.obj process.obj output.obj**

The **operation line** is identical to the command you would type to generate the **target** file.

## Additional Features

**Generalizing Rules.** These steps describe the basis of a MAKE utility. Many MAKE utilities, however, provide you with other capabilities. Primary among these is the ability to generalize rules. For example, instead of specifying the **operation line**

**cc filename.c**

for every **filename.obj**, you can specify the following generalized rule: Unless otherwise specified, every **filename.obj** file is generated by the **cc filename.c** command.

To state this generalized rule, we would modify our sample makefile as shown in Figure 14-3.

```
.c.obj :
    cc $<

test : input.obj process.obj output.obj
       link input.obj process.obj output.obj

input.obj : codes.h keys.h

process.obj : codes.h

output.obj : codes.h
```

**FIGURE 14-3**

The first two lines of our modified **makefile** specify the command **cc filename.c** to create any **filename.obj** file from the corresponding **filename.c** file. The **$<** is a macro that is replaced by the name of the source (**filename.c**) file.

Note that it is no longer necessary to state that **filename.obj** depends on **filename.c**. The generalized rule, in specifying some operation on **filename.c**, informs the MAKE utility that **filename.obj** is dependent on **filename.c**.

**Macro Expansion.**  Many MAKE utilities include an additional macro expansion capability for simplifying the **makefile**. You can specify any replacement by defining it at the head of a **makefile**. This define is called a macro. To define the macro, type the macro name, followed by an equal sign ( = ), followed by the string to replace it with. To use the macro, type a dollar sign ($) followed by the macro name in parentheses.

In our sample **makefile**, we could replace the three .obj files necessary to generate the **test** file with the macro name **OBJECTS**. Our **makefile** would then appear as shown in Figure 14-4. Notice that the macro expansion can be used both in **dependency lines** and **operation lines**.

You can also create a **dependency line** containing multiple **target** files. Figure 14-5 shows an example, again using our sample **makefile**. Figure 14-5 indicates that all files represented by **OBJECTS** (**input.obj**, **process.obj**, and

```
OBJECTS = input.obj process.obj output.obj

.c.obj :
    cc $<

test : $(OBJECTS)
    link $(OBJECTS)

input.obj : codes.h keys.h

process.obj : codes.h

output.obj : codes.h
```

**FIGURE 14-4**

```
OBJECTS = input.obj process.obj output.obj

.c.obj :
    cc $<

test : $(OBJECTS)
    link $(OBJECTS)

$(OBJECTS) : codes.h

input.obj : keys.h
```

**FIGURE 14-5**

output.obj) are dependent upon **codes.h**. The file **input.obj** is also dependent upon the file **keys.h**.

**Other Additional Features.** Additional features found in many MAKE utilities include:

1. Order independence—The utility can handle file creation even when the dependencies are listed out of order. For example, the **dependency lines**

a : b

b : c

c : d

are equivalent to

$$b : c$$
$$a : b$$
$$c : d$$

The MAKE utility with this capability will determine in which order operations need to be performed.

2. Batch file capability—Using a MAKE utility with this capability, you can specify batch file commands within the **operation lines**.

3. Compatibility with hierarchical file systems.

4. Association of file suffixes with directories—For example, you can state the rule that, unless otherwise specified, all files with a **.db** extension are found in the **database** directory.

5. Compatibility with date/time stamping mechanisms other than the operating system's.

6. Invocation flags—flags that allow you to modify the operation of the MAKE utility, without modifying the **makefile**.

7. UNIX compatible **makefile** syntax.

8. Automatic **makefile** generation—utility programs that can read input files of various formats (e.g., C source code files or linkage editor command files) and construct a **makefile** automatically.

## Conclusion

Any substantial application will be modified, often many times and in many different places, before the final executable is created. Modular programming makes it unnecessary to re-compile and re-link the entire application every time a change is made. Program development is much more efficient if only the modified modules are re-generated. With many modules, however, remembering which ones need to be processed for each revision of the application is a risky task. MAKE utilities relieve you of that responsibility, keeping track of modified files and automatically recreating the executable in the fewest possible steps.

## LINT UTILITIES

### Introduction

Static analysis tools (often called **lint** utilities) are a complement to the compiler. Like a compiler, a static analysis tool reports syntax errors in a C program. Unlike a compiler, a static analysis tool will not generate an executable program. It will produce more diagnostic messages than a typical C compiler, however.

Static analysis tools exist because C contains several weaknesses that make compiler detection of all errors a difficult task. Many errors are not detected by the compiler, in some cases because the additional checking is expensive and difficult to perform automatically, and in other cases because the "errors" may be intentional constructs to take advantage of special features of the target machine.

UNIX lint is the oldest static analysis tool for C, sharing much of its code with the Portable C Compiler used in many versions of UNIX. UNIX lint has been ported to virtually every other UNIX system. Later, lint utilities for non-UNIX systems became available, particularly *Pre-C* (Phoenix Computer Products) and *PC-LINT* (Gimpel Software), both for MSDOS-based microcomputers, and *LINT/VMS* (Wizard Systems Software) for VAX/VMS systems. All of these programs perform similar analyses, differing mostly in the method of invoking the program and in the format of the error messages generated.

At this writing, the ANSI committee is endeavoring to eliminate many of the weaknesses of C addressed by static analysis tools. The ANSI standard will not eliminate all need for such tools, however. In the descriptions of lint functions later in this chapter, we have indicated which issues are likely to be addressed by the ANSI standard.

## The Weaknesses of C Addressed by Static Analysis Tools

C's weaknesses fall into two major categories and one minor category. The major categories are multiple-source file checking and data type conversion. The minor category is operator precedence rules.

Multiple-source file checking includes verifying that all function calls include the correct number and type of parameters specified in the function definition. It also includes checking that global variables are properly declared at all places in a source program.

Data type conversion problems include a long-standing practice in C of treating pointers and integers as equivalent entities. Many C programs assume that pointers can be safely copied to and from integers. Other programs often assume that pointers to one kind of data can be safetly converted to pointers to a different kind of data. For example, a program may use a character pointer to step through a complex data structure, then convert that pointer to an integer pointer, so that the integer may be extracted or manipulated. On some machines this practice is safe, while on others it could cause a program failure. As this example indicates, data-conversion problems are primarily a problem of program portability. The ANSI standard is likely to correct such problems by requiring pointer type conversion capability in all C compilers.

Operator precedence problems result from C's numerous operators. Operator precedence refers to the rules for determining the order in which operations are performed when an expression contains several operators (without parentheses to group them clearly). The expression $a = b + c * d$ is reasonably intuitive in its operator precedence, interpreted as $a = b + (c * d)$. The precedence of multiplication over addition is a familiar algebraic rule. The expression $a = b + c \ll d$, however, is less obvious. Its correct interpretation in C is $a = (b + c) \ll d$.

## What Static Analysis Tools Can Do

Static analysis tools can help a programmer in several ways. Probably the most useful function of a static analysis tool is in discovering program bugs. These tools can discover several types of bugs, but perhaps the most important class is the detection of function calls with mismatched parameters.

Portability is another feature that static analysis tools can help verify. With rapidly shifting hardware technology and the rising number of independent software vendors, portability is becoming increasingly important. While portability in general is difficult to guarantee, many portability problems can be detected automatically.

Static analysis tools can also help you increase a program's readability. By explicitly stating type conversions, grouping expressions with parentheses, and eliminating unreachable or redundant code, you make your programs more readable. Static analysis tools point out these areas for your revision.

The completeness of the analysis performed is a major strong point of these tools. Hand-checking a large program is nearly impossible, and is certainly a waste of human resources. The diagnostics produced by an analysis highlight the parts of a program which are suspect, vastly reducing the programmer's checking time.

Static analysis tools do have limitations. The tool is separate from the compiler, and rarely as closely bound as UNIX lint and the Portable C Compiler. This opens the possibility of minor differences, non-standard extensions, and even different bugs between the compiler and the static analysis tool. Since a major area being checked by the tool is portability, however, this incompatibility is not as severe a problem as it may seem. Clearly, the compiler must be the final judge of what constitutes an acceptable program. The static analysis tool is usually limited to a portable dialect of C. As a general rule of thumb, use the compiler first to verify the acceptibility of the program, then use the static tool to verify portability and to check for further errors passed over by the compiler.

A more fundamental limitation of a static tool is the fact that many program bugs issue from the dynamic behavior of the program. For example, a static tool can detect that a program divides by a literal zero, but it is theoretically impossible to discover statically whether any division could involve a division by zero. The common problem of recognizing the use of an invalid pointer value is also impossible without running the program.

Static tools thus do not eliminate the need for debuggers or interpreters, but instead complement them (as well as the compiler).

**Analyses Performed.** Static analysis tools operate in two phases. The first phase analyzes each individual source file of the system. The second phase takes information culled from each source file and cross-checks function calls. Different tools vary in the details of how the two phases are connected, and how a library of non-C functions can be incorporated into the analysis.

Since many of the analyses done are heuristic and may create spurious error messages, static analysis tools typically include the ability to suppress diagnostics either for an entire analysis, or on a statement by statement basis. Statement-by-statement suppression is usually accomplished via C commands that have specially defined meanings to the static analysis tool. For example, the comment /* **NOTREACHED** */ indicates a statement that is never reached in the program execution.

Each static analysis tool varies slightly as to which conditions are detected, and in the exact wording of error messages. The following list, then, contains general descriptions of the types of analyses performed by these tools.

*Strict Type Checking.* As discussed earlier, many C programs are cavalier about moving data between objects of different types. Mixing different sizes of integers and mixing pointers with integers are both common practices. If you know the compiler and the machine well, such actions can be harmless, and sometimes necessary. For example, the **malloc()** function is the accepted portable method for dynamically allocating memory. The function, however, returns a pointer to a character. A C program may need blocks of storage for many different types of objects, however: arrays of integers or floating point values, or various types of structures. In the informal documentation for **malloc()**, the pointer returned is guaranteed to be usable for any data type. The difficulty arises in the formal language which requires that the return value of **malloc()** be converted to the pointer type needed by the program. On most machines, it is harmless simply to assign the value of **malloc()** to a pointer of any type. The implicit conversion usually does not change the value, and the documentation states that any such conversion is safe. Static analysis tools check for such explicit casting in changing the pointer type, and typically report a warning if some suspicious (i.e., not explicit) conversion is taking place.

The ANSI standard will require the programmer to explicitly cast a value from one type to another. A conversion of pointer types without a cast is a compiler-reported program error in ANSI C.

The size of variables of type **int** is unclear. On a given machine under a given compiler the size is well defined, but in different machines the size may vary. Most machines define **int** to be the same size as either **short** or **long**. The greatest difficulty in mixing **short**, **int**, and **long** data arises when a value is converted to or from these types. On some machines, converting **long** values to **int** values results in the loss of significant digits (because **ints** are narrower than **longs**). On other machines, converting **ints** to **shorts** produces the same problem. As in mixing pointers, an explicit cast, checked for by the static analysis tool, will make the programmer's intent clear.

*Variable Usage.*  If a variable is declared but never used in a program, at least some memory is wasted. Most compilers do not remove such variables from programs. Unused variables also confuse a reader, who can not easily determine (in a large piece of code) whether the variable is ever used. At worst, unused variables may represent a misspelling of a variable whose use was actually intended.

Similarly, if a variable only appears on the left-hand side of an assignment, its value is never used. In this case, a compiler will almost never detect the uselessness of the assignment, and so generate extra code. In most cases, however, such a useless assignment represents a bug. In both instances, static analysis tools will point out the unused variable.

Also dangerous, but more difficult to detect, is the use of a variable before a value has been assigned to it. Static analysis tools will attempt to determine whether variables are used before being defined. Typically, the algorithm is a forward scan through a function for an assignment of a value before the variable is used. The common C coding style of structured arrangement of code without arbitrary **goto** statements makes this heuristic reasonably trustworthy. Global variables always have a valid value, since they are assigned a value of zero at program start-up if they have not been explicitly initialized otherwise. Local variables, on the other hand, are undefined until assigned. The major difficulty with the common algorithm in detecting this problem is **for** loops. The final expression in a **for** statement is executed after the body of the loop, hence a static analysis tool may erroneously report that a variable is used before it is assigned a value.

*Flow Analysis.*  When both the true and false alternatives of an **if** statement end with **return** statements, the program will never reach the statement following the **if**. Unless the next statement can somehow be reached (e.g., it has a label), the statement will never be executed. Like unused variables, unreachable statements are rarely removed by a compiler, and so take up useless space. Unreachable statements are often indications of a programming error. A static analysis tool will alert you to such statements.

A statement of the form **a + b;** is perfectly legal (assuming **a** and **b** are properly declared), but will have no effect on the program. Many compilers will generate code for this statement, anyway. Like unreachable statements, code with no side-effects is often a programming error. (The example above, for instance, may have been intended as **a = b;**, or perhaps **a += b;**.) A static analysis tool will alert you to these types of statements, as well.

*Function Calling.* Functions return a value by executing a **return** statement with some expression included. If a function returns via **return** statements without expressions, or by "falling through" to the end of the function, no value is generated. If a call to the function tries to use the return value, the results are unpredictable. Any function, therefore, which sometimes returns a value and sometimes does not is quite likely to contain a bug. Detecting whether or not the end of the function is reached is important in detecting value-less returns.Generally, if a function is declared to return some specific type, then all of the returns in the function should contain a value. Static analysis tools will alert you to improperly declared function return values, ignored return values, and absent return values that the calling program attempts to use.

Virtually no C compiler will check whether or not function calls match function definitions. ANSI C partially overcomes this deficiency. The parameters expected by a function can be explicitly declared so that the compiler can check the validity of the function calls. ANSI C does not require these declarations, however, and the compiler can not check whether or not a function declaration actually matches the definition, if the declaration and definition are in separate source files. Static analysis tools check all source files of a program, determining whether each function call contains the correct number of arguments, and that each argument is of the correct data type.

K&R C provides no method for declaring a function that takes a variable number of parameters, such as the **printf()** function. Static analysis tools typically provide a special mechanism for declaring such functions.

**Sample Output.**  Figure 14-6 is sample code containing several of the types of errors detected by static analysis tools. Following the code is the output produced by Pre-C, Phoenix Software's static analysis program.

```
SAMPLE.C

1    static char *inputval;
2
3    main (argc, argv)
4    int argc;
5    char **argv;
6    {
7        int loopi, loopj, k;
```

**FIGURE 14-6**

```
8
9        inputval = calloc(17);
10       for   (loopi = 0; loopj < 17; loopi++) {
11             inputval[loopi] = 'a' + loopi;
12       }
13       if    (loopi = 17)
14             printf("Done\n");
15             return(1);
16       /* Note that the if statement is missing brackets, so the
17          return is not part of the if */
18       inputval == 0;
19       }
20
```

OUTPUT OF PRE-C:

1  Pre-C Version 1.34 From Phoenix Computer Products Corp.
2      Copyright (c) 1984, 1985 Wizard Systems Software, Inc.
3  sample.c:
4  Warning sample.c 9: Non-portable pointer assignment in function main
5  Warning sample.c 10: Possible use of 'loopj' before definition in function main
6  Warning sample.c 13: Possibly incorrect assignment in function main
7  Warning sample.c 18: Unreachable code in function main
8  Warning sample.c 18: Code has no effect in function main
9  Warning sample.c 19: 'k' declared but never used in function main
10 Warning sample.c 19: Parameter 'argv' is never used in function main
11 Warning sample.c 19: Parameter 'argc' is never used in function main
12 Warning sample.c 19: Both return and return of a value used in function main
13 Error sample.c 9: Function 'calloc' return value declared inconsistently
14 Error sample.c 9: Too few arguments in call to 'calloc'

**FIGURE 14-6** (Continued)

## Conclusion

Static analysis tools are a useful and time-saving step in debugging. Functioning, generally, somewhere between a compiler and a debugger, lint utilities isolate many potential errors in a program. By highlighting suspect areas, a lint utility allows the programmer easily to find many of the bugs that are detectable before run time.

# Applied C Appendix
# C Programming Aids

This appendix lists many commercially available C programming aids. (Because of the multitude of products available, we are unable to present a complete list.)

Products are listed in the following categories:
Compilers
General Libraries
Screen Management Libraries
Portability Libraries
Communications Libraries
General Utilities
Database Management Tools
Others

Products preceded by an asterisk (*) are created and/or marketed by *Applied C*'s contributors and reviewers.

## COMPILERS

* *Lattice C Compiler*
* *VAX/VMS Cross Compiler*
* *VAX/UNIX Cross Compiler*
* *6800 C Cross Compiler*
All available from:
      Lattice, Inc.
      P.O. Box 3072
      Glen Ellyn, IL 60138
      (312) 858-7950

* *MWC86 C compiler* for MS-DOS, runs on IBM PC and compatibles
* *MWC68K C compiler* for DEC Rainbow
* *VAX/VMS cross-compiler*
* *COHERENT* operating system for 8086 and Z8000

All available from:
>Mark Williams Company
>1430 West Wrightwood
>Chicago, IL 60614
>(312) 472-6659

* *Toolworks C/80* (CP/M-80) compiler
* *Toolworks C* (MS-DOS) compiler
Both in either integer version or with a MATHPAK, which adds true 32 bit float and
long data types. Available from:
>The Software Toolworks
>14478 Glorietta Drive
>Sherman Oaks, CA 91423
>(818) 986-4885

* Wizard Systems supplies a range of C compilers for 8086 based systems, including
  MS-DOS and BTOS. Available from:
>Wizard Systems Software, Inc.
>11 Willow Court
>Arlington, MA 02174

—*Microsoft C* for MS/PC-DOS (Microsoft Corp.)

—*Megamax C* for the Macintosh, a full-scale development system (Megamax, Inc.)

—*Small-C Compiler 2.1*, for CP/M-80 or MS/PC-DOS (J.E. Hendrix)

—*Elfin Systems C*, for CP/M (Elfin Systems)

—*BDS C*, for CP/M-80 (BD Software, Inc.)

—*Optimizing C86 C Compiler* for MS/PC-DOS (Computer Innovations, Inc.)

—*Series 32000 C Cross Compiler* provides for downloading programs to the DB32000
  development board (JMI Software Consultants, Inc.)

—*QC88*, for MS-DOS
—*Q/C 4.0*, for CP/M
—*QCX* cross compiler
(The Code Works)

—*Eco-C88*, for MS-DOS (Ecosoft, Inc.)

—*Aztec CII*, for CP/M 80
—*Aztec C86*, for PC/MS-DOS and CP/M 86
—*Aztec C80*, for TRS Models 3 and 4

—*Aztec C65*, for Apple DOS 3.3 and Pro-DOS
—*Aztec C68k*, for Macintosh
(Manx Software)

—*DeSmet C* for MS/PC-DOS or Macintosh (C Ware Corp.)

—*Datalight C* for MS/PC-DOS (Datalight)

## GENERAL LIBRARIES

* *C Tools*, a library of IBM PC-specific functions in the areas of graphics, keyboard, and sound. Available from:
  Xor Corporation
  5421 Opportunity Court
  Minnetonka, MN 55343
  (612) 938-0005

* *The Greenleaf Functions* is a general library containing more than 200 functions in C and assembler, for the IBM PC and compatibles. Provides support for DOS, video, string, printer, async, and systems interface. Supports all video capabilities of the PC. Includes printer functions, string functions, time and date functions, and more. Available from:
  Greenleaf Software, Inc.
  1411 Le May Drive, Suite 101
  Carrollton, TX 75007

* *Polytron C Library I* is a collection of useful functions that can be called from Lattice C and assembler. Includes functions for I/O, filename manipulation, wild card expansion, DOS program execution, string operations, and more. Includes source code. Available from:
  Polytron Corp.
  Box 787
  Hillsboro, OR 97123
  (503) 648-8595
  (800) 547-4000 (orders and product information only)

* *C Essentials* is a general C library containing string support functions, DOS access functions, and more.
* *C Utility Library* is a superset of *C Essentials*, adding windowing graphics data entry, and communication functions.
Both available from:
  Essential Software, Inc.
  P.O. Box 1003
  Maplewood, NJ 07040
  (914) 762-6605

—*C Tools* and *C Tools 2*, for the IBM PC and compatibles (Blaise Computing, Inc.)

—*C-LIB*, for the IBM PC and compatibles (Vance info systems)

—*JMI Portable C Library* (JMI Software Consultants, Inc.)

—*Csharp Realtime Toolkit*, for the PDP-11 family and other 8- and 16-bit processors (Systems Guild, Inc.)

—*Applications Programmers Tool Kit*, for Lattice C, Mark Williams C, DeSmet C, BDS C, and others (Shaw American Technologies)

## SCREEN MANAGEMENT LIBRARIES

* *Omniscreen*, a screen management facility with a screen generator and C language interface, and a memory resident screen handler. Available from:
  Omnisoft Associates
  6917 12th Ave.
  Brooklyn, NY 11228
  (718) 680-3259

* *The HAMMER Library*, containing over 150 C routines for the IBM PC, providing screen management, 1-2-3-like menus, data entry routines, and more. Data entry routines can be used individually or as part of a full screen of fields. Available from:
  O.E.S. Systems
  1906 Brushcliff Road
  Pittsburgh, PA 15221
  (412) 243-7365

* *Essential Graphics* is a graphics library for serious software developers. Available from:
  Essential Software, Inc.
  P.O. Box 1003
  Maplewood, NJ 07040
  (914) 762-6605

—*C View Manager*, a screen development system for the IBM PC and compatibles (Blaise Computing, Inc.)

—*Vitamin C*, a library of screen management functions
—*VCScreen*, an interactive screen painter/code generator for use with the *Vitamin C* library
(Creative Programming Consultants)

—*Small-Tools Package 1.2*, a set of sixteen text processing tools written in Small-C for CP/M-80 or MS/PC-DOS (J.E. Hendrix)

—*Windows for C*, a toolkit for all screen management tasks. For PCDOS, PC/XENIX, or UNIX.

—*Windows for Data*, a library of data entry functions that operate within windows. For PCDOS, PC/XENIX, or UNIX. (Vermont Creative Software)

## PORTABILITY LIBRARIES

* *The PORT PACKAGE*, a collection of C routines for porting programs between personal computers such as the IBM, Apple, Commodore, and CP/M systems. Available from:

 Pugh-Killeen Associates
 1 Bowdoin Street
 Newton Highlands, MA 02161
 (617) 964-9045

## COMMUNICATIONS LIBRARIES

* *The Greenleaf Comm Library* is an interrupt driven, ring-buffered asynchronous communications library. It contains over 100 functions in C and assembler to facilitate communications at up to 9600 baud, with up to 8 ports at a time, using ASCII or XMODEM. Available for all major C compilers, for the IBM PC and most machines with MS-DOS and an 8086 processor. Includes source code, examples, demo programs, and more. Available from:

 Greenleaf Software, Inc.
 1411 Le May Drive Suite 101
 Carrollton, TX 75007

—*C Asynch Manager*, a library of communications tools for the IBM PC and compatibles (Blaise Computing, Inc.)

## GENERAL UTILITIES

* MS/PC-DOS productivity tools for the professional programmer including C source analyzer, overlay linker, symbolic debugger, macro-text editor, symbolic performance analyzer, and more. Debugger and performance analyzer written by Purart, Inc. All available from:

 Phoenix Computer Products Corporation
 320 Norwood Park South
 Norwood, MA 02062
 (800) 344-7200

* *PolyMake* is an application program generator/maintainer patterned after UNIX Make. Automates the construction of an application from its component parts by invoking the user's compiler, assembler, linker, librarian, or other translator to generate a new version when one or more of the components is modified.

* *PolyLibrarian* and *PolyLibrarian II* are object module librarians that allow the construction, modification, augmentation, and investigation of object module libraries to be used by object code linkers. *PolyLibrarian* supports MS-DOS compatible libraries; *PolyLibrarian II* supports MS-DOS libraries and Intel format libraries.

All available from:

    Polytron Corp.
    Box 787
    Hillsboro, OR 97123
    (503) 648-8595
    (800) 547-4000 (orders and product information only)

* *C-terp* is a C interpreter that serves as a debugging and development environment for the IBM PC and true compatibles. Current variants support Lattice C, Computer Innovations C86, Microsoft 3.0, Mark Williams, and MANX Aztec C compilers, and provide for linking of object modules created by these compilers.
* *PC-Lint* is a diagnostic facility for C programs and runs on MS-DOS machines. It will find bugs, glitches, and inconsistencies in programs.

Both available from:

    Gimpel Software
    3207 Hogarth Lane
    Collegeville, PA 19426
    (215) 584-4261

* *Faster C* replaces your linkers by keeping the Lattice C or C86 library and any other functions you choose in memory. It also enables you to call active functions interactively to speed program debugging, and includes many options for configuration and control. Available for PC-DOS, IBM-AT, and any 256K MSDOS system.
* *BRIEF* is a programmer's editor offering the features most asked for by professional programmers: Full UNDO, compiler-specific support, unlimited file size, reconfigurable keyboard, and more. Can be customized to suit your coding style—create any command and assign it to any key.

Both available from:

    Solution Systems
    335-D Washington Street
    Norwell, MA 02061
    (617) 659-1571

* *UBACKUP* is a utility for systems backup, restore, and media management for UNIX and UNIX-derivative operating systems.
* *USECURE* is a utility for system security management and audit trail capabilities for UNIX and UNIX-derivative operating systems.
* *SPR* provides superior print spooling and batch job scheduling for UNIX and UNIX-derivative operating systems.
* *UCONTROL* is a complete UNIX systems management environment.

All available from:
UNITECH Software, Inc.
8330 Old Courthouse Road
Suite 800
Vienna, VA 22180
(703) 734-9844

* *Make*, patterned after the UNIX Make facility. Works for code written in any programming language. C source code included. Available from:
Softfocus
1343 Stanbury Drive
Oakville, Ontario
CANADA L6L 2J5
(416) 825-0903
(416) 844-2610

—*BSW-Make*, an implementation of the UNIX Make facility for MS-DOS and VAX/VMS (The Boston Software Works)

—*ESP* (*Entry System for Programs*), a language-directed editor for C and/or Pascal (Popular Programs, Inc., formerly Bellesoft)

—*C EXECUTIVE*, an operating system for embedded applications (JMI Software Consultants, Inc.)

—*FirsTime*, a syntax-directed editor for the Lattice, Microsoft, C-86, and several other compilers (Spruce Technology Corp.)

—*C-PACK*, a collection of CP/M utility programs
—*ICX Toolkit* for CP/M or MS-DOS allows manipulation of ISIS-II disks and full ISIS emulation under CP/M
—*The ZAS Software Development Packages* for the Z-8000 and the Z-8 in MS-DOS, ISIS-II, CP/M-80 or 86 formats
(Western Wares)

—*CPP*, an enhanced version of the C language preprocessor program for CP/M 80, CP/M 68K or MS-DOS (Edward K. Ream)

—*Periscope I* and *Periscope II*, comprehensive debugging systems for the IBM PC, XT, AT, and close compatibles (Data Base Decisions)

—*Instant-C*, a high performance interpreter/compiler for MS/PC-DOS and CP/M-86 (Rational Systems, Inc.)

—UNIX-like utilities for PC-DOS, including lex, yacc, and prep (The Austin Code Works)

—*Dr. Shaw's DOS Shell*, a UNIX-like shell for MS/PC-DOS, includes many UNIX-like commands (Shaw American Technologies)

## DATABASE MANAGEMENT TOOLS

* *PHACT-dbrm* is a library of multi-keyed ISAM functions. *PHACT-query* and *PHACT-report* are high-level tools to access, report, query, and manipulate PHACT databases. Available from:
    PHACT Associates, Ltd.
    225 Lafayette St.
    Suite 1005
    New York, NY 10012

* *BTree Library* provides high speed random and sequential access, multiple keys, and variable length records. C source code included.
* *ISAM Driver* greatly speeds application development by combining the ease of use of a database manager with the flexibility of a programming language. Supports multi-key files and dynamic index definition. C source code included.
Both available from:
    Softfocus
    1343 Stanbury Drive
    Oakville, Ontario
    CANADA L6L 2J5
    (416) 825-0903
    (416) 844-2610

—*C-Index/Plus*, a data management function library (Trio Systems)

—*INFORMIX-SQL*, a relational database management system
—*INFORMIX-ESQL/C*, a development environment for database applications
—*C-ISAM*, a B+-Tree access method
(Relational Database Systems)

—*Unify*, a fourth generation UNIX relational database management system for application developers (Unisource Software Corp.)

—*Btrieve*, a key indexed file management system (ISAM) for use with all programming languages (SoftCraft)

—*db_VISTA*, a network model database management system for Lattice, Microsoft, Computer Innovations, DeSmet, Mark Williams, and Aztec C compilers under MS-DOS, and most UNIX systems (Raima Corporation)

—*FABS* (Fast Access B-tree Structure) for Lattice C (Computer Control Systems, Inc.)

—*c-tree*, B+ tree file handler for MS-DOS, UNIX, XENIX, CP/M, Macintosh, and other operating systems (FairCom)

## OTHERS

* The Programmer's Shop carries hundreds of programmer's aids, and provides programmer services including product information and comparison, newsletter, bulletin board, and more.
  The Programmer's Shop
  128-D Rockland Street
  Hanover, MA 02339
  (617) 826-7531
  (800) 442-8070

* *Homebase*, an integrated DOS environment. Available from:
  Amber Systems, Inc.
  (408) 996-1883

* *The Lattice TopView Toolbasket*, a library of general purpose functions for writing C programs under the IBM TopView environment. Created by Strawberry Software, Inc.
Available from:
  Lattice, Inc.
  P.O. Box 3072
  Glen Ellyn, IL 60138
  (312) 858-7950

—*Exec* implements program chaining using the standard DOS program loader (Blaise Computing, Inc.)

—*H.E.L.P. for ANSI C* and *H.E.L.P.*, C programming environments for MS-DOS or Macintosh (Everest Solutions)

—*BASTOC*, a BASIC to C language translator (JMI Software Consultants, Inc.)

—*The C Users' Group*, an international information exchange for non-commercial distribution of public domain software written in C.

# Index